STUDIES IN HISTORY, ECONOMICS AND PUBLIC LAW

Edited by the
FACULTY OF POLITICAL SCIENCE
OF COLUMBIA UNIVERSITY

NUMBER 457

RESPONSIBILITY OF STATES FOR ACTS OF UNSUCCESSFUL INSURGENT GOVERNMENTS

BY

HAIG SILVANIE

RESPONSIBILITY OF STATES
FOR ACTS OF
UNSUCCESSFUL INSURGENT GOVERNMENTS

BY

HAIG SILVANIE

AMS PRESS
NEW YORK

COLUMBIA UNIVERSITY
STUDIES IN THE
SOCIAL SCIENCES

457

The Series was formerly known as *Studies in History, Economics and Public Law.*

Reprinted with the permission of Columbia University Press
From the edition of 1939, New York
First AMS EDITION published 1968
Manufactured in the United States of America

Library of Congress Catalogue Card Number: 68-58622

AMS PRESS, INC.
New York, N.Y. 10003

To

MY WIFE

SARAH ROCHE SILVANIE

PREFACE

It is a settled rule of international law that the state is responsible for acts of insurgent governments which ultimately succeed in establishing themselves in power as the government. Responsibility for acts of unsuccessful insurgent governments, however, is more difficult to determine. It appears that until recent years international tribunals took the view that unsuccessful insurgent governments were in no sense agents or "authorities" of the state, and could not, therefore, bind the state or render it liable for their acts. Only one important exception was recognized, and that exception dealt with taxes and customs duties collected by unsuccessful insurgents. In such cases it was uniformly held that taxes and duties could not be collected for a second time by the restored government. Aside from this, international tribunals were unwilling to admit that unsuccessful insurgent governments were agents of the state in regard to any other act.

During the recent Mexican arbitrations, however, state liability for acts of unsuccessful insurgent governments was extended to include not only taxes and customs duties but also certain categories of contractual and tortious acts. The state was held liable for insurgent acts of governmental routine, including ordinary commercial contracts, and for all discretionary acts benefiting the state, such as a loan used to meet the maturing obligations of the state or a forcible taking of property for the use of a starving population of a city or town under insurgent control. On the other hand, no insurgent acts done in aid of rebellion, such as the purchase of arms and munitions, the borrowing of money for civil war purposes, and the granting of concessions and the forcible taking of property the proceeds of which were actually used to support the insurgent government, were regarded as benefiting the state and therefore binding on the state.

In this study, which was carried on under the direction of Professor Joseph P. Chamberlain of Columbia University, an attempt has been made to state the rule of international law dealing with state responsibility for acts of unsuccessful insurgent governments and to point out changes, past developments, and the present tendencies in the law. The author is under a deep debt of gratitude to Professor Chamberlain, and owes great debt to Professor Charles Cheney Hyde and Professor Philip C. Jessup of Columbia University, who gave continuous advice and made many valuable suggestions during the preparation of this book and who read the manuscript in its final form and suggested changes which revealed how closely and searchingly they had scrutinized it.

The author also desires to express his sincere thanks to his wife, Sarah Roche Silvanie, for patience and fortitude, and for the very hard work of preparing the manuscript for the press and painstakingly reading the proofs; and to his friends, Miss Rose Roche, Mrs. Mary Humphrey, Miss Isabel Hogan and Miss Alice Hogan, for assistance in typing and in proof reading.

HAIG SILVANIE

NEW YORK CITY,
APRIL 6, 1939.

CONTENTS

CHAPTER I

INSURGENT LOANS

As a general rule the state is not bound by loans made to an insurgent government except in case of success of the revolutionary movement. This rule applies both in the case of insurgents who attempt to overthrow the titular government and establish themselves in its place and in the case of insurgents who propose to secede and create a new state out of a part of the territory of the old state. If the insurgent government succeeds in establishing itself in power either as the government of the old state or as the government of a new state created by secession, such loans are maintained as obligations of either the old or the new state.[1] If, however, the revolutionary movement collapses, such loans do not become obligations of the state and the creditors will lose their money. This principle is stated by Judge Moore as follows:

> Nothing is better settled in law than the principle that those who lend money to insurgents take the risk of their failure. This is also common sense. Such a loan, whether prompted by the hope of gain or by sympathy with the cause, is in the nature of a bet that the insurrection will succeed. If the cause is lost, equally so is the stake; and neither victor nor vanquished can be reproached.[2]

1 The principle that the state is bound by the acts and contracts of the government of a successful revolution has been discussed in the following cases: the case of the Amory concessions, Arbitration between Great Britain and Costa Rica, 1923, *A. J.*, 1924, 147; *Dreyfus Brothers (France) v. Peru*, Franco-Chilean Arbitral Tribunal, 1901, *Decisions*, 290 *et seq.*; *Day and Garrison (U. S.) v. Venezuela*, United States and Venezuelan Claims Commission of 1885, Moore, *International Arbitrations*, IV, 3548 *et seq.*; *Hopkins case*, General Claims Commission of 1923, United States and Mexico, *Opinions*, 1927, 42 *et seq.*; *Garcia case*, *ibid.*, 146. For other cases see, Moore, *Int. Arb.*, III, 2859 *et seq.*; Ralston, *Venezuelan Arbitrations of 1903*, *passim*.

2 See John Bassett Moore's letter to the editor of the *N. Y. Times* dealing with the Confederate debt, *N. Y. Times*, July 25, 1932.

A loan contract with an insurgent government which fails of success is a contract with a debtor which dies, leaving, in contemplation of international law, neither heirs nor assets. The state is not bound by such a contract because it is not a party to it and because, as it will be seen in subsequent discussion, "unsuccessful insurgents are not the agents of the state which suppresses them." [3] And in case of failure of insurgents to secede, no new state is actually created to undertake the obligations arising from a loan contract with such insurgents.

In the past loans have been made to unsuccessful insurgents who were attempting either to subvert a government or to establish a new state, and in both cases such loans were held not to bind the disturbed state. In the *Cucullu case* [4] the United States and Mexican Claims Commission of 1868 held that Mexico was not bound by a loan made by an American citizen to Zuloaga and his partisans who were carrying on a civil war against the constitutional government in 1858. The Commission noted that during the period under consideration there were in fact two coexisting and yet conflicting governments in Mexico, one the constitutional government and the other the Zuloaga government which was ultimately the unsuccessful one, and said:

Who authorized Cucullu to decide which of these two pretenders was "the government of Mexico?" If he took for the government that which was not such he was bound to know that he ran that risk; that he intrusted his interests to the contingencies and result of the civil war; that he took sides with one of the belligerents, and that he could not promise himself that the acts of the one would be respected or legalized *by the other* belligerent. If the precedent be established that the government which becomes consolidated after a civil struggle takes upon itself the obligations contracted by its enemy, the condition of those who speculate in affording assistance to revolutionists would be made too favorable and advan-

3 Hyde, *International Law*, I, 538.

4 Moore, *Int. Arb.*, III, 2873-2881; IV, 3477-3483, *infra*, p. 42.

tageous, and a premium would be offered to those who engage political exiles in enterprises against the authorities of their country and furnish them with the means necessary to participate in the civil war.[5]

A similar decision was rendered by the same commission in the *Stuckle case*[6] involving a loan made to the Maximilian government by an American citizen. During the Venezuelan arbitrations of 1903 the principle that the state is not bound by loans made to unsuccessful insurgents was applied by the United States and Venezuelan Commission in the *Jarvis case*[7] and by the Netherlands-Venezuelan Commission in the *Henriquez case*.[8] The latter case has a more direct bearing on the question under consideration here. The essential facts in this case may be summarized briefly much as they were presented to the Commission. The claim against Venezuela was made in behalf of a subject of the Netherlands for a sum of money " for goods and cash voluntarily loaned or delivered to revolutionary chiefs or their official subordinates, commencing with the so-called de facto government of General Rivera, in the State of Falcon, in June, 1902." Before the tribunal both parties agreed that General Rivera was a revolutionary chieftain warring against the constitutional government; that he was in control of that portion of the Republic of Venezuela of which the claimant was an inhabitant during the time mentioned; that it was a revolution in fact; and that the funds and effects furnished General Rivera and his subordinates in the State of Falcon went for the support and benefit of the revolutionary forces only. The claimant, however, insisted that the Rivera government was the *de facto* government of the State of Falcon, and that he was therefore obliged to recognize its authority; and that, " being a de facto government, the Republic of

5 *Ibid.*, IV, 3482-3483.

6 Moore, *Int. Arb.*, III, 2935, *infra*, pp. 20-25.

7 Ralston, *Ven. Arb. of 1903*, 145, *infra*, p. 47.

8 *Ibid.*, 896.

Venezuela is responsible for the loans and goods furnished to the superior powers then in control of that State." [9] Aside from this, no other ground for the claim has been stated. It is possible that the Government of the Netherlands submitted the claim to the Commission on the ground that the loan in question was a forced loan exacted by the insurgent government in control of the State of Falcon; but this is not clear, and at any rate such a contention would have been contrary to the facts in the case.[10] In any event, the commissioners failed to agree and the case thus came before the umpire for his opinion and decision. Umpire Plumley pointed out that there was no evidence that

> General Rivera held any office de facto or de jure under the authority or by the consent of the Republic of Venezuela. Indeed, it is recognized and admitted that such government as there was under him was in direct opposition to the constitutional Government, and was seeking the life of that Government. So far from having the authority to pledge the Government of the Republic of Venezuela for moneys or goods, every dollar received in value by General Rivera was to be used for the destruction of the Government, which it is now sought to charge with its payment.[11]

He then took special notice of the fact that there was " no claim or proof that the loan of the money or the delivery of the goods was in fact compulsory "; but that, on the contrary, it was a claim " resting upon a basis of contract voluntarily entered into

9 If it was the intention of the claimant here to argue that Venezuela was liable, as a federal state, for acts and contracts of an insurgent government in control of a component state, this point was not discussed either by the Commission or by the umpire.

10 The assumption that this might have been a forced loan was answered by the umpire to the effect that even if such was the case, which would be the strongest position to which this claim could be assigned, " it would not then occupy such relation to the constitutional Government as would require its payment out of the treasury of such Government " because the insurgents did not have the right to act in the name and on behalf of Venezuela. Ralston, *Ven. Arb. 1903*, 898.

11 *Henriquez case*, *ibid.*, 896, 897.

between him and those who as revolutionists had received his money and goods." He therefore held that "as resting on such voluntary contract it would have no standing whatever before this Commission." On this point he said:

While the government of General Rivera might have been a de facto government for certain municipal purposes within the State or District, when, for the time his was the supreme force, he had power to compel respect and obedience, it lacked all of the characteristics of a de facto national government that could speak and act in the name of Venezuela. . . .

A de facto government which would give this claim a position before this Commission must be one recognized as such for the Republic of Venezuela, and not one temporarily in authority in a State or district under revolution and against the will and purpose of the de jure and de facto government of the nation. Such a rule may work occasional hardship in the individual case, but it is the unvarying rule of international law, and taken as a whole works beneficially to the nation at large. Insurrections and revolutions are to be deplored, and the cases of especial hardship resulting within the territory subject to such conditions may call for sympathy, but they can have no right of compensation from the national treasury. Insurrections and revolutions more than all other forms of belligerency are always against the will of the constituted government and originate without its ability in any way to prevent them. To hold the government responsible for the means by which its life is sought would be destructive of all governmental conditions.[12]

The principle thus stated has been applied also to loans made to unsuccessful insurgents who were attempting to secede and establish a new state in international law. During the Civil War the Confederate Government issued certain "cotton-loan bonds" in England, and a large number of British subjects purchased these rebel bonds with the expectation of big profits. The fact that cotton was hypothecated in favor of the bondholders seems to have given the assurance that the loan would be repaid out of the proceeds of the cotton whatever the ulti-

12 *Henriquez case*, Ralston, *Ven. Arb. of 1903*, 896, 899.

mate outcome of the conflict. At the time many people in England were under the definite impression that the Confederate Government was actually within reach of final victory; they were certain at any rate that in the event of the restoration of peace without victory the rebel States would insist that the United States undertake the financial obligations arising from this particular bond issue as a condition of peace. After the Civil War, when it was clear that the Government of the United States not only would not assume the rebel debt [13] but that it had also appropriated for its own use the cotton which was pledged as security, the British bondholders attempted to induce "Her Majesty's Government to intervene on their behalf with the Government of the United States and obtain from them payment of the bonds issued by the late *de facto* Confederate Government." [14] The matter was referred by the Foreign Office to the Law Officers of the Crown for an opinion on the question as to whether the British Government should intervene and make representations to the Government of the United States. In his capacity as a Law Officer, Sir Robert Phillimore advised the Foreign Office against such intervention chiefly on the ground, *inter alia,* that the United States is not bound "by the principles, rules and precedents of international law to pay to the Foreign Creditor debts owing to him from the Confederate Government." He denied that the British recognition of Confederate belligerency had created any new right in that respect, and said:

13 From the beginning the United States denied liability for the rebel loan as being a hostile act and "a direct engagement with armed insurgents." Mr. Seward, Sec. of State, to Mr. Adams, Min. to England, April 10, 1863, *For. Rel.* 1863, I, 210-211; Mr. Adams to Lord Russell, April 28, 1863, *For. Rel.* 1863, I, 239; Mr. Seward to Mr. Adams, March 13, 1865, *For. Rel.* 1865, I, 205-206; Same to same, March 13, 1865, *For. Rel.* 1865, I, 202. See also article XIV, sec. 4, of the amendments to the Constituion of the United States, adopted in 1868.

14 For the text of the bondholders' memorial to the Foreign Office see Report of Sir Robert Phillimore, Law Officer of the Crown, to Lord Stanley, Feb. 13, 1867, H. A. Smith, *Great Britain and the Law of Nations*, I, 412.

Her Majesty proclaimed a strict neutrality and enjoined it upon her subjects, admonishing them that if they aided either belligerent they would do so at their own peril—and without any claim upon her assistance, if evil consequences ensued to them therefrom.

To furnish a belligerent with money is to render him the most material aid, to supply him with the very sinews of war. Let me moreover suggest some tests by which both the duty of the neutral Government towards its subjects, and the *jus victoris*, may be tried.

If the money, *in specie*, advanced by the Memorialists to the Southerners had been captured on its way out to them?—If the United States Army had seized the money *in specie* in the Treasury of the Confederates? If instead of money munitions of war, ships, cannons, and the like had been furnished by the Memorialists, and the United States Army had seized these articles for which Cotton Bonds had been given as a security, and afterwards the very Cotton itself which was pledged for their payment? In any or all of these instances the unfitness of any intervention on the part of Her Majesty's Goverment would be apparent:—but would not be easy to distinguish, in principle, the right of Her Majesty's Government to demand, on behalf of the Memorialists, from the United States repayment of the money, which had actually reached the hands of the Confederate Government, and been expended by them; from the right to do so, when the money had been captured on the high seas, or on land, or when the loan had been contracted by an exchange—immediate or promised of commodities (e. g.—So much munitions of war for so much Cotton) and these commodities had been seized *jure belli* by the Conqueror. . . .

The creditors, in this case, entered of their own free-will into a speculation which, if the Confederates had prospered, would have been lucrative, but which their failure has rendered the reverse.[15]

15 Report of Sir Robert Phillimore, Law Officer of the Crown, to Lord Stanley, Secretary for Foreign Affairs, February 13, 1867, H. A. Smith, *Great Britain and the Law of Nations*, I, 413-416.

One of the reasons offered by the bondholders for British intervention on their behalf was that under the American federal system the States were sovereign entities capable of contracting debts, and that since during the Civil War they were conquered the conqueror should therefore pay the debts of the conquered. On this point the Law Officer said: "I am of opinion, that Her Majesty's Government ought not to accede to the request of the

Although the conclusion reached here to the effect that the British Government should not intervene because the United States was not bound by the rebel loan appears to have been final in so far as diplomatic representation was concerned, the question nevertheless did not rest there. Ultimately the British Government was induced to bring the matter before the British-American Mixed Claims Commission of 1871. The Commission, however, accepted the principle expressed in the opinion cited above as to the nonliability of the United States by rendering the following decision in the *Barrett case*: [16]

> The Commission is of opinion that the United States is not liable for the payment of debts contracted by the rebel authorities. The rebellion was a struggle against the United States for the establishment in a portion of the country belonging to the United States of a new state in the family of nations, and it failed. Persons contracting with the so-called Confederate States voluntarily assumed the risk of such failure and accepted its obligation, subject to the paramount right of the parent state by force to crush the rebel organization and seize all its assets and property whether hypothecated by it or not to its creditors.[17]

Memorialists. It might be enough to say that Her Majesty's Government could not do so without to a certain extent pronouncing judgment upon the difficult question of Foreign Constitutional Law with respect to the limits of the Sovereignty of each State and their relation to the Supreme Government of the United States which in great measure gave rise to this very war. . . . Her Majesty's Government must therefore necessarily assume as the basis of their right to intervene that the very proposition of American Constitutional Law as to which this fierce controversy has arisen, and which has practically been solved by force and conquest after a bloody civil war, is nevertheless incontrovertible in the sense contended for by the Confederates and their Creditors . . . that the War which they have waged, and in which they have conquered, was unlawful, and contrary to the principles and laws of their own internal constitution. It is obvious that it is not competent to Her Majesty's Government to take this course" (*ibid.*, 413-416).

As to the question of federal liability for acts of an insurgent State see, *Montijo case*, Moore, *Int. Arb.*, II, 1421, 1439-1442; *Hanna case, ibid.*, III, 2982; *Wyman case, ibid.*, III, 2978; *De Brissot case, ibid.*, 2949.

16 Moore, *Int. Arb.*, III, 2900; Hale's *Report*, 154.

17 *Barrett case*, Moore, *Int. Arb.*, III, 2900, 2901.

From the foregoing it thus appears that the state is not bound by loans made to unsuccessful insurgents for purposes of the civil war in which they were engaged. In view of the nature of the cases discussed, this is the only conclusion reached and the only point decided. Loans made to unsuccessful insurgents for other than a belligerent purpose, such as a loan used to build a lighthouse or to pay interest on the national debt, may, as will be seen presently, produce different effect; but the principle stated above as to loans used for civil war purposes appears to be uniformly accepted. As to such belligerent loans, it has been held in effect that persons who voluntarily advance money to insurgent governments put their resources at the service of the party at war against the titular government, either because they sympathize with its ideals or because they expect to realize business profits. In either case, however, they act in aid of rebellion and render material help to the revolution. Such help may be regarded as detrimental to the state when it serves to interfere with the effort made by the state through existing governmental agencies to suppress the insurgent movement. In a word, what serves to increase the burden of suppressing an insurgent movement, the state, in consequence of the failure of that movement, must regard as detrimental to itself and as not calculated to impose upon it a new financial obligation.

II

While the principle that the state is not bound by loans made to an unsuccessful insurgent government for civil war purposes is doubtless well established and uniformly accepted, the question arises whether the state is bound (1) by unsuccessful insurgent loans which do not possess that character, or (2) by unsuccessful insurgent loans which, though intended for a belligerent purpose, present special circumstances and exceptional conditions. In the past a number of such claims have been made on the plea that they constituted exceptions. In cases where it was alleged (1) that the loan was used for projects of public utility, or (2) that it was secured by hypothecation of insurgent property, or (3) that its proceeds were wholly or partly intact either in the treasury of the insurgent government or in the hands of trustees in foreign countries, the claimants attempted to take such cases out of the operation of the general rule. It is therefore important to know how far exceptions to the principle stated above may be established by claims of this character.

1. *Loans used for projects of public utility.* In the *Stuckle case* [18] the Government of the United States contended that Mexico was liable for moneys and military supplies furnished by an American citizen to the government of Maximilian on the ground that such moneys and supplies were used for a public purpose and not for belligerent purposes against the constitutional government. It appears that the claimant made a contract with an agent of the usurper Maximilian in Yucatan, Mexico, "for a certain amount of supplies for troops raised, as it is stated, to fight against the Indians, then making inroads upon and distressing the Yucatan people." It is not clear from the facts whether a sum of money was also furnished, but the decision of the umpire does make reference to a loan. This point is not essential, however, in view of the fact that the principle is the same both in the case of a loan of money or in the case of a sale of goods on credit. A portion of the money due for these supplies was paid, apparently by the government of Maximilian, a portion remained unpaid, and this unpaid portion the United States asked the Republic of Mexico to pay for the benefit of Stuckle. Although Yucatan was at that time occupied by French troops for and in the name of Maximilian, who styled himself Emperor of Mexico and was acknowledged as such by a portion of the Mexican people, no attempt was made to hold France responsible for the claim as the actual military occupant. For the purpose of this claim Maximilian and the French troops were apparently treated as part of the insurgent movement in Mexico, and the claim was therefore lodged

18 Moore, *Int. Arb.*, III, 2935.

against Mexico. The United States argued in favor of Mexico paying the demanded sum for the benefit of the claimant on the ground that the government of Maximilian was " an authority or the authorities of Mexico " to which the money and supplies were furnished; that it was, " for the time being, the *de facto* government, no other government existing, or no other body of men possessing or wielding *public power*, or *authority*, in those regions; and every fair engagement, nay, every laudable contract, made with the temporary or *de facto* government necessarily, and in the spirit of true justice, passes over from the *de facto* government to the restored lawful authority, with all its inhering obligations." [19] In order to show that the claimant's contract was a " fair engagement " and a " laudable contract," the United States argued that " the money advanced by Stuckle was to provide for volunteers raised to fight against barbarous Indians, not against the lawful authorities of Mexico. These troops, as it were, fought for civilized men at large, against butchering savages." [20] The true basis of the instant claim was reported in Stuckle's own words as follows:

> Although the Government of Mexico does not recognize the legality of debts contracted in Mexico by a government which to-day does not exist, the Government of the Mexican Republic is bound by right and equity to satisfy the claim of the debt in question, contracted with a foreigner (meaning with himself) and for a purpose which not only was not damaging to the government of the republic, but which on the contrary was connected with the public interest of the country and with the defense of the national territory. . . . Consequently the sum claimed by the undersigned refers to a special object of public utility entirely deprived of a political interest.[21]

It is clear that both the Government of the United States and the claimant Stuckle expressly admitted that as a rule Mexico

19 *Stuckle* (*U. S.*) *v. Mexico*, Moore, *Int. Arb.*, III, 2935.

20 *Ibid.*, 2935.

21 *Ibid.*, 2936.

was not bound by loans made to the government of Maximilian, but they insisted that this particular loan was an exception since it was used for an object of public utility. Nevertheless, the Mexican Government, without discussing this particular issue, disclaimed any liability on the ground that the claim was not founded " in any act done by the authorities of Mexico " but was in fact based " on a contract for a loan with an enemy of Mexico, or a rebel, or one that acted for a usurper openly at war with the Republic of Mexico." [22]

The American and Mexican Commissioners, presumably unable to agree, referred the matter to the umpire " for his final award on the whole case." As the first umpire of the American-Mexican Mixed Claims Commission of 1868, Lieber dismissed the case with a reasoning as follows:

> It is urged that Stuckle furnished money and commodities for a *corps* destined to fight against ruthless Indians. This is possible, though we have no strong proof of the extent of that war. But whether we have or not, does not alter the law of the case. The things were furnished to a *corps* of armed men fighting under the usurper's flag, and contracted for with the authorities of a temporary government at war with that government which is now called upon to make payment to the United States on account of Stuckle. . . . The law of war, and the whole law of nations, of which it is a branch, forbid taxing the Republic of Mexico with the payment of the claim made by the United States in behalf of Stuckle. . . . My individual opinion is that it would be an evil day for America when the United States should be paid this claim for Stuckle by Mexico.[23]

22 *Stuckle Case*, Moore, *Int. Arb.*, III, 2935.

23 *Ibid.*, 2937-2938. In the course of his opinion, Lieber made a comparison between the Stuckle loan and the Confederate loan underwritten by Messrs, Emile, Erlanger & Co. of Paris, as follows: " What he (Stuckle) furnished was for a portion of the 'imperial army', in open hostility with Mexico, and now to come and claim payment for unpaid sums from that very Mexico against which claimant had furnished many of those things which soldiers stand in need of seems to me very much as if the ghost of Erlanger, the German banker, naturalized in Paris, were to rise and demand payment of

The learned umpire pointed out that Stuckle went into the business with his eyes wide open. He had heard from a relation of his that "a good deal of money might be made by shipping provisions to Yucatan for the troops to be raised by the occupying authorities; that is, by the 'imperial government'," and he took full advantage of that information. Probably he thought, as very many others did at the time, that the Mexican Republic was doomed to perish. Whether he did think so or not, however, does not affect the argument of this case, it was said. He knew at least that, in defiance of the laws of war, he was going to contract with and lend money to a government which was carrying on *de facto* war with the constitutional government of Mexico. He thus committed a hostile act against Mexico and took a bad risk, and under the circumstances there could be therefore no just ground for the liability of Mexico for his loan to the government of Maximilian.[24]

The Commission in this case was called upon to decide the definite and specific question whether Mexico was bound by a

the loans he most obsequiously made to the so-called Southern Confederacy, because Jefferson Davis and his consorts were the government *de facto* in the Southern States of this country, and the United States dissolved that government and took upon itself *ipso facto* the obligations of the Southern Confederacy. No slur whatever is intended; no comparison between the two men made. The umpire from the time when he was chief in the Archives Bureau knows the character of Erlanger, through his cringing letters to Davis; of Stuckle he has no knowledge whatever, except that which appears from the case under consideration. I simply speak of the validity of engagements with an enemy or rebel when brought before the lawful government of the assailed belligerent against whom the loan was made." *Stuckle case,* Moore, *Int. Arb.*, III, 2937.

24 Moore notes that under the convention of July 4, 1868, "Claims against Mexico growing out of the acts of the Maximilian authorities were dismissed by the commissioners in *Rodolfo Dressel v. Mexico,* No. 540; *American and Mexican Steamship Company v. Mexico,* No. 448; *George F. Knacke v. Mexico,* No. 455; *Henry Peeler v. Mexico,* No. 845. In the case of *Humphrey E. Woodhouse v. Mexico,* No. 595, the claim was dismissed by Sir Edward Thornton, on the ground that the injury alleged was committed by a person who was shown to have been in the service of the imperialists." *Int. Arb.*, III, 2938.

loan made to a local *de facto* government but used for an object of public utility, that is, to fight against ruthless Indians. The umpire dismissed this important question by a brief comment to the effect that " we have no strong proof of the extent of that war," and that " whether we have or not, does not alter the law of the case." He then went on to decide the case by applying the principle that the state is not bound by loans made to an unsuccessful insurgent government, although that principle, as already seen, should strictly apply only to insurgent loans used for civil war purposes. The decision thus turned out to be a convincing argument in favor of the general rule already discussed. He took the position that the general rule was " the law of the case " and that proof or no proof Mexico was not bound by the loan in question chiefly because the deal was with an enemy or rebel government fighting against the constitutional government of that country. For the purpose of this case, therefore, the umpire expressly rejected the proposed exception to the general rule.

In view of the fact that this is the only case in which the question of the public use of unsuccessful insurgent loans has been raised as the sole issue before an international tribunal,[25] it is to be regretted that neither the Commission nor the umpire deemed it worthwhile to discuss the possibility whether a different decision would have been rendered had the claimant been in a position to furnish " strong proof " in support of his claim that the loan was used for an object of public utility. It was perhaps impossible for the claimant to furnish more positive and convincing proof that the military supplies in question were

25 See, however, the *Cucullu case* where the claimant argued that the loan was to be used " in the service of the nation," although in fact the money was advanced by an American citizen to certain partisans of the insurgent Zuloaga government in the United States for a military expedition to aid insurgents in Mexico. Apparently the argument was not seriously intended, because what the claimant really meant was that money advanced to Zuloaga to overthrow the Mexican Government was money used " in the service of the nation." However, the decision in this case was rendered on an entirely different ground. Moore, *Int. Arb.*, III, 2873; IV, 3477. *Infra*, p. 72.

used solely against ruthless Indians. Such a failure to prove the allegation would have been sufficient ground for dismissing the case.

Nevertheless, the theory that exceptions should be made to the principle of nonliability in cases where the insurgent loan was used for an object of public utility, or where the state was in any way benefited by it, has its merits. In fact, it has a limited sanction in state practice. On at least two occasions states have undertaken obligations arising from unsuccessful insurgent loans actually applied to the public debt. In 1832 the restored government of Portugal made a distinction between two kinds of loans issued by the revolutionary government of Don Miguel. Two so-called internal loans the proceeds of which were apparently used by the Miguel government for the payment of the state debts were maintained.[26] An external loan, on the other hand, the proceeds of which were intended to finance the civil war was declared invalid and void.[27] The same distinction was applied by Mexico in dealing with the Huerta loan of 1913. This particular loan has an immediate bearing on the question under discussion and therefore requires consideration here.

The government of General Huerta came into power on February 19, 1913, as a result of the overthrow of the federal administration of President Madero in the capital of Mexico. Huerta was the military commander of the Mexican capital, charged with the protection of the administration of President Madero against the revolutionary activities of General Reyes and General Felix Diaz, when on February 18, 1913, he revolted and joined cause with Madero's enemies. He imprisoned both President Madero and the Vice President and compelled them to tender their resignations; he then took control of the federal machinery of government and declared himself pro-

26 This is on the authority of Rougier, *Les guerres civiles et le droit des gens*, sec. 133; Alglave et Renault, *De le personalité de l'Etat en matière d'emprunt*, 1880, *passim*; Politis, *Les emprunts d'Etat en droit international*, ch. II.

27 For a discussion of the Miguel loan of 1832 see, *infra*, p. 32.

visional president of Mexico.[28] But although within a few hours he thus established himself in the federal administration, his regime faced armed opposition almost from the very beginning. On the day he assumed the presidency of Mexico, General Carranza, who was governor of the State of Coahuila, officially declined to recognize him as "Chief of the Executive power of the Republic, which he alleges to have been conferred upon him by the Senate," [29] and shortly thereafter followed the armed conflict between Huerta and Carranza.[30] There is no doubt, of course, that during the early part of the civil war which ensued Huerta was in control of the larger part of Mexico. This and the fact that he dominated the federal machinery of government in the capital, including the foreign office and the treasury, were perhaps the main reasons why his government was recognized by certain foreign powers within the first four months of his revolution.[31] In the opinion of many people Huerta's government at this early stage was the government of Mexico.[32]

28 *For. Rel.*, 1913, 721 *et seq.* In order to give constitutional sanction to his assumption of power, Huerta forced the provisional acting president to appoint him the ranking minister in office and resign immediately thereafter, which thus made Huerta president according to the letter of the Mexican Constitution. The General Claims Commission of 1923 between the United States and Mexico points out, however, that irrespective of this fact Huerta's power was a mere usurpation, and goes on to say that this arbitrary act was confirmed by the Mexican Congress from which Huerta's antagonists had fled and which could not actually muster a quorum. *Hopkins case, Opinions,* 1927, 42, 43. See also *For. Rel.*, 1913, 721.

29 See text of the decree of February 19, 1913, issued by Carranza in his capacity as governor of the State of Coahuila, *For. Rel.*, 1913, 721.

30 *For. Rel.*, 1913, 734, 765.

31 Huerta's government was not recognized by the United States chiefly because of an executive policy inaugurated by President Wilson to the effect that his administration would recognize no government in the countries south of the Rio Grande which came into power as a result of revolution. See President Wilson's Annual Message to Congress, December 2, 1913.

32 The General Claims Commission of 1923, United States and Mexico, apparently had a difficult task in deciding whether the Huerta government was or was not the government of Mexico. For certain purposes the Commission treated it as an unsuccessful insurgent government. *Hopkins case, Opinions,* 1927, 42, 48.

However, the fact remains that during his brief career he never succeeded in getting complete control over all Mexico and his government in fact never achieved the status of a general *de facto* government of that country. For the purpose of this study, therefore, the Huerta government will be treated as the government of an unsuccessful revolution.

At the height of his power, that is, sometime between February and June, 1913, when "he was paramount in the north, the center, and the south of Mexico,"[33] Huerta floated a bond issue in the name of Mexico notwithstanding uprisings against him in several States and in many parts of the country. Subscriptions for this loan came chiefly from foreign bankers, including a private banking firm in the United States.[34] There were three series of this bond issue, designated as A, B, and C series bonds. After the fall of Huerta, the Carranza government refused to recognize the liability of Mexico for this bond issue, including all of the three series. This was in line with his earlier decrees issued in 1913 and in 1916 to the effect that in case of his ultimate success he would not recognize the validity of the acts and contracts done by General Huerta "in his character as Chief of the Executive power of the Republic" of Mexico.[35] When Obregon came into power as the result of the revolution of 1920, he was urged by the international bankers to undertake the payment of these bonds as an obligation of Mexico. At first it was the intention of these bankers to induce

33 The phrase is that of the General Claims Commission of 1923, United States and Mexico, *Hopkins case, Opinions*, 1927, 42, 49.

34 On June 2, 1913, the American ambassador to Mexico telegraphed to the Secretary of State of the United States as follows: "Mexican loan of 200,000,000 pesos has been definitely concluded. Speyer Brothers share in this loan as creditors and also directly through their European houses." *For. Rel.*, 1913, 806.

35 Carranza's decree of February 19, 1913, reads in part as follows: "General Victoriano Huerta is not recognized in his character of Chief of the Executive power of the Republic, which he alleges to have been conferred upon him by the Senate; and none of his acts and orders in that capacity are recognized." *For. Rel.*, 1913, 721.

the Obregon government to assume liability for all of the three series of bonds, but the final result was in fact a compromise. Ultimately Mexico assumed liability only for the series A bonds, with the bankers presumably foregoing their claims for the series B and C bonds.[36] The reason advanced for the willingness of the Obregon government to admit the obligation of the first series of bonds but to repudiate the other two series of the same issue was that the proceeds of the one were applied to the payment of the interest on the preexisting debt of Mexico, while the proceeds of the others were used for the purchase of arms, munitions, and the like, in order to maintain in power the Huerta administration and to carry on civil war.

The principle invoked in this instance in maintaining one series of bonds and repudiating other series of bonds of the same issue is doubtless subject to different interpretations. In referring to it in the *Hopkins case*,[37] the General Claims Commission of 1923 between the United States and Mexico refrained from expressing an opinion as to the propriety of application of a legal principle in such form, but seems to have regarded it as a good illustration of a cleavage between acts of an impersonal character done by the government itself as an abstract entity and acts of a personal character done by a revolutionary administration in support of the particular persons administering the government for the time being. After making

36 The agreement of 1922 between the Obregon government and the international committee of bankers concerning the settlement of the external debts contracted by Huerta in behalf of Mexico did not make a provision for and expressly excluded "such bonds of the Huerta issues (following so-called issue 'A') which are held by bankers as collateral," that is, series B and C Bonds. See text of the agreement, *Commercial and Financial Chronicle*, Sept. 9, 1922, 1155.

The Mexican view was made clear prior to this agreement. Mexico refused to recognize any obligations arising from "debts contracted during Huerta's usurpation, including the Packing House loan." *Ibid.*, July 1, 1922, 17. See also the *Current History Magazine*, Vol. 15, 360; Vol. 16, 911, 1019; Vol. 17, 353.

37 *Hopkins case, Opinions*, 1927, 42. See *infra*, Ch. III.

the distinction between acts of an unsuccessful insurgent administration in its personal aspect, which it held not to bind the state, and acts of government routine, which it held to bind the state, the Commission said:

> The same cleavage was recognized in connection with the financial transactions of the Huerta administration by later administrations of the Government of Mexico. The series of Mexican bonds issued during the Huerta regime, the proceeds of which were applied to the payment of the interest on the preexisting debt of Mexico, have been uniformly recognized as valid, while other series of the same issue, the proceeds of which are claimed to have been applied to the maintenance in power of the Huerta administration or to the purchase of arms, munitions, and the like, have been repudiated. The Commission here expresses no opinion with respect to the application made by Mexico of the principle invoked in recognizing as valid one series of bonds and repudiating another series of the same issue. The latter is referred to here only to point out that the principle which the Commission applies in this case has been recognized and invoked by the Government of Mexico under administrations of unquestioned regularity and validity.[38]

What in effect the Commission did was to treat the act of the Huerta government in issuing the series A bonds, which was used to pay interest on the public debt and for which Mexico assumed liability, as an act of government routine[39] and therefore valid and binding; while it regarded the same government's act in issuing the series B and C bonds, which were used for civil war purposes and for which Mexico assumed no liability, as an act in aid of rebellion and therefore invalid and void. This is doubtless good law, and shows the recent trend in the development of the law as applied to acts of unsuccessful insurgent governments. At the time Lieber decided the *Stuckle case*[40] the generally accepted theory was that un-

38 *Hopkins case*, General Claims Commission of 1923, United States and Mexico, *Opinions*, 1927, 42, 46-47.

39 *Infra*, Ch. III.

40 *Supra*, p. 20.

successful insurgent governments were not "authorities" of the state and therefore could not bind the state. This is a fair deduction from the language of the early cases decided by international claims commissions dealing with acts and contracts of such governments. In recent years, however, this theory has been subjected to very considerable change.[41] On the theory that an unsuccessful insurgent government is not wholly alien to the state, international tribunals no longer hesitate to hold the state bound by a greater number of acts and contracts of such governments than was done in the nineteenth century. Indeed, there is no good reason why an international tribunal, when faced with a clear cut issue of this sort, should not hold the state bound by an unsuccessful insurgent loan used for a purpose of public utility, as contrasted with an insurgent loan used for civil war purposes by which, as already seen, the state is not bound. Such a result may be predicated on two grounds. First, that it is only just and equitable that the state should make compensation in cases where there is convincing evidence that it derived benefits from an unsuccessful insurgent loan, instead of being injured by it. Secondly, following the course suggested by the American-Mexican General Claims Commission of 1923, that such a loan may be deemed to be an act of government routine and therefore binding on the state.

2. *Loans secured by hypothecation of insurgent property.* After the American Civil War the British bondholders of the Confederate States loan were apparently convinced that they had a good claim against the United States because of the fact that the loan in question, though used for a belligerent purpose, was nevertheless secured by Confederate cotton captured by the Federal Government. As it has been seen, this was one of the chief grounds of their appeal to the British Government to intervene on their behalf with the Government of the United States and obtain from them payment of the bonds issued by

41 Silvanie, "Responsibility of States for Acts of Insurgent Governments," *American Journal of International Law*, Vol. 33 (1939), 78, 90-103.

the Confederate Government.[42] Failing in that effort, they brought the matter before the British-American Claims Commission of 1871. In the *Barrett case* [43] a British claimant alleged that in 1864 he purchased and was still the possessor and absolute owner of certain "cotton-loan bonds" of the Confederate States of America, and asked for recovery specifically on the ground, *inter alia,* that the Government of the United States in 1865 "seized all the public assets of the said Confederate States and especially a very large quantity of cotton, hypothecated by the said Confederate States government for payment of the said cotton loan, and thus prevented those States from paying their cotton loan bondholders." The Commission, however, held that the United States was not bound by the debt of the Confederate Government, and said:

Persons contracting with the so-called Confederate States voluntarily assumed the risk of such failure and accepted its obligations, subject to the paramount right of the parent state by force to crush the rebel organization and seize all its assets and property whether hypothecated by it or not to its creditors. Such belligerent right of the United States to seize and hold was not subordinate to the right of creditors of the rebel organization, created by contract with the

42 *Supra,* p. 18. Newspaper reports of the Confederate bondholders' meetings in 1865 make very interesting reading. In these meetings the following questions were discussed: (1) Whether the contractors of the loan, Messrs. Emile, Erlanger & Co. of Paris, or their agents in London, Messrs. Schroeder, had money in hand to pay the coupons. (2) Whether the Confederate States had any property on which the bondholders might have a preferential lien, as against the Federal Government. This was apparently on the basis of the decision in the *United States v. Prioleau* (1865), 13 Law Times Reports 92 (3) Whether each State member of the Confederacy was liable for a proportional share of the debt. (4) Whether the Federal Government was liable as conqueror of the Confederate States and possessor of their property, presumably on the theory that the Confederate States were not in rebellion, but as independent states had right of war in the sense of international law and were conquered. See *London Daily News,* Sept. 6 and 16, 1865; *London Morning Post,* Oct. 19, 1865; *For. Rel.,* 1865, I, 529-535, 620-622.

43 *Moore, Int. Arb.,* III, 2900; Hale's *Report,* 154.

latter; and when such seizure was actually accomplished, it put an end to any claim of the property which the creditor otherwise might have had. We are therefore of opinion that after such seizure the claimant had no interest in the property, and the claim is dismissed.[44]

No other decision was possible in this case, in view of the fact that the rebel loan in question was used for a belligerent purpose and therefore created no obligation binding on the United States.

3. *Loans the proceeds of which are wholly or partly intact.* Can the creditors of an unsuccessful insurgent government claim exceptional treatment in cases where the whole or a part of the proceeds of a loan is found intact either in the insurgent treasury or in the hands of trustees in the creditors' own country. This question has never been presented to international tribunals for adjudication. However, it was an important consideration in the final settlement of both the Miguel loan and the De Valera loan. The first resulted in a prolonged controversy and a compromise between Portugal and Miguel's foreign creditors; the second was decided by courts in the United States and in the Irish Free State.

The Miguel loan of 1832 is one of the earliest and doubtless one of the most widely discussed cases involving the question of the liability of the state for foreign loans and financial contracts of an unsuccessful insurgent government.[45] It appears that on the death of King John VI of Portugal his elder son, Don Pedro, who was already emperor of Brazil, became also king of Portugal. Don Pedro, however, decided to surrender

44 *Ibid.*, 2900, 2901.

45 See especially Alglave et Renault, *De la personalite de l'Etat en matiere d'emprunt*, 1880, 18-30. These writers are the most consistent advocates of the liability of Portugal for the Miguel loan perhaps because of their purported connection with the case as counsel to the bondholders. See also Calvo, *Droit international*, I, sec. 102; Politis, *Les emprunts d'Etat en droit international*, Ch. II, 145-156; Rougier, *Des guerres civiles et le droit des gens*, sec. 136.

his Portuguese crown to his daughter Maria, a little girl of seven years of age, with the understanding that she should become the wife of his younger brother, Don Miguel, who was made regent in the minority of Dona Maria. Miguel, however, promptly repudiated his promises and by means of a coup d'etat in 1828 declared himself king of Portugal and thus became the actual sovereign in opposition to the legitimate claims of Pedro and Maria. Portugal was brought under the control of the Miguel government, with the exception of the islands of the Azores, which were and remained under the control of the legitimists headed by Pedro, who returned from Brazil to carry on war against Miguel. The civil struggle thus commenced in 1828 lasted until 1833, although for the first four years the legitimists had only the Azores under their control. Miguel continued to be the ruler of the Portuguese mainland until July 1832, when the legitimists succeeded in invading the mainland and in gaining a foothold in Oporto. A year later, July, 1833, they defeated Don Miguel and reestablished the old government on behalf of Dona Maria.[46]

After his coup d'etat Don Miguel floated two internal loans in 1828 and in 1831 respectively, and one external loan in 1832. The proceeds of the two internal loans were evidently used for the payment of state debts. The proceeds of the external loan, however, were intended to finance the civil war. This particular loan was issued in October 1832, three months after the legitimists succeeded in invading the Portuguese mainland, and when the government of Don Miguel was in real danger of being utterly crushed, as it was in fact crushed during the succeeding year. In view of the precarious financial conditions of the Miguel government, it is a wonder that any of these bonds were sold at all in foreign markets. As early as 1830, when the authority of Don Miguel was admittedly stronger, in commenting on the financial conditions of Portugal the *Annual Register* had the following to say about the prospects of a loan issued by Miguel in that year:

46 *Annual Register*, 1828-1833, *passim*.

He brought out a loan for 25,000,000 of francs, to be paid in twenty-five years, at the rate of 500,000 francs every six months. Nobody would touch it in Lisbon; tricks were tried to give it a name in foreign markets; but no monied man would have any thing to do with Miguel and his securities. In fact, the branches of revenue offered as securities for the loan, were already otherwise appropriated, or, like almost all the other branches of revenue, anticipated for several years to come.[47]

That this financial diagnosis was correct is proven by the fact that in 1831 the Miguel government had to resort to a forced loan to obtain money.[48] How is it, then, that he could market a foreign loan in 1832 when both politically and financially the position of his government was even more precarious? This is one of the mysteries of the situation which is difficult to explain. At any rate the loan of 1832 was issued and the bonds were marketed mainly in Paris and to a lesser extent in London. During the civil struggle the legitimist government of Dona Maria at the Azores repeatedly declared that in case of its restoration it would not recognize the validity of the loans issued by the Miguel government in the name of Portugal.[49] Manifestly this applied to the internal loans as well as to the foreign loan of 1832. When that government was restored, however, it undertook the financial obligations arising from the two internal loans, but refused to recognize the foreign loan. Its position concerning the foreign loan seems to have been confusing. In the first place, while formally declaring that it was not bound by the loan, it nevertheless made a definite promise as a matter of generosity to return to the foreign lenders any funds representing the unused balance of the loan found in the public treasury. In the second place, when it occupied Lisbon in July 1833 and found money and drafts of the loan in the treasury,

47 *Ibid.*, 1830, 298.

48 *Annual Register*, 1831, *passim.*

49 Calvo, *Droit international*, I, sec. 102; Alglave et Renault, *op. cit.*, 30; Politis, *op. cit.*, 147.

not only did it fail to return such funds to the interested parties as promised, but sent agents to Paris and London to collect the rest of the payments due on the loan.[50]

In view of the failure of the restored government to adopt the loan, the foreign creditors of Don Miguel undertook the task of bringing about diplomatic intervention of their respective governments to obtain recognition of the loan as a public debt of the Portuguese state. They contended that the Miguel government was in fact the government of Portugal as the result of his successful coup d'etat of 1828; that his government was in full and undisputed control of the Portuguese mainland for over four years; that many of the foreign powers recognized it as the government of Portugal,[51] and therefore internationally it had the right to represent Portugal; that Don Pedro's movement in 1832 was in fact a revolt against Miguel who was the established government then and had been since 1828; that since under international law the government of a successful revolution is bound to respect the obligations of the preceding government de facto or de jure, Don Pedro was therefore bound by the foreign loan of the defeated Miguel government; and finally, that since the restored government recognized the validity of the two internal loans of the Miguel regime, it was therefore bound to recognize also the loan of 1832 because it was issued by the same authority.[52] However, the Government of Portugal absolutely refused to be bound by the loan. Failing in their main purpose, the foreign creditors presented two specific demands: first, they should be at least allowed to get hold of the properties of Don Miguel, which were already taken over by the restored government and incor-

50 See Politis, *op. cit.*, Ch. II, 147; Rougier, *op. cit.*, sec. 136.

51 "The Pope, the Emperor of Russia, and President Jackson were the only authorities on earth which ever recognized Dom Miguel as King of Portugal." Mr. Buchanan, Sec. of State, to Mr. Rush, March 31, 1848, Moore, *Digest*, I, 124.

52 For a good presentation of the viewpoint of the foreign creditors, see Alglave et Renault, *op. cit.*, 30-33, and *passim*.

porated into the public domain of the Portuguese state; secondly, that the sums found in the public treasury as the unused balance of the loan should be returned to them. A great deal of international financial pressure was brought to bear on the Portuguese Government to enforce these two demands. Eventually the credit of Portugal became so endangered that in 1892, sixty years after the date of the original loan, the government of that country decided to meet only the foreign creditors' second demand and return to them the sums found in the public treasury representing the unused balance of the loan at the time the legitimist government entered Lisbon in 1833.[53]

This case raises a number of very interesting questions. One important question is, was Portugal bound by the Miguel loan of 1832? If not, did the fact that it undertook the obligations arising from the two internal loans make any difference? According to the view adopted by the succeeding Portuguese Governments after the restoration of Dona Maria, the Miguel government was and always remained the government of an unsuccessful revolution. Although the question whether the Miguel government was or was not in fact the government of Portugal will perhaps remain a matter of opinion, the Portuguese view would seem to be supported by international law. The period from 1828 to 1833 was manifestly a period of civil war for Portugal. So long as the legitimist government had even a small part of the Portuguese territory, such as the Azores, to call its own, and so long as it was either carrying on or actively preparing to carry on war against Miguel, it could not be considered as utterly crushed. By the same reasoning the Miguel government could not be considered as the government of Portugal. On the assumption that this view is correct, it follows that Portugal could not be held bound by the loan of 1832 since the loan itself was issued to finance the civil war at a time when the legitimists had already invaded the mainland and when the

53 Rougier, *op. cit.*, sec. 136; Podesta Costa, "Efectos internacionales de la actuacion de los gobiernos de facto," *Revista de la Facultad de Derecho*, Buenos Aires, 1924, Vol. III, 422.

Miguel government was fighting for its very existence. It is true that the restored government undertook the obligations of the two internal loans issued by Miguel in 1828 and 1831. But this act may be justified on quite different grounds, and can not be urged as a reason for the maintenance of the loan of 1832. In the first place, the proceeds of the two internal loans were used for the payment of the state debts and justice and equity required, as already seen, that Portugal should be bound by them.[54] In the second place, there might have been important political considerations inducing the restored government to undertake the obligations of these two loans, regardless of any legal duty to do so. By such an act Don Pedro, who was never very popular with the Portuguese people, might have intended to unify public opinion in his favor and in support of his government. Under no circumstances, therefore could the foreign creditors claim the maintenance of the first two loans as a reason for the maintenance of the loan of 1832, which was used for belligerent purposes against the legitimist government.

Another important question is, was the Government of Portugal in any way obligated to hand over the property of the Miguel government to the foreign bondholders in consideration of the loan? Did the bondholders have a preferential claim to such property as against the restored government? These questions have been definitely settled in the *Barrett case*,[55] and need no extended discussion here. There is no doubt that the bondholders had no prior claim to the properties of Miguel either as an individual or as a government. By his act of rebellion Miguel forfeited his private property to the Portuguese state, subject only to preexisting claims of private creditors of Miguel as an individual. The bondholders' claim did not fall within this category since the Miguel loan was not a private loan. As to the property of the Miguel government, the law is clearly

54 *Supra*, p. 30.

55 *Supra*, p. 18.

established that the claim of the restored government to such property is a paramount claim and is not subordinate to the right of creditors of the rebel organization.

And lastly, did the bondholders have a right to the unused balance of the loan found in the public treasury? Although in the instant case the unused balance of the loan was ultimately returned to the lenders, it is believed that it was done as a matter of expediency and not because the government admitted a legal obligation to do so. It is not clear on what ground restitution may be claimed for a loan made voluntarily in aid of rebellion. In case of a forced loan the restored government may be said to be under an obligation to make restitution to individuals of money and property forcibly taken by the unsuccessful insurgent government but recovered by it during or at the close of the civil war.[56] But in case of a loan voluntarily made to insurgents in pursuance of their political aims that principle does not operate. Lenders in such a case can not be regarded as victims of the insurgents; they are, on the contrary, persons who connive with the rebellion and thus identify themselves with the insurgents.

In the De Valera loan case [57] the main issue was in many respects quite similar to that raised in the Miguel loan case, although there existed also important differences between the two situations. In this instance the money was advanced by persons in the United States for the express purpose of helping

56 Some writers contend that although the restored government can legitimately take over property and money of unsuccessful insurgents, it nevertheless should make restitution if such property and money belong to others. This solution, it is said, is derived from a general principle of equity according to which he who, without just cause or legal formality, obtains property through the effort of some one else, must give back the property or its equivalent to the titular owner. These writers, however, fail to limit the application of this principle to forcible taking of property. See Podesta Costa, *op. cit.*, 426; Rougier, *op. cit.*, sec. 136.

57 As to the facts of the De Valera revolution and of the loan under consideration see, *Fogarty and Others v. O'Donoghue and Others* (1926), Irish Reports, 531; *Irish Free State v. Guaranty Safe Deposit Co.*, 222 N. Y. Supp. 182.

the so-called Dail Eirean government to establish an independent Irish republic in 1919 and 1920. The De Valera revolution, however, failed of immediate success and no such republic was in fact established; although as an ultimate result of this insurgent movement the Irish Free State was later created. Part of the loan was taken to Ireland and either actually used for belligerent purposes or banked there; the balance of the subscriptions was deposited in a New York bank with De Valera and others as trustees. After the final settlement of the Irish question in 1922, no attempt was made by the American bondholders of this Dail Eirean government loan to ask either the British Government or the Government of the Irish Free State to undertake the repayment of the money thus advanced. In view of the fact, however, that unused balances of this loan still existed in the hands of trustees both in Ireland and in the United States, the Government of the Irish Free State brought two actions, one in its own courts and the other in the courts of the United States, to take possession of the money. In *Fogarty and Others v. O'Donoghue and Others,*[58] decided by the Irish courts, the Free State Government claimed possession of the funds in Ireland both by title paramount, on the ground that it was in fact the continuation of the very Dail Eirean which raised the money, and by derivative title, on the ground that it was the successor of the original *de facto* government or of the revolutionary group. It also consented to undertake the obligations arising from the loan and to make provisions for its repayment.[59] The Irish court rendered its decision in favor of the plaintiff government and the defendants were ordered to deliver to the Minister of Finance of the Irish

58 (1926) Irish Reports, 531.

59 The Government of the Irish Free State kept its promise and in April 1935 it began to make the first repayment to the American bondholders of about $5,200,000, including interest of 25 cents on each dollar. The original loan amounted to about $5,800,000 raised by an aggregate of 309,000 subscriptions. Part of this money, as it will be seen, was returned to the subscribers in 1930 by decision of the New York Supreme Court. See the *N. Y. Times,* March 28, 1935.

Free State all the moneys, securities, and other property received by them on behalf of the revolutionary Dail Eirean government. This decision was predicated chiefly on the ground that the Dail Eirean government which originally raised the money in 1919 and in 1920 ultimately became the government of Ireland in the person of the Free State Government, that the latter was in fact the continuation of the former and could therefore claim the funds in question by paramount title.[60] In effect, the court regarded the revolutionary Dail as the government of a successful revolution and not as a mere unsuccessful insurgent government. As such, this case therefore has no immediate bearing on the question under consideration here. In the *Irish Free State v. Guaranty Safe Deposit Company*,[61] decided by the New York Supreme Court, the Free State Government claimed possession of the funds in the hands of trustees in New York again by title paramount and by derivative title, but this time it was unwilling to undertake the obligations arising from the loan and would not take the funds subject to an accounting with the trustees. The court held that the plaintiff Free State Government was not entitled to the funds in question because it was neither the continuation nor the successor of the revolutionary Dail which originally raised the money. The court further said that even if the Free State Government had derivative title to the funds, it could not be awarded possession thereof in an action in equity, where it did not adopt the loan contract nor submit itself to the equitable jurisdiction of the court. Similarly, the trustees were denied further possession of the funds on the ground that the insurgent government existed no longer. The case was therefore dismissed and the funds returned to the subscribers.[62] This was in line with the con-

60 See especially opinion of Judge FitzGibbon, *Fogarty and Others v. O'Donoghue and Others* (1926) Irish Reports, 531, 565.

61 222 N. Y. Supp. 182.

62 The New York Supreme Court appointed receivers who paid to one portion of the subscribers about $2,500,000, or about 58 cents on the dollar, which represented the balance of the loan in New York banks. When the

tention of the two committees of bondholders who were allowed to intervene. It was the position of these bondholders' committees that if the court was to decide in favor of the plaintiff government, the Free State should be required to adopt the original loan contract with the insurgents, which provided for the repayment of the money "after the freeing of the territory of the Republic of Ireland from Britain's military control"; otherwise, it was said, the funds should be returned to the subscribers.[63]

The result obtained in these cases goes to show that if the unused balance of an unsuccessful insurgent loan is found in the creditors' own country, their courts will make restitution regardless of the question whether such loan was intended for belligerent use or not. Such courts consider it a primary duty to protect the interests of their nationals first. Doubtless this was the intent of the decision of the New York Supreme Court in returning to the subscribers the balance of the De Valera loan found within the jurisdiction of the United States. However, if the unused balance of an insurgent loan is found in the insurgent treasury by the restored government, the right of the lenders to such balance would seem to depend largely on the character of the loan in question. If the loan was for a belligerent purpose, the balance will not be returned to the creditors by the restored government the result in the Miguel case notwithstanding, since such a loan must be regarded as an act in aid of rebellion. If, on the other hand, the loan was

entire loan was repaid in 1935, the difference, plus the regular 25 per cent interest, was paid back to these 1930 claimants. See *N. Y. Times*, March 28, 1935.

63 In the instant case one of the assumptions of the New York Supreme Court was that legally the Free State Government was the successor of the Government of Great Britain and Ireland and not that of the revolutionary Dail. If so, the claim for the funds in New York should be considered to have been made by the British Government through its successor in Ireland. This view will put this case in the same category as the Confederate property cases decided in England after the Civil War. See the *United States v. Prioleau*, 13 Law Times Reports, 92; *United States v. McRae*, 20 Law Times Reports, 476.

for a purpose of public utility having no relation to the civil conflict, the lenders, as already seen, may have a right to the maintenance of the whole loan contract, since it can not be contended that such a loan was detrimental to the state. At any rate, their right to the unused balance of such loan appears to be just and equitable.

III

In a number of cases dealing with loans made to unsuccessful insurgent governments the state has been charged with liability expressly on the alleged ground that such insurgent government was the government of the state and therefore entitled to act in its name. In such cases the question whether the state is or is not bound by such loan becomes fundamentally a question of evidence. The burden of proof is on the creditors to show that the loan in question was made to an insurgent government which was already in control of the state at the time of the loan or established itself in power shortly thereafter. The question therefore has been raised as to what constitutes revolutionary success. Does the possession of the capital indicate that the insurgent government is the government of the state? Is recognition of the insurgent government by a foreign power or powers a proof of revolutionary success? Is a foreign creditor protected by the fact of recognition of the insurgent government by his own state?

In the *Cucullu case* [64] a claim was made by an American citizen against Mexico for the payment of money advanced to the revolutionary Zuloaga government on the ground that that government was in fact the government of Mexico. The loan was made at New Orleans on February 2, 1858, at about the beginning of the Zuloaga revolution, to certain partisans of Zuloaga who were then living in the United States and who wished to return to Mexico and take part in the revolution. The money was to be used "in the service of the nation," and was

64 Moore, *Int. Arb.*, III, 2873; IV, 3477.

to be repaid in installments from the proceeds of the maritime custom-houses whenever the revolutionary party should capture any. The funds were in fact used to enable certain generals who had been driven into exile by the Mexican Government and who were " so much needed by General Zuloaga to return to the scene of the pending struggle and play a useful part in establishing the new government and in capturing the maritime custom-houses," all of which were held at the time by the constitutional government. Part of the loan was paid to each of the exiles presumably for transportation purposes, and the balance invested in munitions of war for the use of the Zuloaga government against the government established under the Mexican constitution of 1857.[65]

The United States and Mexican Claims Commission of 1868 held that Mexico was not bound by the loan on the ground, *inter alia,* that at the date of the loan contract the Zuloaga government was not and never did become an " authority " of the Mexican nation, that is, the government of Mexico.[66] The Commission pointed out that in order to consider an insurgent government an " authority " of the state, it should be a *de*

65 For the facts in this case see especially the opinion of Commissioner Wadsworth, Moore, *Int. Arb.*, IV, 3477-3480. The American and Mexican Commissioners rendered separate but concurring opinions.

66 The claim was dismissed for another reason which has no direct bearing on the main question under consideration here. The Commission pointed out that the loan was used " to provide the means for a hostile enterprise from the shores of the United States against the constitutional government of Mexico," and raised the point that by the *lex loci* the contract itself was invalid since it was made in violation of the neutrality laws of the United States. It was thus contended that the loan was used for an unneutral purpose, that is, to provide means for a military expedition. It was also pointed out that the hostile enterprise was in violation of the treaty between the United States and Mexico as well as in violation of the American neutrality laws. The American Commissioner said: " It is certain that the municipal courts of the sovereign whose laws have been violated, bound to uphold the laws by their decisions, will treat the contract as a nullity." Both Commissioners expressed the opinion that for these reasons the Government of the United States should have declined to present the claim. *Cucullu* (*U. S.*) *v. Mexico*, Moore, *Int. Arb.*, IV, 3478-3481.

facto government in general control and fully established. It was shown that the Zuloaga government was never in general control of Mexico, nor did it receive the " habitual obedience " of the " bulk " of the people of the United Mexican States.[67] The facts disclosed that on January 11, 1858, General Zuloaga, who had been in command of a brigade in the Mexican capital, inaugurated a revolution against President Comonfort and after a conflict of nine days defeated and drove him out of the capital on January 20, 1858. He immediately named a junta called " representatives of the States," but " who were simply truculent followers of Zuloaga resident in the city," and this junta named him president on the 21st of January. On the 22nd of January all the diplomatic representatives of the foreign powers at the capital, except the American minister, recognized his government. The American minister followed this example on the 27th of January.[68] It also appeared that " the regular army almost entirely supported the Zuloaga rebellion; the great riches of the clergy were profusely employed in its favor; the old monarchical party, in which there

67 After stating that an insurgent government should be in possession of the " sovereignty " of a state before it can be regarded as the government, Commissioner Wadsworth said: " When may this sovereignty be said to exist? Perhaps Mr. Austin, in his lectures on jurisprudence, has expressed this notion of sovereignty as concisely and accurately as anyone: ' If a determinate human superior, not in a habit of obedience to a like superior, receives *habitual* obedience from the *bulk* of a given society, that determinate superior is sovereign in that society, and the society (including the superior) is a society political and independent.' (Vol. I, p. 226.) Says Wheaton: ' The habitual obedience of the members of any political society to a superior authority must have once existed in order to constitute a sovereign state.' (Dana's ed., p. 34.) This habitual obedience of the members of a political society (of the ' bulk ' of them) must, in fact, exist, to constitute a government." *Cucullu case*, Opinion of Wadsworth, Moore, *Int. Arb.*, III, 2876-2877.

68 In the instant case the Commission was under the impression that the American minister's recognition of the Zuloaga government was not approved by his government. Opinion of Wadsworth, Moore, *Int. Arb.*, III, 2873-2881. However, in later cases it was shown that this was a mistake and that approval had been given. See especially *McKenny case, ibid.*, 2881-2885; *Jansen case, ibid.*, 2902-2931.

were some able and influential men, constituted the nucleus of the rebels"; and that the revolutionary movement was "seconded in the capitals of some of the states, and the leaders of these local movements assumed the characters of governors of said States, and made themselves obeyed in proportion to the armed forces they could employ."[69] But although Zuloaga was in control of the capital and of certain other parts of the republic, his government never succeeded in getting general control of Mexico, On the contrary, an immense majority of the people took sides with President Juarez, who as vice-president and chief justice succeeded to the presidency under the constitution of 1857 after the fall of President Comonfort, and under his direction they fought until they finally triumphed and reestablished the constitution of 1857.

As evidence of the existence of the Zuloaga government as the supreme government of Mexico the claimant apparently relied chiefly on the fact that it was recognized as such by almost all the diplomatic representatives of the foreign powers, including the claimant's own state. The Commission, however, refused to attribute any constitutive force to recognition, and denied that recognition alone could create a government. It said in effect that recognition in this instance was due to the fact that the Zuloaga government was in control of the capital and of the federal machinery of government in Mexico and not because it was the established government. It maintained that neither the possession of the capital nor recognition by foreign powers is sufficient evidence of the existence of an insurgent government as the government of the state, and said:

Recognition is based upon the preexisting fact; does not create the fact. If this does not exist, the recognition is falsified. It may entail unpleasant consequences upon the power which improperly accords it, but can not increase or diminish the rights or obligations of the other government struggling to maintain its supre-

69 *Cucullu case*, Opinion of Palacio, Mexican Commissioner, Moore, *Int. Arb.*, III, 2880-2881.

macy. If, therefore, the Zuloaga government in Mexico was the government *de facto*, it was because the facts existing at the time made it so. If it was a government, *the* government in Mexico, it was because it claimed and possessed the sovereignty over that independent nation we call " the Republic of the United Mexican States " . . .

It will be seen how absurd it is to claim that on the 27th day of January 1858 the " habitual obedience " of the " bulk " of the people of the United Mexican States had been shown to the . . . armed pretension of the Zuloaga brigade. . . . In the light of subsequent events, at least, no man can doubt that the vast majority of the Mexican people refused obedience to Zuloaga and adhered to the constitutional government, making good their rights by force of arms.

It will not change this essential and controlling fact to plead a custom amongst foreign diplomatic representatives in Mexico whereby the possessor of the capital was always recognized. It is to be hoped that no such custom had been established. If any such existed, it was simply flagitious. It offered encouragement to every bully at the head of a brigade to overthrow the government of the country, and made foreign representatives morally responsible for many of the misfortunes of Mexico. Such unwarranted conduct, however, on the part of the agents of the foreign governments could not and did not transfer this habitual obedience of the bulk of the people to the leaders of revolt in the capital.[70]

The Commission thus reached the conclusion that since the attempt of the revolutionary Zuloaga government " to establish itself as a government in fact, by force of arms, over the established and *de facto* government " of Mexico failed, neither its possession of the capital nor its recognition by foreign powers could give it at any time the status of a government in general

70 *Cucullu case*, Opinion of Wadsworth, American Commissioner, Moore, *Int. Arb.*, III, 2876-2877.

The Mexican Commissioner concurred in this view and expressed a similar view as follows: " The recognition of a new government made by foreign powers only shows that said powers *believe* that such a government is really a government. If this *belief* is not correct, it will not produce any result." Opinion of Palacio, Mexican Commissioner, *ibid.*, 2880.

control. It held, in effect, that in case of an unsuccessful revolution an insurgent loan of a foreign creditor, such as Cucullu, could not be protected by the mere fact of recognition of the insurgent government by his own state. Accordingly, the claim of Cucullu against Mexico was dismissed and disallowed on the ground that the claimant failed to prove that the Zuloaga government was in fact the government of Mexico.

In the *Jarvis case* [71] a claim was made against Venezuela for the cost of certain bonds issued to an American citizen by the revolutionary government of General Paez while it was in temporary control of the Venezuelan capital and of the federal district of Caracas. Here again the question at issue was one chiefly of proof as to whether the Paez government was or was not the government of Venezuela by virtue of the fact that it was in control of the capital and of the central machinery of government in that country. Briefly stated, the facts are that General Paez, returning to Venezuela from abroad apparently because of a pending civil conflict, was proclaimed "supreme civil and military chief of the Republic" at a public meeting of the citizens of Caracas on August 29, 1861. On September 10, 1861, he took possession of the government in Caracas and his government continued to be in control of that region until June, 1863. It was never recognized by the United States as the government of Venezuela. It appears that there were in fact two distinct governments in Venezuela during this period, one headed by Paez and another by General Falcon. On April 24, 1863, an agreement was reached between the representatives of the Paez and Falcon factions terminating the existence of the two separate governments in Venezuela and providing for a national assembly, which convened on June 17 following and appointed General Falcon president. The Falcon government was subsequently recognized by the United States. Ten days prior to the agreement with the Falcon faction to end the civil conflict, the Paez government gave certain bonds to Jarvis in

71 *Jarvis (U. S.) v. Venezuela*, Ralston, *Ven. Arb. of 1903*, 145.

consideration of his financial aid rendered to General Paez in 1849, in the latter's unsuccessful attempt in that year to overthrow the then existing Government of Venezuela. It seems that, while in exile, in 1849 Paez undertook an expedition from the United States to overthrow the constitutional government of that country. In aid and furtherance of this enterprise, Jarvis furnished General Paez with money, a steamer, and munitions of war and other equipment; but the expedition was unsuccessful, and Paez was captured and sent out of the country again to return for the same purpose in 1861. It was in consideration of this earlier service rendered by Jarvis for which the bonds in question were issued. These bonds were issued " in conformity with the resolution of the Treasury Department " of the Paez government in 1863, which resolution stated that Jarvis was to be compensated for the money he had advanced to the insurgents in 1849.[72]

In the *Cucullu case* it was noted that the United States and Mexican Claims Commission of 1868 disapproved the preferment by the United States of a claim which was based on a contract made in violation of its own neutrality laws.[73] Manifestly mindful of this, and in view of the fact that the original consideration for issuing the bonds in the present case might create complications, the American Government on behalf of Jarvis sought to limit the instant claim and asked for a decision expressly upon the merits of the case in regard to the bonds issued by the Paez government in 1863. It argued that " the

72 The resolution referred to the events of 1849 and said: "the service rendered by Mr. Jarvis in the period mentioned was very opportune, since its object tended to defend the cause of morality under the auspices of the illustrious citizen, overthrowing the ominous domination that oppressed the Republic . . . it would not be just nor right that that foreigner who so generously contributed to aid, with uncommon disinterestedness, the triumph of the same cause, whose principles this day prevail under the administration of a great number of citizens who fought for it, should suffer damages for the default of the payment of a claim to a certain part sacred." *Jarvis case*, Ralston, *Ven. Arb. of 1903*, 145, 146.

73 *Supra*, p. 43, note 66.

nature of the original consideration is immaterial; that the claim is upon the bonds of 1863, not upon the contract of 1849." After thus defining the issue, it went on to say that Venezuela was bound by the bonds in question because it was issued by the *de facto* government of that country, thus contending that the Paez government in 1863 was in fact the government of Venezuela.

Since the issue was raised in this form, the American-Venezuelan Claims Commission of 1903 undertook to ascertain, *inter alia,* the capacity of the Paez government to issue bonds in the name and on behalf of Venezuela.[74] This, it was said, was a question of fact as to whether that government was or was not the government of Venezuela at the time the bonds in question were issued in 1863. The facts showed that the Paez government was never in general control; that it was merely an insurgent government in possession of the capital and of the province of Caracas. Obviously such partial control even of the central machinery of government was not sufficient to make an insurgent government the government of the state. The Commission said that on this point

the decision of the political department of the United States Government on November 19, 1862, that there was no such conclusive evidence that the Paez government was fully accepted and peacefully maintained by the people of Venezuela as to entitle it to recognition must be accorded great weight as to the fact, *and is*

74 Aside from rendering a decision on the merits, the Commission in this case held also that the Paez bonds could not be discussed apart from the original consideration. As to this, it pointed out that the bonds were issued in consideration of the aid rendered to the unsuccessful Paez expedition of 1849 by Jarvis in violation of his duty to his country and in disobedience to its neutrality laws and the treaty then existing between the United States and Venezuela. Accordingly, it held that "a subsequent contract made in aid and furtherance of the execution of one infected with illegality partakes of its nature, rests upon an illegal consideration, and is equally in violation of the law." *Jarvis case*, Ralston, *Ven. Arb. of 1903*, 145, 150. Under this construction, Venezuela would have been absolved from liability for the bonds even though the Paez government had been found to be the government of that country in 1863.

in any event conclusive upon its own citizen. And certainly the evidence that the Paez government was "submitted to by the great body of the people" was no stronger on April 14, 1863, when the Jarvis bonds were issued and, when as a matter of historical fact, it was encompassed by its enemies and tottering to its fall.[75]

Accordingly, the claim was dismissed on the ground, *inter alia,* that sufficient evidence was not furnished by the claimant to establish that in 1863 the Paez government was the government of Venezuela; and that in fact that government was an insurgent government in local control only and therefore did not possess the capacity to act in the name and on behalf of Venezuela.

It follows from the foregoing that in order to hold the state bound by an insurgent loan expressly on the ground that the insurgent government was the government of the state, it is not sufficient to prove that the insurgent government was in control of the capital and a part of the territory of the state or that it was recognized by foreign powers. To prove that an insurgent government was the government of the state and therefore acted in its name it is necessary to show that the civil war terminated in its favor; that the titular government was destroyed and dispersed; that the whole country became under the control of the insurgent government; and that the success of the insurgent movement was a matter of public notoriety. In case of secession, the claimant must prove that the civil war was at an end at the time of the loan or ultimately came to an end in favor of the seceding party. In every case it must be established that the success and the stability of the revolutionary government was a historical fact. If a claimant submits convincing proof to this effect, an international tribunal will not hesitate to render a decision in his favor.[76]

75 *Jarvis case*, Ralston, *Ven. Arb. of 1903*, 145, 150.

76 *Supra*, p. 1, note 1.

IV

The discussion thus far has been confined to loans made by private persons to unsuccessful insurgent governments. Loans made by governments of foreign states to insurgents may now be considered. Foreign government loans to insurgents, like loans made by individuals, may also be divided into two classes: first, loans used for civil war purposes, that is, to fight the titular government; secondly, loans used for a purpose of public utility and having no relation to the civil conflict.

To the first class belong loans made by a foreign government when for reasons of its own it decides to help the insurgent party with arms and money. As example mention may be made here of the financial and military aid given by France to the colonists in America during the Revolutionary War of 1776 and by the Government of the United States to the Cuban insurgents during the Spanish-American War. In such a case, of course, a foreign government loan is an act of intervention and an act in aid of rebellion. As is the case with private loans of a similar character, if the insurgent government collapses, the disturbed state can not be held bound by such loan; if it succeeds, those who derived benefits from the loan must undertake its obligations. In view of the fact that a loan of this character made by a foreign government to insurgents is chiefly an act of intervention, a discussion of its political consequences is beyond the scope of this study.

To the second class belong two loans made by the Government of the United States to two insurgent governments in Russia, one to the Provisional Government of Russia in 1917 and the other to the *de facto* Armenian Republic in 1920, the territory of which was confined to the Russian portion of Armenia and was entirely within the territorial limits of Russia. Both of these loans were for public purposes, having no relation to the civil conflict. The loan to the Provisional Government was for war supplies to fight the German armies; the Armenian loan was for relief. In view of the fact that these loans were not intended to be used for civil war purposes, it is necessary to determine their legal status and as to whether Russia is bound by them.

It should be recalled that the Provisional Government came into power in the early days of March 1917 as a result of the overthrow of the titular government of the Russian Emperor. On March 12 the revolution broke out in Petrograd in the form of bread riots on the part of factory workers and people in general. The Emperor immediately issued an order to prorogue the Duma; but the Duma refused to recognize or obey this order, took the direction of the government in its own hands, and appointed an Executive Committee to be head of the temporary government.[77] On March 15 the Emperor abdicated for himself and his son in favor of his brother, the Grand Duke Michael.[78] The Grand Duke, however, declined the throne unless it was offered him by the people through a constitutional convention.[79] Since there was a delay in calling a constitutional convention, the Grand Duke was thus eliminated and the direction of the government remained in the hands of the Executive Committee of the Duma which came to be known as the Provisional Government of Russia under the Premiership of Prince Lvov who was eventually succeeded by Kerensky sometime during the latter part of July, 1917.[80] The Provisional Government, which was in control of all Russia, was in turn overthrown by the Soviet Government in November 1917.[81]

The Provisional Government was recognized by the Government of the United States on March 22, 1917, within about

77 The American Ambassador to Russia to the Secretary of State, March 14, 1917, *For. Rel.*, 1918, Russia, I, 1; March 17, *ibid.*, 3-4; March 18, *ibid.*, 5-6; American Consul at Petrograd to the Secretary of State, March 20, 1917, *ibid.*, 7-11.

78 *For. Rel.*, 1918, Russia, I, 3.

79 The American Minister to Sweden to the Secretary of State, March 19, 1917, *ibid.*, 6-7.

80 *Ibid.*, Ch. IV, 159 *et seq.*

81 *For. Rel.*, 1918, Russia, I, Ch. V, 224 *et seq.*

a week after it was formed.[82] Shortly thereafter, in conformity with an act of Congress enabling the Treasury at Washington to advance money to the Allies to carry on war against Germany, the Government of the United States made a loan of about 325,000,000 dollars to Russia under the Provisional Government. Of this sum an advance of about 175,000,000 dollars was made under the Premiership of Lvov prior to July 1917, and an advance of about 150,000,000 dollars was made under the Premiership of Kerensky after July 1917.[83]

When the Soviet Government came into power in November 1917, it issued a series of decrees repudiating, *inter alia,* all foreign loans and financial obligations undertaken by previous Russian governments, including the United States Government loan to the Provisional Government.[84] The United States, as well as other interested foreign states, has steadfastly denied the right of the Soviet Government to repudiate the public and private foreign financial obligations of Russia. In 1918 the American Ambassador to Russia joined the diplomatic envoys of other nations in making the following declaration:

In order to avoid any misunderstanding in the future the representatives at Petrograd of all foreign powers declare that they consider the decrees regarding the repudiation of Russian state loans, the confiscating of property of all kinds and other analogous

82 The Secretary of State to the American Ambassador to Russia, March 20, 1917, *For. Rel.*, 1918, Russia, I, 12; The American Ambassador to the Secretary of State, March 22, 1917, *ibid.*, 12. The Government of the United States was the first to grant recognition to the Provisional Government. The Allied recognition followed shortly after.

83 According to the *Foreign Relations* the following loans were made: to the Lvov Ministry, $100,000,000 on May 16, 1917, and $75,000,000 on July 9, 1917; to the Kerensky Ministry, $100,000,000 on August 23, 1917, and $50,000,000 on October 12, 1917. *For. Rel.*, 1918, Russia, I, *passim*. But apparently the Provisional Government took advantage of this advance only to the extent of about $185,000,000, as this figure is being mentioned in the current discussions.

84 As to the text of the Soviet decree declaring that "absolutely and without exception all foreign loans are annulled," see *For. Rel.*, 1918, Russia, III, 29-33.

measures as without value as far as their nationals are concerned; and the said representatives reserve the right to claim from the Russian Government at an opportune time damages for all loss which these decrees may cause their nationals.[85]

From 1917 to 1933 the United States followed a policy of non-recognition toward Soviet Russia.[86] During this long period of years the question, *inter alia,* of the American loan to the Provisional Government remained in abeyance. Since the American recognition of the Soviet Government in 1933, however, this loan has been a subject of diplomatic discussion.

Is Russia bound by this loan and what are the real bases of such liability? The answer to this question depends on two considerations: first, whether the Provisional Government was or was not the government of Russia at the time this loan was made; second, whether the character of the loan is such that it would bind Russia regardless of the status of the Provisional Government. If the Provisional Government was in complete control of Russia, that country would be liable under the principle of international law that a state is bound by acts of its government *de facto* or *de jure*. And, again, if the loan had no relation to the civil conflict and was used for an object of national importance, the presumption is that Russia is bound by it even if the Provisional Government be considered a mere insurgent government which did not attain general control.

It is generally understood that the Soviet Government is of view that the Provisional Government was not in a position to

85 *For. Rel.*, 1918, Russia, III, 33.

86 The reasons underlying the nonrecognition policy of the United States toward Soviet Russia have been summarized in a pamphlet entitled "The Recognition Policy of the United States" issued by the Foreign Policy Association, Information Service, no. 3. It contains texts of declarations made in regard to the Russian situation by Secretary of State Colby, Secretary of State Hughes, and President Coolidge. As to these declarations see also Department of State press releases. See also N. D. Houghton, 'Policy of the United States and Other Nations with respect to the Recognition of the Russian Soviet Government, 1917-1929," *International Conciliation*, no. 247.

act in the name and on behalf of Russia because it was not a definitely established government in supreme control of that country. But the facts point to the very interesting conclusion that the Provisional Government both under Lvov and under Kerensky was in general control of Russia. It should be remembered that the revolution took place in Petrograd, the capital of Russia at that time, and to a lesser degree in Moscow. The rest of that vast country was quiet, and there was hardly any bloodshed anywhere. At the time the main force for making or breaking a government was the army, and from the first the army sided with the Duma and the Provisional Government. After the abdication of the Emperor and the formation of the new government, all of which was a matter of only a few days, the American ambassador reported that the rest of the country was quiet and had apparently submitted to the new government.[87] The behavior of the great bulk of the Russian people during the existence of the Provisional Government from March to November 1917 could be interpreted only as being friendly to the new regime. All these indicate that the Russian people submitted to the new government and that that government was in fact in general control of the country. The important fact is that during the period in question there was no other government in Russia acting in opposition to the Provisional Government. It is true that there existed in Petrograd a so-called Council of Workingmen's and Soldiers' Deputies, and that the constant shift of ministers of the Provisional Government both under Lvov and under Kerensky, the change of the premiership from one to the other, the numerous government crises during the short period of only about seven months, and many other events of a similar nature, may be traced directly to that Council.[88] But the important thing is

87 "The six days between last Sunday and this have witnessed the most amazing revolution. . . . Absolute quiet prevails here and throughout Russia so far as known." The American Ambassador to the Secretary of State, March 18, 1917, *For. Rel.*, 1918, Russia, I, 5-6, and *passim*.

88 The American Consul at Petrograd to the Secretary of State, April 10,

that the Council was not a government, and that it more often acted with the Provisional Government rather than against it. In view of these facts, the conclusion is inescapable that the Provisional Government was the sole government of Russia during the short period of its existence, that it had control over all Russia, and that it was therefore in a position to undertake financial obligations in the name and on behalf of that country. It is true that after a short period of existence it was ultimately overthrown. But from the viewpoint of international law complete control of the governmental machinery of the state justifies the claim of the possessor of that control that it may fairly hold itself out to the outside world as the government of that state; and that the acts which it commits during such period may also be fairly allowed to be those of the state which it thus represents. On this score, therefore, the claim of the United States against Russia for the repayment of the loan made to the Provisional Government in 1917 is based on solid ground.

But let it be assumed that the Provisional Government was a mere unsuccessful insurgent government. It is believed that even in that case Russia would be bound because of the nature and the character of the loan in question. The Soviet Government can not contend that it was a hostile loan for the purpose of financing a civil war. The purpose of the loan was unique; it was made for a worthy public object, that is, to carry on the war against Germany. It was clearly stipulated that "in case of the discontinuance of war the credits will of course cease to be extended." [89] Now, if it is just and equitable that Mexico should repay a loan made by private persons to the

1917, *For. Rel.*, 1918, Russia, I, 21-24; same to same, April 30, 1917, *ibid.*, 34; the American Ambassador to Russia to the Secretary of State, April 17, 1917, *ibid.*, 25-27; same to same, May 4, 1917, *ibid.*, 40; same to same, July 19, 1917, *ibid.*, 161-162; the American Consul at Petrograd to the Secretary of State, May 8, 1917, *ibid.*, 42.

89 The Secretary of State to the American Ambassador to Russia, May 17, 1917, *For. Rel.*, 1918, Russia, III, 9-10.

Huerta Government in 1913 to meet maturing obligations of the national debt,[90] it appears to be equally just and equitable that Russia should repay the United States Government loan to the Provisional Government to carry on an already existing international war. On the assumption that both the Huerta government in Mexico in 1913 and the Provisional Government in Russia in 1917 were unsuccessful insurgent governments which happened to be in control of the central machinery of government in both countries, it follows that financial obligations created by these two governments would be analogous. For the purpose of the American loan of 1917, which was used for a national object and was not detrimental to the state, the Provisional Government therefore should be regarded as acting for and in the name of Russia although opinion may differ as to whether it was the government or not. On this score, also, it thus appears that the claim of the United States is justified on every ground of law and fact.

As to the Armenian loan, briefly the facts in this case are as follows. After the collapse of the Provisional Government in Russia in November 1917, the people of Armenia, like the peoples of other Russian succession states, declared their independence and maintained a semblance of self-government with a more or less organized government of their own in the southern portion of the Caucassus. For over three years this region was divested of Russian control due chiefly to the fact that the Soviet Government was engaged in a bitter civil war against the forces of Kolchak, Denikin, and others, and was therefore unable to reach the border nationalities. In 1919 the Supreme Council of the Allied powers decided to establish an independent Armenian Republic and in principle recognized its independence. The new republic was to combine the so-called Russian Armenia, which had already declared its independence from Russia, and the so-called Turkish Armenia; and President Wilson was formally requested to designate the boundaries

90 *Supra*, p. 29.

between the new Armenian Republic and Turkey. It is also significant that at about this time the Soviet Government also made a declaration in principle recognizing Armenian independence. Meanwhile, in view of the famine which prevailed at that time in a large part of Central and Eastern Europe, the Government of the United States decided to recognize " the *de facto* government of the Republic of Armenia " and to make a loan of about ten million dollars to that government to be spent chiefly for relief purposes. Ultimately the project for an independent Armenian Republic fell through by the reestablishment of control over the territory in question by the Soviet Government. The loan made by the Government of the United States is still credited to the so-called Republic of Armenia in the reports of the Secretary of the Treasury at Washington. Although no diplomatic action has been taken in this matter, it nevertheless raises a number of interesting questions in view of the American recognition of Soviet Russia. Is it possible to hold Russia liable for this loan and on what grounds? The Government of the United States may, of course, advance the argument that at the time of the loan Armenia was in fact an independent republic, and that the subsequent conquest of that new state by Russia necessarily raises a question of state succession and therefore liability on the part of Russia. This gives rise to a question of fact. Was Armenia in fact an independent republic in 1920? There seems to be little doubt that it was independent. Since Russia was torn by civil conflict, the people in this little border territory were entirely ignored and left unmolested. They took advantage of this situation, formed a government of their own, and became a politically organized community for the time being. But here a distinction should be made between control and permanency. The *de facto* government was in control of the territory in question and was apparently independent, but it was neither a stable nor a permanently established international entity. If the so-called Republic of Armenia is to be regarded as being in fact independent in 1920, there can be no doubt as to the liability of Russia especially in view of the non-belligerent and non-military object of the loan. If, on the other hand, it is to be decided that Armenia was not in fact independent and did not constitute a state in the sense of international law, that the Soviet Government was engaged at the time in a civil war against its enemies which included the *de facto* government of the new republic, and that the subsequent conquest of that country amounted to nothing more than a mere subjugation of seceding insurgents in the same way that the Federal Government conquered the Confederate States, the Government of the United States will be put in a most embarrassing position of recognizing and loaning money to rebels who were unsuccessfully attempting to establish a new state. Since the act of recognition in such a case is an act of intervention, Russia can not be held bound by the loan although it was made for relief purposes and not for a military object.

CHAPTER II

CONCESSIONS AND ALIENATIONS OF STATE PROPERTY

THE question whether concessions involving natural resources and contracts for the sale and alienation of the public domain and other state property by the government of an unsuccessful revolution are or are not binding on the state would seem to depend chiefly on the character of each transaction. It is generally admitted that an insurgent government may use national property found within the territory over which its immediate control extends and it may sell the fruits thereof accruing during the period of the civil war.[1] As to concession contracts and alienations involving the public domain and other

1 During the Civil War the following instructions, *inter alia*, were issued to the United States Military authorities: "A victorious army appropriates all public money, seizes all public movable property . . . and sequesters for its own benefit or of that of its government all the revenues of real property belonging to the hostile government or nation. The title to such real property remains in abeyance during military occupation, and until the conquest is made complete." Instructions for the Government of the Armies of the United States in the Field, April 24, 1863, Moore, *Digest*, VII, 278.

On July 18, 1898, President McKinley issued, *inter alia*, the following order to the Secretary of War: " It is conceded that all public funds and securities belonging to the government of the country in its own right, and all arms and supplies and other movable property of such government, may be seized by the military occupant and converted to his own use. The real property of the state he may hold and administer, at the same time enjoying the revenues thereof, but he may not destroy it save in the case of military necessity. All public means of transportation, such as telegraph lines, cables, railways, and boats, belonging to the state, may be appropriated to his use, but, unless in case of military necessity, they are not to be destroyed." Moore, *Digest*, VII, 261, 262.

"Article LIII. An army of occupation can only take possession of the cash, funds, and property liable to requisition belonging strictly to the State, depots of arms, means of transport, stores and supplies, and, generally, all movable property of the State which may be used for military operations." Convention respecting the Laws and Customs of War on Land, The Hague, July 29, 1899.

public property of the state and extending beyond the period of insurgent occupation, it appears that, as a rule, the state is not bound. This is especially true in cases where a concession or alienation is in some way detrimental to the interests of the state or is done by unsuccessful insurgents in pursuance and in aid of their political aims. In cases, however, where a concession or alienation is not detrimental to the state and may be regarded as "a fair and reasonable exercise of the authority under which it was made," [2] especially when the other party to the contract acted in good faith and made expenditures for permanent improvements accruing to the benefit of the state, the presumption is that the state may be exceptionally bound. In case of insurgent loans an attempt was made to distinguish between insurgent loans in aid of rebellion by which the state was said not to be bound, and insurgent loans used for a purpose of public utility by which the state may be bound. There is no reason why the same principle should not prevail in case of insurgent concessions and alienations of public property.

The few cases decided by international claims commissions deal solely with insurgent concessions and alienations of the type which have been held not to bind the state. Besides, they present a rather confusing picture as to the issues involved. The question whether the state is bound by such transactions was at no time the only or even the main issue in these cases. It appears that, in practically every case, the unsuccessful insurgents involved apparently assumed to act for the state in accordance with the existing local laws as to concessions and alienations of public property, since they neither abrogated such laws nor promulgated laws of their own; but in every case the mode of exercising their authority as to such contracts happened to be in violation of the *lex loci*. The commissions held, therefore, that since the old laws were still in operation in the insurgent territories, and since insurgent concessions and alienations in question were in violation of such laws, the state was not bound.

2 *New Orleans v. Steamship Company*, 20 Wall. 387, 395.

The question whether unsuccessful insurgents could bind the state in the matter of concessions and alienations was discussed in a general way, but no definite conclusions appear to have been reached on this point independently of the other issue just stated. In cases where the commissions intimated that such insurgents could not bind the state, it appears that the proceeds of the concessions and alienations in question were used for civil war purposes by the insurgents, though the commissions failed to discuss this last point.

In the case of *Beales, Nobles and Garrison (U. S.) v. Venezuela,*[3] decided by the United States and Venezuelan Claims Commission of 1885, the claim involved two contracts made by the revolutionary Paez government with certain American citizens for the purpose of granting concessions for a steamship service and for a project of immigration and colonization which involved the alienation of extensive lands in Venezuela. From 1861 to 1863 General Paez held possession of the capital and the province of Caracas against the faction which he had succeeded in displacing but which nevertheless controlled other parts of the country outside of the province of Caracas. Sometime during the winter and early spring of 1863, and just before his government came to an end by an agreement with the other faction under which General Falcon became the President of the Republic,[4] Paez gave a power of attorney to the Venezuelan consul in New York authorizing him to enter into contracts in behalf of Venezuela with certain citizens of the United States for the establishment of a steamship service between New York and La Guayra and for a scheme of immigration and colonization of foreigners in the Republic of Venezuela.[5] Under this power the consul made two contracts with

3 Moore, *Int. Arb.*, Vol. IV, pp. 3548-3564.

4 *Supra*, p. 47.

5 The power of attorney given by Paez provided in part that "the said consul will act without any limitation, only following as far as possible the instruction to be communicated to him by my secretary general . . . and, to remove at once any objections which might be urged against the validity

the claimants Beales and Nobles, who acted in behalf of a stock company to be formed in the future. According to one contract a steamship line was to be established using steamers "suitable for carrying the mails, twenty-five passengers and six hundred tons merchandize"; giving preference to "the effects, articles, and properties of the Government of Venezuela over all other cargoes and passengers, to be paid for, however, at the usual rates charged to merchants or private individuals"; and carrying officers and troops of the government at reduced rates.[6] According to another contract the claimants agreed to bring into Venezuela immigrants and colonists for which they were to receive a large portion of the territory of that country, along with the conveyance of a fee-simple title to all the mines within the limits of the lands thus ceded, including not only mines "of metal but also those of petroleum, asphaltum, marble, coal and others." For the first year the contractors were entitled to one thousand acres of land for each colonist settled, "for each 1,000 acres two persons in the second year, three in the third, four in the fourth, and so successively one person for each year up to the number of ten in the space of ten years, so that for each 1,000 acres there shall be ten persons within ten years."[7]

of the terms in which this authority is granted, I, Jose Antonio Paez, Supreme Chief of the Republic of Venezuela, hereby approve *now and for all times whatever may be contracted for* by Simon Camacho, consul of Venezuela in New York, with respect to the said contracts." *Case of Beales, Nobles, and Garrison*, Moore, *Int. Arb.*, IV, 3549.

6 This contract also provided that two young men selected by the government were to be carried free of expense in order to receive practical instruction in navigation and the management of steam machinery; and that free carriage was to be provided for seeds, plants, and other articles of similar nature not exported for profit. "For these services and some others Camacho agreed that Venezuela should pay $50,000 in gold coin of the United States yearly, payable in monthly installments . . . to be deducted from the 40 per cent duty belonging to the government on the *imports* and *exports carried* by the steamers . . . this payment of $50,000 shall continue for three years only . . . after which time the sum of $30,000 shall be paid for the period of twenty-seven years." *Case of Beales, Nobles, and Garrison*, Moore, *Int. Arb.*, IV, 3549-3550.

7 Language of the Contract quoted by the commission, Moore, *Int. Arb.*, IV, 3555-3556.

. . . if at the end of ten years, they had not furnished ten emigrants, but only the half of that number they were at liberty to buy, at the rate of fifty cents an acre, the excess of land remaining over and above the number of emigrants agreed to be supplied. Not only so, but if they saw fit to introduce no emigrants at all, if they believed that the purchase of all the lands within the limits ceded to the colony at a half dollar an acre in Venezuelan currency, would pay them better than the turning of a " constant stream of immigration " into Venezuela, they were at liberty to abandon the colonization scheme altogether and turn the contract into a land speculation pure and simple.[8]

In effect this so-called immigration and colonization contract was apparently nothing more than a mere concession of vast tracts of Venezuelan lands to the contractors who were given " the right every year to select in the part of the republic where they may see fit 100,000 square acres of land, either in one parcel or in divided portions . . . provided that within two years from the date of such selection of lands the contractors shall have placed two colonists for each 1,000 square acres." On this point the commission commented as follows:

Drawn up in solemn form, acknowledged before a notary, and sealed, too, this instrument has all the exterior legal requisites, both at the civil and common law, to protect it from criticism and assault for want of consideration, but it is in fact no contract mutually binding upon the parties; but the concession of a privilege by Venezuela to be availed of or not, and when or never, as Messrs. Beales and Nobles in their discretion saw fit.[9]

After the dictatorship of General Paez in Caracas came to an end in 1863, the Government of Venezuela under President Falcon annulled these contracts and ultimately a claim for damages was brought against Venezuela before the American-Venezuelan Claims Commission of 1885. The United States based this claim on the general proposition that the state is

8 Summary of provisions of the contract by the commission, *ibid.*, 3557.

9 Opinion of the commission, by commissioner Findlay, *ibid.*, 3557.

bound by acts of its *de facto* government, and argued that the Paez government was the government of Venezuela at the time it granted to Camacho, the Venezuelan consul in New York, the power to make the contracts under consideration. The Commission conceded that "a *de facto* government can bind the state in a matter of private contract between it and the citizens of another state, and that good faith as between nations binds the state as a personality to fulfull the terms of its private contracts, or pay damages for their non-fulfillment"; but categorically denied that "the government of Paez was such a government." It said:

The argument of the learned counsel for the United States and the claimants was addressed largely to establishing the proposition that a government *de facto* was invested with the same authority to conclude binding contracts as a government *de jure*, and having succeeded in this, then proceeded upon the pure assumption of the petition that the Government of Venezuela was a government *de facto*, when this power was granted; but this, it is not necessary to say, is not only the very question at issue, but the duty of establishing the affirmative rests upon the petitioner . . . in a case like this . . . the petition must be treated as if it had averred in terms that the power, in virtue of which these contracts were executed, was . . . the medium through which the undisputed authority of the state was conveyed, and by which it was bound. A man claiming under a deed must prove it, and if there is any question as to the power of the grantor to do the deed he must establish that also. The mere fact of execution is a matter of formal evidence, but the right to do the act of which the paper instrument usually called the deed supplies the proof, is the essential issue in controversies of this character. Treating this petition, then, as . . . asserting the actual authority of Paez to issue such power, as the foundation stone on which this claim is erected, we are confronted by the general denial which Venezuela has interposed to the petition. . . . The question is thus raised whether conceding that a *de facto* government . . . has the same authority to bind the state as a government *de jure*, the Paez government can lay claim to such a character, and on this question the burden of proof is on the claimant.

It would be enough to say that they have not discharged this obligation, but from the references we have made to the origin and character of this government it would seem reasonably clear that if the claimants had assumed to carry such a burden they must have failed in the undertaking.[10]

The Commission then pointed out that the control of the Paez government did not in fact extend beyond the capital and the province of Caracas, and said:

This government lasted about twenty months, and was succeeded by the Falcon administration, which was also in possession of the capital when the contracts were annulled. How much of the habitual respect of the bulk of the people outside of the province of Caracas it managed to acquire before its overthrow we have no means of knowing, but, if the preamble of the decree just quoted affords any reliable evidence of the condition of affairs at that time, there is not much ground for believing that the Paez government was founded on any tenure more reliable than the ability to maintain its authority for a limited period within a circumscribed district of the country.[11]

It also showed that the United States, treating the matter of recognition as a question of fact only, "refused to recognize the government of Paez as the *de facto* government of the state, rebuked its minister for attempting to do so, and promptly repudiating his act." On this point, it said:

While the failure or refusal of the United States to recognize the government of Paez is not binding upon us as a court in determining the question whether that government was a government *de facto* or not, the necessity of determining that question, in some way as an essential prerequisite absolutely vital to the correct determination of the main issue involved, is just as binding and imperative, as it would be upon any other tribunal empowered to adjudicate the question. In the absence of presumptions, which, in the condition the country was at the time, cannot be made

10 *Case of Beales, Nobles and Garrison*, Moore, *Int. Arb.*, IV, 3561-3562.

11 *Ibid.*, 3559.

in favor of the lawfulness of the government, resort must be had to evidence to establish its true character, as any other fact in doubt is required to be proved, and on this question of *fact* the failure of the United States to recognize the Paez government is a fact which cannot be ignored.[12]

Having thus disposed of the issue raised by the United States, the Commission then proceeded to decide the case on an entirely different ground. It said, that contrary to fact, even assuming that the Paez government was the government of Venezuela, it nevertheless could not make contracts of this character by executive order alone because the power to make such contracts was expressly reserved to the Venezuelan congress under the Constitution of 1858, which was still in force. On this particular point, it said:

Recurring now to the question of the lawfulness of the power it may be more than doubted whether Paez, if he had been supreme chief, both *de facto* and *de jure*, could have granted such a power. It appears that the constitution of the 31st of December 1858 was in force when he assumed this character. Title IX of this constitution concerns the power of *congress*, and among these powers, as prescribed in article 64, is the power to decree what may be convenient for the administration, preservation, and alienation of national property, to assist in the immigration and colonization of foreigners, and to encourage by means of legislation and by contracts the navigation and canalization of rivers, the opening of roads, and other works, provided they be of national utility (sections 13, 16, 30). This is a clear devolution of the authority exercised by Paez upon the legislative department of the government, and unless we assume that the supreme chief for the time being in possession of the capital and of the province of Caracas, had supplanted completely the constitution, and could exercise in own person the functions of the executive as well as the legislative department it is very clear that the authority granted to Camacho was an excess of power in itself as to both contracts . . . [13]

12 *Case of Beales, Nobles and Garrison*, Moore, *Int. Arb.*, IV, 3560-3561.

13 *Ibid.*, 3548, 3558.

On the whole our conclusions are that by the constitution of Venezuela the lawful and undisputed government of that country could not, by its executive department alone, have granted the power in question, and therefore the grant by Paez was without lawful authority, even if the *de facto* character of his government had been established, as to which there is not only a failure of proof but the evidence seems the other way.[14]

In the case of the *Georgiana* and the *Lizzie Thompson*,[15] the United States claimed damages from Peru for the seizure and condemnation of two American vessels who had obtained permits from the revolutionary Vivanco faction to load and transport guano which was a government monopoly. The question involved chiefly the right of Vivanco and his revolutionary party to dispose of guano under or claimed to be under their temporary control. It appears that in 1856 a revolt occurred at Arequipa, a city in the southern part of Peru, and the insurgents declared General Vivanco, who previously had been an unsuccessful aspirant for political power, to be president in opposition to the titular government. The revolutionary movement met with a cold reception from the people and made no great progress on land, but it nevertheless secured essential aid in the revolt of the Peruvian fleet which evidently consisted of about three vessels. On these three vessels Vivanco embarked his troops, about two thousand in number, took possession of the Chincha Islands for the purpose of availing himself of the guano deposits there, and then decided to proceed to the coastal towns and ports in the hope of gaining support. He did not succeed in this enterprise, however, and in the port of Callao he was repulsed with such loss that he was forced to retreat to Arequipa where he remained until the end of the revolution. Eventually two of the three war vessels returned to obedience to the titular government; but the remaining vessel under the command of General Rivas ran from port to port in the south-

14 *Ibid.*, 3563.

15 Moore, *Int. Arb.*, II, 1593.

ern Peru, with Rivas assuming to be collector of customs, commandant-general of marine, secretary of the treasury, and superior chief of the south, administering the affairs of whatever port he happened to be and sold guano, protecting the purchasers in the loading of it. He finally established himself in the port of Iquique, with his chief, Vivanco, at Arequipa, about ninety miles from the coast. In October 1857 the Peruvian army proceeded south, and in March 1858 it took Arequipa. Vivanco escaped in the guise of a friar, and the insurrection thus came to an end. The minister of the United States at Lima reported that Vivanco's conduct had from the beginning been weak and indecisive.[16]

In January 1858, less than two months before the collapse of Vivanco's insurrection, the naval forces of the titular government of Peru seized the two American vessels, the bark *Georgiana* and the ship *Lizzie Thompson,* while they were loading guano, which according to the then existing law was the sole property of the Republic of Peru and the sale of which was a government monopoly. It appears that the two vessels went to Iquique in the regular course of trade, and found the port under the administration of General Rivas, one of the leaders of the revolutionary movement. After discharging their cargoes, they received licenses from the Vivanco faction and were cleared at the custom-house for the purpose of loading guano under charter to private parties, one of which happened to be the French vice consul whose act was later officially disavowed. They commenced loading only a few days before their seizure by the forces of the titular government. They were taken to Callao, where the masters and their vessels were ordered for trial by a decree of the Peruvian council of ministers, with the collector of that port sitting as judge of contraband and confiscations. Both vessels were condemned and ultimately sold at public auction for the reason of their dealings with the revo-

16 For a detailed statement of these facts, see Moore, *Int. Arb.*, Vol. II, pp. 1593-1595.

lutionary party for contraband trade in guano and because of their otherwise illegal operations.

The Government of the United States protested against these proceedings and made a formal demand upon the Government of Peru for compensation.[17] During the diplomatic controversy which ensued the American argument dealt very largely with the right of a revolutionary occupant to dispose of the public property of the state. In denying the right of the Peruvian Government to seize and condemn the vessels, the Government of the United States maintained that since for nearly two years Peru had been in a state of civil war, and since the revolutionary party had succeeded in getting control of certain parts of the country, had appropriated the tangible and available property of the nation as a means of carrying on war, had issued bonds, and had seized upon the public moneys in the custom-houses, it therefore had jurisdiction as a government *de facto* over the territory it held, the jurisdiction of the titular government at Lima being for the time and place divested. If the insurgent government had the power to govern the territory under its control, it also had the right to make laws and to determine questions of internal administration touching the sources of public revenue situate there, such as the guano deposits. It followed as a consequence that the laws of the titular government of Peru for the regulation of the trade of guano had no practical application to the place of capture which was under insurgent control; and that, at any rate, it was argued, " the true construction of these regulations, their repeal or suspension, or modification or application, are questions of administration to be determined by the existing administrative power," that is, the insurgent government, " to whose decision foreigners must submit." It was further said that during the civil conflict the two American vessels had a right to enter any

17 The sum of $155,714.35 was demanded on account of the two vessels. Cases of the *Georgiana* and the *Lizzie Thompson*, Moore, *Int. Arb.*, Vol. II, 1597.

port of the Peruvian Republic open to foreign commerce and not blockaded, for the prosecution of their commercial enterprises; and that it was their duty after such entrance to obey the authorities they might find established there. When, therefore, the revenue officers at Iquique, acting under the authority of the *de facto* government, gave the necessary permission for the purchase of guano at the places indicated and at the time subject to the control of that government, the American captains had the right to go there and to take that article on board their vessels for freight, in conformity with the provisions of their charter parties; and the subsequent transfer of the possession of these places while the vessels were engaged in this employment could justly work no forfeiture for acts previously done under these circumstances, nor subject the officers or crew to punishment.[18]

The Government of Peru admitted that the Vivanco faction was in possession of a certain portion of the national territory, and that foreign vessels had the right to carry on trade in ordinary commercial articles with the insurgent ports not under

18 Cases of the *Georgiana* and the *Lizzie Thompson*, Moore, *Int. Arb.*, II, 1596-1601.

The Secretary of State submitted to the Peruvian Government an opinion of Attorney-General Black rendered in support of the American view. In this opinion Judge Black conceded the possession of full sovereign rights to a rebellious party, even where "the rebellion is but partially successful." It was said that the parties to a civil war were "to be regarded for the time as distinct political societies," and that "a revolutionary party, like a foreign belligerent power, is supreme over the country it conquers as far and as long as its arms can carry and maintain it." Judge Black came to the conclusion that since there was in fact a civil war in Peru, and since Vivanco was in *de facto* possession of the port of Iquique and had "officered and organized the local government of the port and the city and the guano deposits, the jurisdiction of the party headed by Vivanco was perfect, and an American vessel trading to the port was bound to conform to its decrees." In doing so, it was contended, the two vessels "were guilty of nothing for which the other party to the civil war could punish or molest them afterward," and therefore "the whole proceeding of the Peruvian Government against the two vessels was contrary to the law of nations, and repugnant to the prinactual blockade; but it emphatically denied the right of the insurgent government to dispose of the guano deposits of the state for two reasons. First, it contended that the bare fact of possession of state property by the chiefs of a revolution did not authorize the citizens of other nations to deal with them at once as the owners of what they thus held. In this respect it sharply disagreed with the American definition of the rights of a revolutionary occupant and regarded it to be a dangerous doctrine on the part of the United States to ascribe to insurgents, who had no more than the shadow of a *de facto* government at the ports where the American vessels were loading guano and who were shortly after defeated and dispersed, the same powers within the territory temporarily controlled by them as belonged to the permanent government. Secondly, it pointed out that the whole transaction between the two American vessels and the insurgents in respect to guano was in violation of the *lex loci*. According to the Peruvian law, it was said, the guano deposits at Punta de Lobos and Pabellon de Pica, where the two vessels were captured, were state property and their sale a government monopoly; that the commercial regulations of Peru, promulgated in 1852, provided, *inter alia,* that vessels should take in guano for foreign trade only in certain ports of the Chincha Islands; that such vessels must be under contract with the government or its agents; and that vessels found at anchor on the coasts of other islands with guano on board or in the process of loading guano should be confiscated and their captains and crews tried for contraband trade. In addition, a decree promulgated by the national convention of the Peruvian Republic during the Vivanco revolution in 1857 provided: " That all the guano exported and thereafter to be exported from the Chincha Islands or from any other deposit of Peru by disturbers of the public order or by virtue of contracts made with them or with their agents shall at all times be subject to

ciples of natural justice." Opinion of Attorney-General Black, Moore, *ibid.*, 1602-1604.

be claimed back as stolen national property, and the parties responsible therefor shall be civilly and criminally prosecuted in conformity with law." [19]

After thus stating its laws as to guano, the Peruvian Government said that the capture and embargo of the two American vessels and the arrest and imprisonment of their captains and crews

> were caused by the vessels having been surprised at Punta de Lobos and Pabellon de Pica in the criminal and scandalous contraband of guano, in contravention of the fiscal laws, commercial regulations, and coasting ordinances which severally prohibit foreign vessels not only such illicit trade but even access to the ports, landings, and guano deposits without a special permit from the government under the penalties there enacted—penalties which, in addition to the civil part, extend to personal punishment against the perpetrators of such offenses.[20]

The vessels in question, it was said, "were met at points interdicted, not only without permits from the lawful authorities of the republic, but in the act also of doing that which, under the laws, no authority of the government, however legal it may be, can lawfully allow." As to this, it was shown that while the permits granted by the insurgents to the two vessels

> merely authorize them "to proceed south to take in guano," neither of the charter parties makes mention of any point south; but on the contrary the contract with the *Lizzie Thompson* grants the privilege to the charterer of naming any of the ports of Peru, provided that it be not one more to the north of Callao, and therefore embracing the Chincha Islands. Again, the contract for the *Georgiana* gives to the freighters a free choice of any of the ports on the whole coast of Peru, north as well as south. An irresistible consequence from these facts is that neither the charterers nor the chartered vessels had any intention of confining themselves to the

19 Cases of the *Georgiana* and the *Lizzie Thompson*, Moore, *Int. Arb.*, II, 1596-1597.

20 *Ibid.*, 1595-1596.

southern ports, where alone there was the least shadow of an authority *de facto* standing in opposition to the government of the nation, whilst it was evident that the captains had lent themselves to the schemes of the insurrectionists and had joined in accompliceship with them to defraud the treasury of the republic, ready as they were to carry out their project, wherever the most inviting and least dangerous opportunity might offer.[21]

While admitting that, as a rule, the two vessels had the right to trade with insurgent ports not under actual blockade, the Peruvian Government said, however, that

the vessels did not simply obey the alleged *de facto* authorities; they proceeded to contract with them for the purpose of despoiling the national property, in spite of the laws of the republic as to guano. In entering the port of Iquique and in leaving it on a lawful voyage, they would have exercised the perfect right. When they went so far as to take possession of the national property, they appealed to a possible right of war, and took the incidental hazards, as participants in the violence committed by the revolutionists. They dealt with the revolutionists not as a mere *de facto* authority, but as the Government of Peru, possessing power to deal with guano in defiance of the national laws. Peru could justly reclaim the guano on the *jus postliminii*.[22]

It was further pointed out that under exactly identical circumstances both Chile and France had recognized the rights of the Republic of Peru in this matter. The Government of Chile had refused to intervene in behalf of three Chilean vessels which were seized by the forces of the titular government of Peru at the same time as the two American vessels and for the same offense, and had notified Peru of its decision. Similarly, the French consul at Iquique, who had chartered the *Lizzie Thompson* to load and transport guano by permission of the insurgent government, had appealed to the French chargé at

21 Cases of the *Georgiana* and the *Lizzie Thompson*, Moore, *Int. Arb.*, II, p. 1602, note 2.

22 *Ibid.*, p. 1605.

Lima for his official intervention; but instead of granting the request the chargé demanded of the consul the surrender of his office, and notified the Peruvian Government that it had acted within its rights in seizing the vessel chartered by the consul.[23]

After a prolonged controversy, which in fact resulted at one time in a rupture of diplomatic relations between the United States and Peru,[24] the two governments finally decided to submit the question to arbitration. The King of Belgium was named as "arbiter, umpire, and friendly arbitrator," with "the most ample power to decide and determine all the questions both of law and fact." But His Majesty, after examining what had been published on the controversy, was compelled to decline the role of arbitrator because he

> perceived that the arbitration would be "of a very delicate nature by reason of the special circumstances" of the case, and that the question of fact as well as of equity was complicated by a question of law which it would be difficult to decide at a distance from the place at which it arose, and without having a perfect knowledge of local legislation, which it was not easy to obtain so far away.[25]

In an interview with the American Minister to Belgium, he amplified his reasons and added that

23 Peru also communicated to the Government of the United States an opinion of Mr. Reverdy Johnson, in which it was maintained: (1) that the two American vessels at the time of the seizure were engaged in loading guano from deposits which belonged to the Republic of Peru, was a government monopoly, and had for years constituted the principal source of its revenue. (2) The authority to load was not obtained from the titular government of Peru which alone had the right to grant it, but from insurgents who were not even recognized as belligerents. (3) Until the titular government is defeated, and foreign governments have recognized the insurgents as the government or at least as belligerents, such titular government is to be treated as the government of the state. Moore, *Int. Arb.*, II, 1606.

24 Diplomatic relations were broken off in October 1860, but were resumed when Lincoln became President. Moore, *Int. Arb.*, II, 1608-1610.

25 The *Georgiana* and the *Lizzie Thompson*, Moore, *Int. Arb.*, II, 1611-1612.

He had looked into the case, and he must say that he did not think we had the strongest side of it; indeed, he would have been constrained, had he accepted the position of arbitrator, to decide it against us, and that his desire not to make a decision unfavorable to us had been a motive for declining to accept the trust which had been, in so flattering a manner, offered to him.[26]

In view of these reasons, the Government of the United States decided to accept the unofficial but adverse opinion of the arbitrator and to treat the claim as finally disposed of.[27]

It should be remembered that the main question in this case was whether the Peruvian Government had a right to seize and condemn the *Georgiana* and the *Lizzie Thompson* for loading guano under permits from the insurgent authorities and in ports which were not open to foreign trade under the existing Peruvian laws which were not abrogated by the insurgents within the territory under their control. Apart from this, the question whether Vivanco did or did not have the right, regardless of such laws, to dispose of the guano was raised by the United States as a defense to justify the conduct of the two vessels. Now, the question arises whether the unofficial opinion of the arbitrator in this case should be deemed to dispose of these issues adversely to the United States.

As to the main issue, that is, the question of violation of the *lex loci,* it is believed that the arbitrator's unofficial verdict that the United States did not have "the strongest side of it" is substantially correct. In this respect, the Peruvian Government argued that the two vessels were not only "participants in the violence committed by the revolutionists" and "had lent themselves to the schemes of the insurrectionists and had joined in accompliceship with them to defraud the treasury of the repub-

26 The American Minister to Belgium to the Secretary of State, Moore, *Int. Arb.*, II, 1612.

27 See the note of the Secretary of State of the United States to the Peruvian Government stating that the incident was closed in view of the arbitrator's unofficial opinion. Moore, *Int. Arb.*, II, 1612.

lic," but that they had violated the existing law by loading in ports which were not open to foreign trade. They were therefore guilty, it was said, of the offenses with which they were charged and for which they were condemned by the Peruvian courts. This argument was never refuted by the Government of the United States. It is assumed that the captains of the two vessels were familiar with the existing Peruvian laws and regulations as to guano, and they must have known that they were acting illegally when they applied to the insurgents and received licenses to load guano in ports which were not open to foreign trade even in time of internal peace. There is no evidence that Vivanco had abrogated the existing laws as to guano and had issued new regulations of his own for territories under his control. Presumably, therefore, the existing Peruvian laws prevailed even in insurgent territories. So long as the titular government of Peru was still in power, being in control of the greater part of the country and of the machinery of the central government the Government of the United States and its citizens were bound under international law to regard the titular government as the government of Peru and to respect its laws as to the regulation of guano even in the islands under temporary insurgent control. Since the insurgents did not change such laws, American citizens had no right to assume that they were changed by the mere fact of insurgent occupation of the islands. Under these circumstances, American merchants had a right to deal with the insurgents when the latter acted in conformity with the existing laws which they had not abrogated; they could not contract with such insurgents when the latter acted in violation of the existing laws as to guano. It seems, therefore, that the Government of Peru was justified in considering the whole transaction both as a breach of its own laws and as an act in aid of rebellion.

It is believed that had Vivanco acted in conformity with the Peruvian laws as to guano, the result may have been quite different; it would have changed the whole course of the Peruvian argument. At any rate, the two vessels may have escaped seizure and condemnation on the ground that they were dealing with the government in local control in the ordinary course of commerce.

And again, the American case would have been stronger also had the insurgents abrogated the existing law as not applicable to territory under their control and had they promulgated laws of their own as to the loading of guano. In such a case, the argument that the laws of the titular government did not apply to territory under insurgent control would have been worthy of most serious consideration. But since the old laws continued in the insurgent territory, that argument had no application.

This reasoning, as to insurgent concessions and alienations done in violation of the *lex loci,* is equally applicable to the case of the Paez concessions in Venezuela, stated above. In that case also Paez assumed to act in behalf of Venezuela, but Venezuela was held not to be bound because his act was shown to be in violation of the existing constitution which he had not abrogated.

However, apart from considerations of local law, in the case of the *Georgiana* and the *Lizzie Thompson* the United States, as already seen, also raised the question that Vivanco had a right to dispose of the guano under his control in accordance with regulations of his own. Should the arbitrator's unofficial opinion in this case be deemed to be also adverse to the United States on this point? In referring to the ultimate result obtained in this case, Judge Moore states that

> it is probable that this result should be understood to affect not the general proposition stated by Mr. Cass when applied to ordinary commercial intercourse, but rather the broad interpretation sought to be given to them in ascribing to insurgents, who were afterwards defeated and dispersed, the same powers within the territory temporarily controlled by them as belonged to the permanent government.[28]

28 Moore, *Digest*, I, 44.

He observes that in effect the Department of State did not recognize any limitation to the right of insurgents in temporary occupation of a place to dispose of the public property there situate, and that in one of the diplomatic papers of Secretary of State Cass it was expressly declared that when the place where the guano was deposited "was conquered from its previous rulers, all authority and jurisdiction over it, legislative, executive and judicial, so far as foreigners were concerned with it, passed to and became vested in the conqueror." [29] In view of this definition of the rights of the revolutionary occupant by the Department of State, Moore concludes:

As the argument thus set forth assumed the absolute power of the revolutionary occupant as by right of conquest over the territory occupied by him, it was undoubtedly superfluous, on the assumption that that view was correct, to discuss the right of such an occupant to dispose, in whole or in part, of the national property, whether consisting of guano deposits or of anything else of value. And it is quite true that down to the middle of the eighteenth century the practice of belligerent nations was in accord with the theory that all kinds of property, coming into the hands of one of the parties to the war, vested in him as conqueror and were subject to his absolute disposal, so that he might even alienate or cede the occupied territory while the issue of hostilities remained undecided.[30] But since that period this rule has been either abandoned or subjected to very considerable limitations both in theory and in practice; and in view of this change the validity of the seizure of the *Georgiana* and the *Lizzie Thompson* may be said in some measure to have depended on the answer to be given to these questions: (1) To what extent does a recognized belligerent possess the right to dispose of the public property in territory which he temporarily occupies? (2) Under what circumstances must a revolutionary chief be recognized by the titular government as possessing that right? (3) Are guano deposits belonging to the nation to be considered as property over which the belligerent

29 For an extract from the diplomatic papers of Secretary of State Cass to this effect see, Moore, *Int. Arb.*, II, 1606-1607.

occupant's right of disposal is unlimited? (4) If not, to what extent may he dispose of them.[31]

It is a settled rule, of course, that a foreign military occupant's right to dispose of state property in occupied territory is limited.[32] As a matter of general principle " the contracts of the conqueror touching things in conquered territory lose their efficacy when his dominion ceases." [33] But exceptions to the general principle may be made in cases where a concession or alienation, though made for a term exceeding the period of occupation, may nevertheless be deemed to benefit the state.[34] Reasoning by analogy, it is believed that such exceptional treatment may also be given to insurgent concessions and alienations which are not done in aid of rebellion and are not detrimental to the state, especially when the concessionnaire or purchaser has acted in good faith and has involved himself in heavy expenditures and improvements enriching the state. Indeed, since the relation of an insurgent government to the state is closer and more personal, it follows that the law as to the maintenance of insurgent concessions and alienations of this character is based on better consideration.

30 Hall, *Int. Law*, 4th ed., 482 *et seq.*

31 Moore, *Int. Arb.*, II, 1607-1608.

32 "Article LV. The occupying State shall only be regarded as administrator and usufructuary of the public buildings, real property, or forests, and agricultural works belonging to the hostile State, and situated in the occupied country. It must protect the capital of these properties, and administer it according to the rules of usufruct." Convention respecting the Laws and Customs of War on Land, The Hague, July 29, 1899. See also *supra*, this chapter, note 1.

33 *New Orleans v. Steamship Company*, 20 Wall. 387, 395. See especially the dissenting opinion of Justice Field in this case, *ibid.*, 397 *et seq.*

34 *New Orleans v. Steamship Company*, 20 Wall. 387, 393-395. In this instance the Supreme Court of the United States took the case out of the general rule expressly on the ground that a lease of water-front property made by the military occupant, that is, the United States army of occupation, was not detrimental to the city; that the city had benefited by it; and that the restored city authorities had made "no offer of adjustment touching the lasting and valuable improvements made by the company."

In the *Raborg case*,[35] decided by the American-Peruvian Mixed Claims Commission of 1863, the claim advanced by the United States against Peru was somewhat similar in principle to that in the case of the *Georgiana* and the *Lizzie Thompson*, since it also involved the right of Vivanco to dispose of guano under or claimed to be under his temporary control, but the decision was rendered on an entirely different ground. It was during the Vivanco revolution that Raborg, a citizen of the United States living in Lima, Peru, entered into a contract in 1857 in the harbor of Callao with Admiral Vallue-Reistra, representing General Vivanco, by virtue of which he obtained permission to export guano from the Chincha Islands which were then under Vivanco's control. On this concession Raborg paid in advance about $7,000 to the insurgents, and he immediately chartered vessels and involved himself in heavy liabilities for the purpose of carrying out his enterprise. But before he had removed any guano, which was national property under the Peruvian law and the sale of which was a government monopoly, the Government of Peru recovered possession of the islands in question and absolutely refused to recognize his contract with the insurgents. The Commission held the contract to be " null and void " on the ground that both according to the law of nations and the then existing treaty between the United States and Peru, Raborg, a foreigner resident in the latter country and engaged in commerce there, could not make a lawful contract with and advance money to an enemy of the government which protected him and with which his own government was at peace. It said:

> There are no principles of public law more clearly laid down than those which define the duties and obligations of a foreigner resident in a country and engaged in commerce there. Kent says that " if a person goes into a foreign country and engages in trade there, he is by the law of nations to be considered a merchant of that country and a subject to all civil purposes." [36]

35 Moore, *Int. Arb.*, II, 1613.

36 Kent, *Commentary on International Law*, Vol. I, p. 74.

The first article of the treaty between the United States and Peru of 26th July 1851 stipulates that there " shall be perfect and perpetual peace and friendship between the United States of America and the Republic of Peru, and between their respective territories, people, and citizens, without distinction of persons and places."

And yet Henry W. Raborg, a citizen of the United States, residing in Lima, engaged in trade there, and a subject of the recognized government, made a contract with and advanced money to an enemy of that government, by which acts he violated his first and most solemn duty as a neutral and as a citizen of the United States; and at the same time broke the plighted faith of his government, and as an indivdual committed an act of war against the government which protected him and with which his own was at peace.

In the opinion of the mixed commission the contract of Henry W. Raborg is null and void, and they decide that the claim is disallowed.[37]

This decision is substantially correct, and the reasons advanced in its support by the Commission must be interpreted in the light of the special circumstances of this case. It appears that Raborg, while residing in Lima and engaged in trade there, made a contract with the admiral of the insurgent navy in temporary control of the harbor of Callao. Apparently the insurgents were not even in possession of the city of Callao, though they did control the harbor there for a short time. The facts show that at the beginning of the insurrection Vivanco embarked his forces on two rebel vessels, took possession of the Chincha Islands for the purpose of availing himself of the guano deposits there, and then proceeded to Callao. But he did not at first attempt to land there. Instead, he continued his voyage to the north of Callao in the hope of gaining support. Meeting with opposition in the north, he returned, and on April 22, 1857, landed at Callao, expecting to take that city and Lima. But he did not in fact succeed in taking Callao. It

37 *Raborg* (*U. S.*) *v. Peru*, Moore, *Int. Arb.*, II, p. 1614.

appears that the people of that city remained loyal to the titular government, and, under the command of leading citizens, they repulsed Vivanco with such loss that he was forced to retreat to Islay and then to Arequipa, where he remained until his ultimate defeat. It was apparently at the time that Vivanco was attempting to take Callao that Raborg, though a resident of Lima which was under the control of the titular government, made his contract with the insurgents and paid them in advance for the concession. In view of these facts, the Commission's decision that Raborg acted in violation of law and of the treaty of peace and friendship between the United States and Peru appears to be justified.

CHAPTER III

ACTS OF "GOVERNMENT ROUTINE"

In recent years international claims commissions have evinced a growing tendency to distinguish within the insurrectionary line in a disturbed state between the insurgent government on the one hand and the permanent administrative machinery of the civil service on the other hand, and between acts and contracts done by the insurgent government and acts and contracts done by the administrative agencies and bureaus of the government which may continue to function under the rebel jurisdiction. In the *Hopkins case*[1] the General Claims Commission of 1923 between the United States and Mexico formulated this distinction for the first time as follows:

The greater part of governmental machinery in every modern country is not affected by changes in the higher administrative offices. The sale of postage stamps, the registration of letters, the acceptance of money orders and telegrams (where post and telegraph are government services), the sale of railroad tickets (where railroads are operated by the government), the registration of births, deaths, and marriages, even many rulings by the police and the collection of several types of taxes, go on, and must go on, without being affected by new elections, government crises, dissolutions of parliament, and even state strokes. A resident in Mexico who cleans the government bureaus or pays his school fee to the administration does not and cannot take into consideration the regularity or even legality of the present administration and the present congress; his business is not one with personal rulers, not one with a specific administration, but one with the goverment itself in its unpersonal aspect.

The difficulty of distinguishing between the government itself and the administration of that government arises at the point where the voluntary dealings and relations between the individual and

1 *Hopkins (U. S.) v. Mexico*, General Claims Commission of 1923, United States and Mexico, *Opinions*, 1927, 42.

the government agencies assume a personal character in support of the particular agencies administering the government for the time being. To this class belong voluntary undertakings to provide a revolutionary administration with money or arms or munitions and the like. But the ordinary agencies, departments, and bureaus of the government must continue to function notwithstanding its principal administrative offices may be in the hands of usurpers, and in such a case the sale and delivery to these necessary and legitimate agencies of supplies, merchandise, and the like, to enable the government itself in its unpersonal aspect to function is a very different transaction from one having for its object the support of an individual or group of individuals seeking to maintain themselves in office. The character of each transaction must be judged and determined by the facts of the particular case.[2]

The Commission then made an interesting attempt to apply this distinction in the field of international law and relations. In this respect it said:

A similar distinction arises in the field of international law. There are, on one side, agreements and understandings between one nation and another changing or even subverting its rulers, which are clothed with the character of a free choice, a preference, an approval, and which obviously undertake to bear the risks of such a choice. There are, on the other hand, many transactions to which this character is alien. Embassies, legations and consulates of a nation in unrest will practically continue their work in behalf of the men who are in control of the capital, the treasury, and the foreign office—whatsoever the relation of these men to the country at large may be. Embassies, legations, and consulates of foreign nations in such capital will practically discharge their routine duties

2 *Hopkins (U. S.) v. Mexico*, General Claims Commission of 1923, United States and Mexico, *Opinions*, 1927, 42, 44-45.

This distinction was approved by the Claims Commission of 1926 between Great Britain and Mexico in the case of *Mrs. Christina Patton*, where it was said: "Even when a country passes through a period of anarchy, even when an established and recognized Government is not in existence, the permanent machinery of the public service continues its activities." *Opinions*, 1933, 215, 218-219.

> as theretofore, without implying thereby a preference in favor of any of the contesting groups or parties. International payments (for a postal union, etc.) will be received from such government; delegates to an international conference will often be accepted from such government. Between the two extremes here also there is a large doubtful zone, in which each case must be judged on its merits. . . .
>
> In the field of international relations the distinction is apparent. Where preexisting relations with government agencies continued under such circumstances as not to imply either approval or disapproval of the new administration or the recognition of its authority these transactions must be treated as government transactions and binding on it as such rather than transactions had with a particular administration. The routine diplomatic and consular business of the nation continued to be transacted with the agencies assuming to act for the government and which were in control of the foreign office, the treasury, and the embassies, legations and consulates abroad. Even the United States, though placing its stamp of disapproval in the most unmistakable manner on the act of Huerta in usurping authority, kept its embassy in Mexico City open for the transaction of routine business, entrusting it to a charge d'affaires, and maintained its consulates throughout Mexico. Such relations, so maintained, were entirely unpersonal; they constituted relations with the United Mexican States, with its Government as such, without respect to the status of the individual assuming to act for the Government.[3]

In making this distinction between acts of a revolutionary administration in its personal character and acts of purely government routine of the government itself as an abstract entity in its unpersonal aspect, the Commission went further and held acts falling in the first category as invalid and void and acts falling in the second category as valid and binding on the state. Between these two extremes, it was said, there is also a large doubtful zone in which each case must be judged on its merits

3 *Hopkins (U. S.) v. Mexico*, General Claims Commission of 1923, United States and Mexico, *Opinions*, 1927, 42, 45-46.

The General Claims Commission of 1923 was established to deal, under international law, with claims "arising from acts incident to the recent revolutions" in Mexico. In a number of cases it was called upon to decide the question whether Mexico was bound by acts and transactions of unsuccessful insurgent governments. From a careful study of the reported cases it appears that no claims involving the so-called acts of an unsuccessful revolutionary administration in its personal character were actually brought before the Commission. Nevertheless, as examples of this kind of acts the Commission mentioned the borrowing of money and the purchase of arms, munitions and the like, that is, acts in aid of rebellion. The lack of claims involving such acts may be explained by the fact that the law is clear on this point. A foreign citizen who knowingly and voluntarily furnishes an insurgent government with money, military supplies and provisions gambles with his property, and in case of the failure of the insurgent movement, has no redress.[4] The Commission's statement, therefore, that the state is not bound by such acts is merely an expression of a generally accepted view. Almost all of the claims before the Commission, therefore, were for alleged acts of government routine. More specifically, they involved postal money orders issued and ordinary commercial contracts made by different departments and bureaus of the Mexican "Government itself as an abstract entity" functioning under the Huerta and other rebel administrations. Although the Commission apparently had a difficult task in deciding whether the Huerta Government was or was not the government of a successful revolution, however, for the purpose of these cases it regarded that government as an unsuccessful insurgent government.

The claim in the *Hopkins case* was one made by the Government of the United States for the price of six postal money orders purchased by an American citizen in 1914 from the

4 *Supra*, Ch. I. See also the *Henriquez case*, Ralston, *Venezuelan Arbitrations of 1903*, 896; *Jarvis case*, *ibid.*, 145; *Stuckle case*, Moore, *Int. Arb.*, III, 2935; the case of *Mary Lowell*, *ibid.*, 2772.

Mexican Government at its post offices in the States of Sonora and Sinaloa. It was said that all of these money orders were in due time presented to the Mexican postal authorities, but that payment was refused by them. The Government of Mexico made a motion to dismiss the claim on the ground that " these money orders were issued by the Huerta administration, which was illegal, that the acts of such administration did not bind Mexico, and that therefore these orders cannot be made the basis of a claim before this Commission against the United Mexican States." The Commission, however, overruled this contention. It pointed out that although " the assumption of power by Huerta was pure usurpation," and that " from being the military commander of the capital, charged with the protection of the administration of President Madero against the revolutionary activities of Generals Reyes and Diaz to overthrow it, Huerta went over to Madero's enemies," took control of the Federal administration and declared himself provisional president of Mexico, nevertheless, it held that these facts had nothing to do with the postal money orders issued to the claimant. The acceptance of money orders by the postal authorities of Mexico was an " unpersonal " act of government routine and not an act of the Huerta administration in its personal character. As an act of government routine it was held binding on Mexico. In this respect the Commission said:

It is clear that the sale by the Mexican Government to and the purchase by the claimant Hopkins of postal money orders falls within the category of purely government routine having no connection with or relation to the individuals administering the Government for the time being. The facts as developed in the Memorial and the briefs, which are not contested by the Mexican Agent, aptly illustrate the necessity of the distinction here made between acts of the Huerta administration in its personal character and acts of the Government itself in its unpersonal character. From the facts so developed it appears that at the very time these postal money orders were issued the greater part of the States of Sonora and Sinaloa, from which they issued, was dominated by Carranza as First Chief of the Constitutional Army, while the City of Mexico, on which the orders were drawn, was dominated by Huerta. Yet the post offices in these two States under the domination of Carranza continued to issue money orders of the United Mexican States upon the postmaster in the Federal District of Mexico. In other cases that have been submitted to this Commission it is apparent that the Government agencies functioning under the Huerta administration continued to carry out obligations under preexisting contracts and otherwise functioned without reference to the change in the administration. It also appears that when Huerta seized the reins of government which in his capacity as provisional president he undertook to administer he did not change the Government machinery as it had been set up under President Madero, which continued to operate in all its parts in the service of the people, and the great majority of the personnel of all of the bureaus and agencies of the Government remained unchanged and continued to discharge their duties to and in the name of Mexico. At no time did the Government machinery cease to function, notwithstanding the change in the personnel of some members of its executive branch. To the extent that this machinery acted in the discharge of its usual and ordinary functions or to the extent that it received benefits from transactions of an unusual nature, Mexico is bound.[5]

In support of its decision the Commission pointed out that the principle applied by it in this case "has been recognized and invoked by the Government of Mexico under administrations of unquestioned regularity and validity." It was said for instance that in the decisions made by the Carranza administra-

5 *Hopkins* (*U. S.*) *v. Mexico*, General Claims Commission of 1923, United States and Mexico, *Opinions*, 1927, 42, 48-49.

In the final decision in this case the Commission disallowed the claim as to three of the money orders in question in view of the uncertainty in the record with respect to the circumstances surrounding the purchase of these orders; but with respect to the other money orders it was decided that the Government of Mexico shall pay to the Government of the United States on behalf of George W. Hopkins the total amount of the orders, with interest at the rate of six per centum per annum from June 6, 1914, to June 3, 1927, the date on which the last award was rendered. *Hopkins* (*U. S.*) *v. Mexico*, *ibid.*, 1927, 329-331.

tion as to the legality of the acts of the Huerta administration, "such acts as the registration of births, deaths, and marriages were practically undisturbed, because they were performed in the orderly functioning of the Government . . . itself as an abstract entity"; and that the same principle was recognized in connection with the financial transactions of the Huerta administration by later administrations of the Government of Mexico to the effect that "the series of Mexican bonds issued during the Huerta regime, the proceeds of which were applied to the payment of the interest on the preexisting debt of Mexico, have been uniformly recognized as valid, while other series of the same issue, the proceeds of which are claimed to have been applied to the maintenance in power of the Huerta administration or to the purchase of arms, munitions, and the like, have been repudiated."[6] The Commission here evidently intimated that loans used for a purpose of public utility may be assimilated with acts of government routine.

As the Commission held that Hopkins' money order contracts, being contracts of government routine, were unaffected by the character of the Huerta administration and were "binding upon the United Mexican States as such," the question presented itself whether "this binding force has from an international viewpoint been subsequently destroyed" by certain decrees of nullity issued by Carranza on February 19, 1913, and July 11, 1916.[7] This question was answered in the negative. It was said that the decree of 1913, issued by Carranza in his capacity as governor of the State of Coahuila, could have no possible effect on or modify either the rights or duties of the Mexican Union itself; and that the decree of 1916, "even when considered as subsequently invested with the character of a law by the Mexican Congress, could not possibly operate unilaterally to destroy an existing right vested in a foreign citizen

6 *Hopkins (U. S.) v. Mexico*, General Claims Commission of 1923, United States and Mexico, *Opinions*, 1927, 42, 46. For a further discussion of the Huerta loan see, *supra*, p. 29.

7 For the texts of these decrees see *Foreign Relations*, 1913 and 1916.

or a foreign state or a preexisting duty owing by Mexico to a foreign citizen or foreign state." [8]

The principle of the *Hopkins case* was uniformly applied by the same Commission to a number of so-called money order cases arising from the Huerta revolution in Mexico.[9] In all of these cases the facts were the same as those in the *Hopkins case,* and the Commission therefore overruled the Mexican defense to the effect that the money orders could not obligate Mexico because they were issued by an illegitimate authority, that is, the Huerta administration. In the *Cook case,*[10] however, a new defense was attempted. In this case again the claim was made by the Government of the United States in behalf of an American citizen to recover a sum of money stated to be the aggregate amount of numerous postal money orders issued in the years 1913 and 1914 to the claimant, and which were not paid upon presentation to the postal authorities in Mexico. Although the Mexican Government moved to dismiss the claim on the ground that "the money orders in question were issued by an illegitimate authority (the administration of General Huerta) which could not bind the United Mexican States," no contentions on this point were pressed before the Commission

8 *Hopkins (U. S.) v. Mexico,* General Claims Commission of 1923. United States and Mexico, *Opinions,* 1927, 42, 49.

Here the Commission referred to the often reiterated principle that foreign citizens may enjoy both rights and remedies which the state does not accord to its own citizens.

9 The principle of the *Hopkins case* to the effect that Mexico was bound by postal money orders issued during the Huerta regime was applied to the following cases: *George W. Cook (U. S.) v. Mexico,* General Claims Commission of 1923, United States and Mexico, *Opinions,* 1927, pp. 318-324; *Parsons Trading Company (U. S.) v. Mexico, ibid.,* 324-325; *John A. McPherson (U. S.) v. Mexico, ibid.,* 325-329; *National Paper and Type Company (U. S.) v. Mexico,* General Claims Commission of 1923, United States and Mexico, *Opinions,* 1929, pp. 3-5; *Francis J. Acosta (U. S.) v. Mexico, ibid.,* 1929, pp. 121-123; *Singer Sewing Machine Co. (U. S.) v. Mexico, ibid.,* 1929, pp. 123-126; *Esther Moffit (U. S.) v. Mexico, ibid.,* pp. 288-291.

10 *George W. Cook (U. S.) v. Mexico, Opinions,* 1927, 318.

in view of the unfavorable decision in the *Hopkins case*. Instead, the Mexican Government shifted its defense and alleged that according to the Mexican law " the right to collect a postal money order is subject to a statute of limitations of two years after the date of issue, and that a recovery on the orders in question is now barred by that statute." The Commission, however, held in effect that domestic " statutes of limitation are not a bar to international reclamations "; that as a matter of international practice, there is " no rule of international law putting a limitation of time on diplomatic action or upon the presentation of an international claim to an international tribunal "; that " the Mexican Government could not by withholding payment for a period prescribed by a domestic statute of limitation relieve itself from an obligation under international law to make restitution of the value of the orders "; and that since it was " satisfactorily established by evidence that the claimant in the instant case presented his money orders and requested payment within the period during which payment could be made under Mexican law, and that payment was refused by Mexican postal authorities," the Mexican statute of limitations did not therefore apply.[11] Accordingly, Mexico was held bound by unpaid money orders issued during the Huerta administration.

In another group of cases, decided by the same Commission, ordinary commercial contracts for the purchase and sale of goods and merchandise between different departments and bureaus of the Huerta administration and foreign citizens were also held to be contracts of government routine and therefore binding on Mexico. The Mexican Government was held liable, for instance, for certain automobile accessories purchased by

11 *George W. Cook (U. S.) v. Mexico*, General Claims Commisison of 1923, United States and Mexico, *Opinions*, 1927, 318, 319.

The Commission also overruled the Mexican defense as to the applicability of the statute of limitation to commercial contracts, see *Parsons Trading Company (U. S.) v. Mexico*, General Claims Commission of 1923, United States and Mexico, *Opinions*, 1929, 135.

and services relating to the repair of automobiles rendered to the Huerta Government between the years of 1913 and 1914;[12] for printing machinery, paper envelopes, and other goods sold to and purchased by various departments of the Mexican Government between 1912 and 1914, a part of the goods being sold and delivered during the period of the Huerta administration;[13] for certain linotype machine supplies, a book sewing machine together with hooks and eye needles, and various kinds of press boards, sold and delivered to different departments of the Mexican Government in 1913;[14] for a number of school benches ordered and delivered to the Mexican Ministry of Public Instruction and Fine Arts during the period from December 1913 to February 1914;[15] and for household furniture, fittings,

12 *Lee A. Craw (U. S.) v. Mexico*, General Claims Commission of 1923, United States and Mexico, *Opinions*, 1929, 1-2.

13 *National Paper and Type Company (U. S.) v. Mexico, ibid., Opinions*, 1929, 3-5.

14 *Parsons Trading Company (U. S.) v. Mexico, ibid., Opinions*, 1929, 135-137.

In this case Mexico raised the defense based on the Mexican statute of limitations, but the Commission overruled it as well as the defense that the contract was with the Huerta administration. See also *George W. Cook (U. S.) v. Mexico, ibid., Opinions*, 1927, 318.

15 *George W. Cook (U. S.) v. Mexico, ibid., Opinions*, 1929, 266-281.

In this case the Mexican Government denied liability on two grounds: first, because the transaction in question took place with the Huerta administration which it considered to be illegitimate, and secondly, because the contract was entered into not between the Ministry and the claimant company directly, but between the Ministry and an agent of the company personally. It was contended that the company could not, under Mexican law, enforce a contract made by its agent in his own name for the company. The Commission unanimously overruled the first defense on the basis of the Hopkins case, but by a majority opinion sustained the second defense. The majority opinion stated that since in countries, and among these Mexico, where the civil law prevails, the sole fact of a contract having been entered into by an agent in his own name excludes the principal from right of action, the claimant company did not have the right to sue in a case like this the contract of which was governed by Mexican law. (*Ibid.*, 267-268). In his dissenting opinion the American commissioner urged an award on the ground that the company as the real party had in fact furnished the benches in good faith, and that failure of an award would be like confiscation of the property of an alien (*ibid.*, 268-281).

fixtures, equipment and utilities purchased during the same period by departments and bureaus of the Mexican Government.[16] All of these commercial goods and supplies were sold and delivered to the different departments of the Mexican Government by American citizens and corporations; and although Mexico uniformly denied its liability on the ground, *inter alia,* that the transactions in question took place with an illegitimate authority, that is, the Huerta administration, nevertheless, the awards were made in favor of the United States in the light of the decision in the *Hopkins case*. It was held that these commercial contracts were contracts of government routine with the Mexican Government as an abstract entity and had nothing to do with the Huerta administration in its personal aspect.

In the *Peerless Motor Car Company case* [17] the application of the doctrine of liability for acts of government routine was perhaps carried farther than in any other case in this group. It was in fact the first case decided by the Commission involving the question whether Mexico was bound by ordinary commercial contracts of the Huerta administration. In the instant case it appears that a contract for the purchase of two automobile ambulances was executed in 1913 in fulfillment of an order "of the Department of War and Navy, between the Chief of the Military Section" of the Huerta Government and a representative in Mexico City of the Peerless Motor Car Company, an American corporation. In the arguments advanced before the Commission the Mexican Government did not dispute the fact "that the automobiles were manufactured and delivered conformably to the terms of the contract, and that the purchase price has not been paid." But it was contended that Mexico had incurred no international liability for "the nonpayment of

16 *George W. Cook (U. S.) v. Mexico*, General Claims Commission of 1923, United States and Mexico, *Opinions*, 1931, 162-167; *George W. Cook (U. S.) v. Mexico, ibid.*, 1931, 167-168.

17 *Peerless Motor Car Company (U. S.) v. Mexico*, General Claims Commission of 1923, United States and Mexico, *Opinions*, 1927, 303-305.

certain war material admitted by the claimant corporation to have been ordered by, and sold and delivered to an illegitimate administration," that is, the administration of General Huerta. It was further maintained that

> even assuming that the legitimate government of the United Mexican States had subsequently to the sale and delivery of the war material aforesaid to the local de facto administration become possessed of the said war material, no liability could be predicated upon the said respondent government neither in international law, nor equity, nor justice, since the said possession was due to the recognized right that all legitimate governments possess to capture the war material of the enemy.[18]

The Commission, however, rejected the Mexican contention and decided in favor of the viewpoint of the Government of the United States which was based upon the principle laid down in the *Hopkins case* relating to acts of government routine. Although there was a general agreement in rendering the award to the United States, there was nevertheless, no unanimity as regards the reason underlying this decision. The American member of the Commission thought that the contract in this case was a mere transaction of government routine, an unpersonal act of the Huerta administration, and therefore binding on Mexico. He said:

> In the view I take of this case it is unnecessary to consider the point as to the responsibility of Mexico grounded on the contention of the United States that it may be assumed from the record that Mexican authorities in power following the administration of General Huerta made use of the cars delivered by the Company. Nor is it necessary to consider the Mexican Government's contention as to the character of the ambulances as war material. The United States contends, among other things, that the purchase of these motor ambulances was an unpersonal act, and that therefore, under the principles laid down in the Hopkins case . . . the Government of Mexico is liable for the purchase price of the ambulances. I am

18 *Peerless Motor Car Company (U. S.) v. Mexico, op. cit.*, 1927, 303, 304.

of the opinion that the contention is sound, and that an award should therefore be rendered in favor of the United States.[19]

The Presiding Commissioner concurred in the award with respect to the liability of Mexico, but said:

The purchase of ambulances, however, in my opinion is not a part of the ordinary routine of government business. It comes within the doubtful zone mentioned in . . . the opinion in the *Hopkins case*. As such it is much more akin to a transaction of government routine (the one extreme) than to any kind of voluntary undertaking "having for its object the support of an individual or group of individuals seeking to maintain themselves in office" (the other extreme), and therefore should, under the principle laid down in the said opinion, be assimilated to the first group, to wit, the routine acts.[20]

The decision in this case appears to be too broad and therefore it necessarily gives rise to the important question of advisability of establishing proper and more or less well defined limits to the concept of acts of government routine. There is, after all, a real difference between the sale, for instance, of postal money orders or the purchase of school benches and sewing machines by the permanent departments and bureaus of a government, on the one hand, and the purchase by the Chief of the Military Section of the Department of War and Navy of a revolutionary administration of motor ambulances and other supplies which may be considered as particularly useful from a military point of view, on the other hand. The first may well be held to fall within the category of acts of government routine; the second most assuredly is not a part of the so-called ordinary routine of government business. The Mexican contention, therefore, that the ambulances in question should be regarded as war material and that their purchase by the Chief of Military Section of Huerta's army should be

19 *Peerless Motor Car Company (U. S.) v. Mexico, op. cit.*, 1927, 304.
20 *Ibid.*, 304-305.

held as an exception to the general rule had its merits. Huerta's army was composed of men who were actively waging war to establish him in power; his Department of War and Navy was undoubtedly functioning under the guidance and control of persons who were most likely appointed to office by the rebel leader and who were interested in the ultimate success of the revolution. Even by the very definition of the Commission in the *Hopkins case* it is believed that this fact alone was enough to induce the Commission to classify the military purchase of these ambulances under acts of the Huerta administration in its personal character and not under acts of government routine. It should be remembered that in the *Hopkins case* the Commission offered two criteria for acts of government routine. First, it gave a list of what it considered to be acts of government routine, such as the sale of postage stamps, the registration of letters, the acceptance of money orders, the registration of births, deaths, and marriages, and the like. In this instance clearly it is either the nature of the act or the character of the goods and services which is assumed to be the determining factor. Secondly, it distinguished between acts of the ordinary departments and bureaus of the government as an abstract entity in its unpersonal aspect and acts of the insurgent administration in its personal aspect. In this instance, therefore, it is the character of the particular government agency performing the act which is assumed to be the determining factor. On the assumption that both of these are useful criteria in deciding acts of government routine and that it may not be difficult or confusing for an international tribunal in applying them to every conceivable case arising from civil conflicts, it is at least clear that the ultimate result obtained by their application to the instant claim leaves something to be desired. Apparently the Commission proceeded on the theory that the ambulances could be safely regarded as non-military goods. If so, the claimant should have been required to establish that either they could not be used or they were not actually used for military purposes as army transports.

The distinction made by the General Claims Commission of 1923 between two categories of acts performed within the insurrectionary line in a disturbed state is new and doubtless useful from the point of view of international arbitral law. Although it has been generally assumed that the state is bound by certain types of unsuccessful insurgent acts and transactions, prior to the cases discussed in this chapter, international tribunals were not in fact called upon and did not have an opportunity to decide this particular question. However, the question itself is not new in so far as national courts are concerned. It is therefore important to know not only the attitude of these courts in this respect, but to point out the difference, if any, beween the theory of national courts and that of international tribunals regarding it. The discussion here will be confined entirely to the view of the Supreme Court of the United States in the Civil War cases. After the American Civil War the Supreme Court was required in a goodly number of cases to decide between the kind of acts of the Confederate Government and of the separate governments of the revolting States to which effect could be given and the kind of acts to which effect could not be given. Most of these cases were of course decided on the basis of the American Constitutional Law and are not therefore germane to this discussion. For the purpose of this study the main point of interest is the attempt of the Supreme Court to distinguish between the different classes of acts of the rebel governments. In the first place a distinction was made between acts of the Confederate Government on the one hand and acts of the State governments within the Confederacy on the other hand. As to the Confederate Government, the court said that in view of the fact that " from a very early period of the civil war to its close, it was regarded as simply the military representative of the insurrection against the authority of the United States," therefore, " no obligations of a national character were created by it, binding after its dissolution, on the States which it represented, or on the national government ".[21]

21 *Thorington v. Smith* (1868), 8 Wall. 1, 9.

It further said:

> When it was overthrown it perished totally. It left no laws, no statutes, no decrees, no authority which can give support to any contract, or any act done in its service, or in aid of its purpose, or which contributed to protract its existence. So far as the actual exercise of its physical power was brought to bear upon individuals, that may, under some circumstances, constitute a justification or excuse for acts otherwise indefensible; but no validity can be given in the courts of this country to acts voluntarily performed in direct aid and support of its unlawful purpose.[22]

This conclusion is due to the fact that practically all acts done by the Confederate Government were by their very nature acts in aid of the rebellion, such as the borrowing of money, the purchase of goods and military supplies, the sale of property, the issuance of Confederate treasury notes and forced currency, and the like. The nature of the political organization of the Confederate States excluded the participation of the Confederate Government in what we call acts of government routine, since this kind of acts were reserved for the member states.

In dealing with acts of the State governments the court pointed out that they "stand on very different grounds, and

22 *Horn v. Lockhart*, 17 Wall. 570, 580.

On the theory that certain Confederate Government acts would be excused because they were mere impositions, the court held that contracts between private parties within the rebel jurisdiction made in the ordinary course of business and stipulating for payment in forced currency were valid. *Thorington v. Smith*, 8 Wall. 1; *Hanauer v. Woodruff*, 15 Wall. 439; *Delmas v. Insurance Company*, 14 Wall. 661; *Planters' Bank v. Union Bank*, 16 Wall. 483; *Taylor v. Thomas*, 22 Wall. 479; *Wilmington and Welder Railroad Company v. King*, 91 U. S. 3; *Effinger v. Kenney*, 115 U. S. 566. In *Thorington v. Smith*, holding that private contracts made within rebel jurisdiction and stipulating for payments in Confederate currency could be enforced in the United States courts, although the currency itself was an act in aid of rebellion, the court said: "They are transactions in the ordinary course of civil society, and, though they may indirectly and remotely promote the ends of the unlawful government, are without blame, except when proved to have been entered into with actual intent to further invasion or insurrection." 8 Wall. 1, p. 12.

are governed by very different considerations ". In view of the fact that for the most part they " merely transferred the existing State organizations to the support of a new and different national head ", and that " the same constitutions, the same laws for the protection of property and personal rights remained, and were administered by the same officers," it came to the conclusion that a distinction should be made between acts of the individual States to which effect could be given and acts to which effect could not be given. Accordingly, this distinction was made quite clear in a number of cases. In *Texas v. White*,[23] for instance, the court considered the nature of acts which would or would not be given effect to and said:

It is not necessary to attempt any exact definitions within which the acts of such a State government must be treated as valid or invalid. It may be said, perhaps, with sufficient accuracy, that acts necessary to peace and good order among citizens, such, for example, as acts sanctioning and protecting marriage and the domestic relations, governing the course of descents, regulating the conveyance and transfer of property, real and personal, and providing remedies for injuries to person and estate, and other similar acts, which would be valid if emanating from a lawful government, must be regarded, in general, as valid when proceeding from an actual, though unlawful government; and that acts in furtherance or support of rebellion against the United States, or intended to defeat the just rights of citizens, and other acts of like nature, must, in general, be regarded as invalid and void.[24]

And again, in *Horn v. Lockhart* [25] the Court said:

We admit that the acts of the several States in their individual capacities, and of their different departments of government, executive, judicial, and legislative, during the war, so far as they did not impair or tend to impair the supremacy of the national authority, or the just rights of citizens under the Constitution, are, in

23 (1869) 7 Wall. 700.

24 *Ibid.*, 700, 733.

25 17 Wall. 570.

general, to be treated as valid and binding. The existence of a state of insurrection and war did not loosen the bonds of society, or do away with civil government, or the regular administration of the laws. Order was to be preserved, police regulations maintained, crime prosecuted, property protected, contracts enforced, marriages celebrated, estates settled, and the transfer and descent of property regulated precisely as in time of peace. No one that we are aware of seriously questions the validity of judicial or legislative acts in the insurrectionary States touching these and kindred subjects, where they were not hostile *in their purpose* or mode of enforcement to the authority of the National Government, and did not impair the rights of citizens under the Constitution.[26]

It thus appears that the executive, legislative, and judicial acts of the rebel States of the Confederacy were divided by the Supreme Court into two main groups: first, acts in aid of rebellion; second, acts done in the ordinary course of governmental routine. Acts falling in the first category were held to be "invalid and void"; acts falling in the second category were as a general rule treated as "valid and binding". Accordingly, decisions were rendered in line with this distinction. For instance in *Texas v. White*,[27] already cited, an action was brought by the State of Texas after the Civil War claiming ownership to certain bonds which had been conveyed to the defendant by a military board created by an act of the legislature of Texas in 1862 while that State was in rebellion against the United States. The court held that the military board was actually created for rebellious purposes by a rebel legislature and that therefore effect could not be given to its act of conveying the bonds in

26 *Horn v. Lockhart*, 17 Wall. 570, 580.

Statements to the same effect as to the different classes of acts of the rebel States may be found in the following case: *Thorington v. Smith*, 8 Wall. 1; *Hanauer v. Woodruff*, 15 Wall. 439; *Mauran v. Insurance Co.*, 6 Wall. 1; *Delmas v. Insurance Co.*, 14 Wall. 661; *Sprott v. United States*, 20 Wall. 459; *United States v. Insurance Co.*, 22 Wall. 99; *Williams v. Bruffy*, 96 U. S. 176; *Baldy v. Hunter*, 171 U. S. 388. For a brief summary of most of these cases see Moore, *Digest*, I, pp. 41-45, 52-60.

27 7 Wall. 700, *passim*.

question. In the *United States v. Insurance Companies*,[28] however, the same court decided that an act of the legislature of the rebel State of Georgia creating two corporations was a valid act of mere ordinary legislation, and that the corporations thus created had valid existence entitling them to claim and recover the proceeds of cotton captured by the military forces of the Federal Government during the Civil War. The Government of the United States challenged the capacity of the corporations in question to maintain action and argued that they had no legal existence since they were created by Georgia while that State was in rebellion. The court overruled this contention, holding that " all the enactments of the *de facto* legislatures in the insurrectionary States during the war, which were not hostile to the Union, or to the authority of the general government, and which were not in conflict with the Constitution of the United States, or of the States, have the same validity as if they had been enactments of legitimate legislatures.[29]

The ultimate result obtained in these cases by the Supreme Court is not only sound, but it very clearly indicates the source from which the General Claims Commission of 1923 derived its own conclusions concerning the different categories of acts of unsuccessful insurgent governments. The similarity of reasoning in both cases is quite obvious. The Supreme Court made the distinction between acts in aid of rebellion and acts in the ordinary course of governmental routine; the Commission distinguished between acts of an insurgent administration in its personal aspect, which it defined as acts in aid of rebellion, and acts of the government itself in its unpersonal character, which it defined as acts of government routine. Aside from differences in terminology, there seems to be no difference of under-

28 22 Wall. 99.

29 *Ibid.*, 99, 101. In the instant case the Supreme Court simply affirmed the decision of the Court of Claims in the *Home Insurance Company's case*, 8 Ct. Cl. 449, where acts of a *de facto* legislature of a rebel state relating merely to the domestic affairs of the people of the state as a community were declared valid.

standing as to the kind of acts of an unsuccessful insurgent government to which effect should be given or by which the state is bound and the kind of acts to which effect could not be given or by which the state could not be bound. There are, however, two fundamental differences between the two situations. First, the Supreme Court was dealing with a domestic problem primarily under the Constitution of the United States; the Commission was dealing with an international situation under the rules of international law. Second, the Supreme Court dealt chiefly with the legislative acts of the rebel states; the Commission dealt with the administrative acts.

CHAPTER IV

TAXES AND CUSTOMS DUTIES

I

UNDER international law the payment of taxes, customs duties, and other revenues of the state by foreign merchants and taxpayers to an unsuccessful insurgent government in temporary control of the territory where payment is demanded and collection made, renders unreasonable and indefensible the subsequent exaction of a second payment by the restored titular government. This rule has been clearly established by decisions of international tribunals of arbitration and uniformly applied in state practice. In the *Guastini case*,[1] brought before the Italian-Venezuelan Claims Commission of 1903, it was found that the revolutionary authorities in possession of the town of El Pilar in Venezuela "during nine months of 1902, and at least to March 10, 1903," had collected certain license fees which would have been payable to the legitimate authorities had they controlled the town. After the collapse of the revolutionary movement the regular governmental authorities reassumed possession of the district in which the licenses had been paid, and compelled a second payment. The claimant, an Italian citizen resident in Venezuela, asked for a refund of his money for being subjected to double license. The Commission allowed the claim on the ground that the original payment made under circumstances of compulsion to the revolutionary authorities who constituted the government *de facto* in the municipality of El Pilar discharged his obligations toward the titular authorities, and held that the money must be returned to the claimant. It stated the rule applicable to such cases and the reason underlying it as follows:

1 Ralston, *Venezuelan Arbitrations of 1903*, 730. For other questions involved in this case see, *infra*, p. 144, note 30.

> Money paid . . . to the *de facto* authorities in shape of public dues must be considered as lawfully paid, and receipts given by them regarded as sufficient to discharge the obligations to which they relate. Any other view would compel the taxpayer to determine at his own peril the validity of the acts of those exercising public functions in a regular manner . . .
>
> During the period for which taxes were collected by the revolutionary government, the legitimate government performed no acts of government in El Pilar. It did not insure protection, carry on schools, attend the needs of the poor, conduct courts, maintain streets and roads, look after the public health, etc. The revolutionary officials, whether they efficiently performed these duties or not during the time in question, displaced legitimate authorities and undertook their performance. The legitimate government, therefore, was not entitled at a later period to collect anew taxes once paid to insure the benefits of local government which it was unable to confer.[2]

This principle was applied also by the umpire of the British-Venezuelan Claims Commission of 1903 in the *Santa Clara Estates case*,[3] where it was held, *inter alia,* that the collection of taxes by the Government of Venezuela for the period during which it had lost its sovereignty over the territory in question, and could neither render protection nor receive obedience, is indefensible in law, logic and ethics. In stating that the titular government had no right to collect for a second time taxes on property which had already been paid to a revolutionary government in effective control of that portion of the national territory where the claimant's property was located, and that taxes so collected must be returned, the Commission said:

2 *Guastini Case*, Ralston, *Ven. Arb. of 1903*, 730, 750-751. The Commission also added: "We must apply to the facts before us the principle which would be involved if the acting *jefe* civil had been illegally appointed or elected by legal authorities acting improperly. In such case no dispute could possibly exist as to the right of the taxpayer to be protected by payment to such illegal but acting officer." *Ibid.*, 750.

3 Ralston, *Ven. Arb. of 1903*, 397.

It is incontestably true that with the duty to pay public taxes flows the right of protection and the conscientious and careful discharge of all imposed public duties by the Government to which this tribute is made; that with the right to demand and exact revenue for the support of government stands the correlative duty to be competent and willing to discharge its public functions and conserve the welfare of the taxpayer, and that the one cannot rightfully or lawfully exist in the absence of the other; but we have found it to be historically true that the Government of Venezuela was neither competent nor present to perform in any part its governmental functions at the place and within the period in question. They had wholly lost their sovereignty over this district and it was wholly out of their control and independent of the titular government, and the attempt to obtain or the obtaining of a second payment of public dues does not disturb the revolutionary status, which the original payment of taxes to the revolutionary government only makes more emphatic its complete control of the situation during the period in question.[4]

Since the American Civil War, at the close of which no demand was made for a second payment of taxes paid to the Confederate Government, the Government of the United States has uniformly taken the position that the exaction of a second payment by the restored government would be " an act of international injustice " if the original payment of taxes and duties to rebel authorities is in fact made in good faith and not in support of rebellion. The cases and incidents to which this principle has been applied by the United States will be discussed presently; here may be cited only certain statements by the Department of State which have a direct bearing upon the general rule. In 1873 the British Government requested the State Department to authorize the American minister to Mexico to use his good offices towards preventing the exaction by the Mexican Government of duties on goods imported by British

4 Ralston, *Ven. Arb. of 1903*, 401-402. Another important question decided in the *Santa Clara Estates Case* involved the responsibility of Venezuela for tortious acts of insurgents. See *infra*, p. 163.

subjects at Mazatlan, which duties had previously been paid to insurgents there. In authorizing the American minister to take that course, the Department said:

It is difficult to understand upon what ground of equity or public law such duties can be claimed. The obligation of obedience to a government at a particular place in a country may be regarded as suspended, at least, when its authority is usurped, and is due to the usurpers if they choose to exercise it. To require a repayment of duties in such cases is tantamount to the exaction of a penalty on the misfortune, if it may be so called, of remaining and carrying on business in a port where the authority of the government had been annulled.[5]

Again, in 1910, while the Estrada and the Madriz factions were fighting for the control of Nicaragua, the Government of the United States simply insisted that "each faction shall collect duties only for territory under its *de facto* control" and refused "to permit the collection of double duties."[6] On this occasion the Department of State instructed the American consul at Bluefields as follows:

The capture by the Madriz faction of the former custom-house at the Bluff does not affect the fact that Bluefields, with certain adjacent territory, for which goods hitherto passing that custom-

5 Mr. Fish, Sec. of State, to Mr. Nelson, American minister to Mexico, February 11, 1873, *For. Rel.*, 1873, I, 654. See also Moore, *Digest*, I, 49.

Here the Department of State attempted an analogy. In referring to the demand for a second payment of duties, it said: "The pretension is analogous to that upon which vessels have been captured and condemned upon a charge of violating a blockade of a port set on foot by a proclamation only, without force to carry it into effect." *For. Rel.*, 1873, I, 654.

Apparently the effort of the American minister to protect the British merchants was not successful, since he subsequently reported that the Mexican "Supreme Court has decided against Messrs. Kelly & Co., of Mazatlan, in the matter of the double payment of duties concerning which your Department, at the request of the English Government, instructed me to use my friendly offices." Mr. Nelson Am. minister, to Mr. Fish, Sec. of State, May 17, 1873, *For. Rel.*, 1873, I, 669.

6 Mr. Knox, Sec. of State, to Mr. Moffat, American consul, June 19, 1910, *For. Rel.*, 1910, 753.

> house are intended, appears to remain, as heretofore, under the *de facto* control of the Estrada faction. This Government therefore admits the right of the Estrada faction to collect customs for Bluefields, and denies this right to the other faction. Inasmuch as this Government recognizes neither faction as a government of Nicaragua, but merely as in *de facto* control of portions of the country, proclamations on either part which are inconsistent with this attitude are without effect on the United States and its citizens.[7]

And again, when from 1912 to 1917 the insurgent factions of Huerta, Carranza, Villa and many other rebel leaders, succeeded in getting control of certain sections of Mexico at different times and in opposition to each other, and in collecting taxes and customs duties, the Government of the United States took the position that

> under the generally accepted rules of international law American citizens in Mexico are entitled to pay taxes upon their property in Mexico to persons in *de facto* authority and that in determining the question of the proper persons to receive payment of taxes it would appear that they would do well to consider the matter of the local control of the territory in which their properties are situated.[8]

It was further said that the payment of taxes on mines and other properties, owned by American citizens, to insurgents exercising *de facto* authority would be regarded by the United States as completely relieving its nationals from further obligation with reference to taxes so paid.[9] This principle received

7 Mr. Wilson, Acting Sec. of State, to Mr. Moffat, Am. consul, May 31, 1910, *For. Rel.*, 1910, 750.

8 The Secretary of State to Consul General Shankin, March 12, 1915, *For. Rel.*, 1915, 964.

9 The American ambassador informed the Mexican minister for foreign affairs under Huerta as follows: "Acting under the instructions of my Government, I have the honor of calling your excellency's attention to the fact that the revolutionists' forces in control of certain portions of those States which have revolted against the Federal Government are levying taxes on mines and other properties owned by citizens of the United States and that my Government regards the payment of such taxes by its citizens to such

its practical application as early as 1912 when the insurgent government of General Orozco demanded from the manager in Chihuahua of the American Smelting and Refining Company of New York City that payments for freight and all export taxes on shipments should be made to that government and not to the Federal authorities. Accordingly, the taxes in question were paid to the insurgent authorities and the American ambassador was instructed to "lay the matter before the Mexican Government and state that the Government of the United States will regard such payments made for freight and export tax to the persons exercising *de facto* authority as completely relieving the Smelting Company of further obligation in regard to such payments." [10] The same procedure was followed during the revolutionary administrations of Huerta and Carranza; in each case those in control of the Federal machinery of government in Mexico were informed that taxes paid to insurgents in States in revolt against the Federal authorities relieved American citizens from further obligations.[11]

An incident illustrative of the principle under consideration arose between the British Government and the Government of Chile in 1891. During the civil war between Balmaceda and the Congressional party, the Balmaceda Government claimed the right to exercise authority over ports and places which had come under the control of the insurgents. In one case double duties were actually exacted when, after a gunboat belonging to the Balmaceda Government succeeded in entering one of the ports in possession of the insurgents and exacting payment of duty on nitrate loaded for a British company on a British ship,

persons exercising *de facto* authority as completely relieving its nationals from further obligation with reference to taxes so paid. My Government has further instructed its Consuls resident within the districts where the above-mentioned insurrectionary forces are in control that such taxes should be paid under protest and should, in so far as possible, be made a matter of record in each case." *For. Rel.*, 1914, 733.

10 *For. Rel.*, 1912, 908-909.

11 *Infra*, p. 126.

the British merchants were forced to make another payment to the revolutionary authorities in order to secure the shipment of the cargo. Informed of this, the British Government took the position that the payment to the insurgents was correct since they were in control of the port, but said that it was "prepared evenually to support a claim on the Presidential authorities for the repayment of the money levied by their gun-boat, as having been wrongfully exacted." [12] The Foreign Office said:

In the opinion of Her Majesty's Government, the action of the gun-boat was altogether wrongful and irregular, such duties being ordinarily and properly payable to the Customs authorities at the port of clearance; and I have informed you that the amount exacted will be claimed back from the Chilean Government.[13]

From the foregoing discussion we may deduce two distinct reasons for the principle that the state is bound by the payment of taxes and customs duties to insurgents. In the first place, it is clear that since civil government is a necessity even in times of internal conflict, those who actually perform the functions of government in a given locality are entitled of right to demand and receive taxes and duties to insure the benefits of local government. Normally such revenues furnish the only available means to enable an insurgent government to carry on the ordinary governmental functions in the interest of peace and good order among citizens. In the second place, looked upon from the viewpoint of merchants and taxpayers, the maintenance of taxes and duties paid to insurgents is due to the fact that "obedience to the command of the insurgent party in a place subject to its control cannot be regarded as unlawful." [14] Once the authority of the titular government over a certain portion of its territory is suspended, its right to the allegiance or obedience of the inhabitants of such territory is also suspended. And since,

12 *Blue Book*, Chile, I, 151. See also, *ibid.*, 139-145, 151-153.

13 *Blue Book*, Chile, I, 157. For other aspects of this case see *infra*, p. 123.

14 Hyde, *International Law*, I, 543-544. See also *United States v. Rice*, 4 Wheat. 246; *MacLeod v. United States*, 229 U. S. 416.

in a sense, the payment of taxes is a token of allegiance or obedience, and a reward for governmental protection, it follows that " where there is no protection, or allegiance, or sovereignty, there can be no claim to obedience " and therefore to the right of collecting taxes and duties.[15] A taxpayer or a merchant must take governments as he finds them, and pay his taxes or customs duties accordingly. He is not permitted to investigate or to question the right to such taxes and duties of even an insurgent government under whose protection he lives and trades.

II

While it is generally accepted both in law and in practice that the payment of taxes and duties to an insurgent government in local control relieves merchants and taxpayers from a second payment to the titular government, this seems to be subject to a definite condition or limitation. This condition consists of the requirement that such payment is in fact made under command imposed by a *force majeure* which makes obedience a necessity, that is, it is made under compulsion or duress, or under threats to person or property, or under intimidations and sanctions amounting to coercion. To prove that such is the case it is necessary to show that the payment was due; that the person making the payment, or his property, or his agent, was within the territorial limits and under the jurisdiction of the insurgent government; and that the insurgent authorities demanded the payment in question. In the absence of any one or all of these elements such payment may be open to a different legal construction. It may raise the question of voluntary payment, and, therefore, considered to be in support of rebellion. It will be seen that practically all of the international controversies on this subject turn primarily on the question whether the original payment to the insurgents was a voluntary one or one made under compulsion. The success or failure of the titular government to compel a second payment depends solely on proof in establishing one or the other contention.

15 *United States v. Rice*, 4 Wheat. 246.

During a civil disturbance in Colombia in 1885 the insurgent forces took control of the port of Barranquilla and proceeded to collect customs duties on foreign importations. After the collapse of the insurgent movement the titular government issued a decree stipulating, *inter alia,* for a second payment of duties already paid to insurgents, declaring that the original payment of custom-house duties in any place occupied by rebel forces not only could not exempt the importers from their obligations to the national treasury, but that that fact would be a reason for imposing an additional fine in case the required second payments were refused or not made promptly.[16] A protest against this decree was made by the foreign consuls at Barranquilla, who regarded a second payment unjust in view of the fact that the original payment of the duties in question was made on the demand of the insurgents who had control of the town and the custom-house.[17] Meanwhile, the Government of the United States made the question a diplomatic one and in a note to the Colombian minister at Washington it said:

> . . . there can be no question that no government has the right to inflict a punishment (for this double tax, with superadded penalty, amounts to a punishment) on neutral and peaceful merchants who have been compelled by military force to contribute against their will to the revolutionary funds or supplies, as if such merchants were voluntarily aiding and abetting the rebellion.

16 See *For. Rel.*, 1885, 270, for the text of the decree issued on February 10, 1885, by the President of the United States of Colombia. Among other things it stipulates as follows: "The payments of the importation duties that have been made to persons having no legitimate official character in any custom-house or place of the Republic, incidentally occupied by rebel forces, not only does not exempt the respective importers from the obligation contracted by them or their agents in favor of the national treasury, but will be a cause for adding to the debt 50 per cent on the amount of duties erroneously paid, provided the importer or his agents having been advised, deny the immediate payment of the duties occasioned in favor of the public treasury." *Ibid.*, 270-271.

17 For the text of the Foreign Consuls' protest see *For. Rel.*, 1885, 271. See also the note of the American minister to the Secretary of State. *ibid.*, 221-222.

A government is bound to use all proper measures to protect the denizens within its borders from revolutionary acts, and in case it fails to insure such protection, it cannot with any justice hold the citizens of foreign nations responsible for its own weakness and failure to protect them, by imposing on them a penalty or fine for the very occurrences which the government itself was bound to avert. Such a course of action as is authorized by the decree of the 10th of February would be especially objectionable as being a retroactive revenue measure at ports admitted to have been beyond the control of the Government at the time the rebel dues were paid.[18]

To the consuls' protest as well as to the note of the American Government the Colombian authorities replied that the decree in question was not intended to be enforced against neutral foreigners who had paid the duties under compulsion.[19] More specifically, the Colombian minister at Washington informed the Department of State that by a new and supplementary decree issued *ad hoc* the Government of Colombia

has declared that only the importers who freely and voluntarily paid the imposts levied on their imports to the rebels who succeeded in getting possession of some of the said ports of entry, are obliged to make the payment over again, together with a penalty; bona fide

18 Mr. Bayard, Sec. of State, to Mr. Becerra, Colombian Minister, June 1, 1885, *For. Rel.*, 1885, 269, 270; Moore, *Digest*, VI, 995, 996.

A remonstrance against the decree issued by the Government of Colombia on February 10, 1885, providing for a second payment and a penalty in case of default, was also made by the American minister at Bogota. The Colombian minister of foreign affairs, adverting to the circumstance that no American names were on the list of those who were required to make the second payment or were fined under the decree, intimated that it never was intended to be enforced against neutral foreigners, and he afterwards stated that it would be revoked. Mr. Scruggs, American minister, to Mr. Bayard, Secretary of State, October 3, 1885, *For. Rel.*, 1885, 221-222, 229-230; Moore, *Digest*, VI, 997.

19 See the reply of General Acevedo to the consuls' protest *For. Rel.*, 1885, 272; Mr. Becerra, Colombian minister, to Mr. Bayard, Sec. of State, Dec. 3, 1885, *For. Rel.*, 1885, 280; Mr. Scruggs, American minister, to Mr. Bayard, Sec. of State, Oct. 3, 1885, *For. Rel.*, 1885, 221-222.

importers, who were compelled to pay under duress, are in consequence free from all responsibility.[20]

In a last communication on this subject the Department of State at Washington apparently acquiesced in the new arrangement in restricting the application of the decree " to cases where the importers freely and voluntarily paid duties to the rebels "; but expressed the view that " no unreasonable proof will be required of the involuntary character of the payments to the insurgent agents," and that in times of armed insurrection the necessary presumption is that importers yield to *vis major* and pay under duress without being permitted to make or file formal protest against the payment of customs duties to the rebel authorities. On this point the Department said:

. . . the Government of the United States assumes, in respect of this supplementary decree, that no unreasonable proof will be required of the involuntary character of the payments to the insurgent agents. It is well known that in times of armed insurrection, when forced loans and arbitrary extortion are resorted to, the usual forms of protest are not permitted, and the parties levied upon are almost invariably constrained to submit, rather than run the danger of incurring by a show of resistance double burdens and greater loss.

Even under the normal operation of Colombian laws a protest against such levies may entail a penalty. This was the case with the decree against which my note of June 1 last remonstrated, for it assumed to add 50 per cent in the case of those merchants who should refuse payment to the agents of the constitutional Government of duties already paid by them to the insurgents when in sole control.[21]

In the disorganized and unprotected condition of society at the Colombian ports in question during the period referred to, it would be indeed surprising to learn that any American importer there

20 Mr. Becerra, Colombian minister, to Mr. Bayard, Sec. of State, December 3, 1885, *For. Rel.*, 1885, 280.

21 The Sec. of State to the Colombian minister, Dec. 11, 1885, *For. Rel.*, 1885, 281.

had been permitted to make or file formal protest against the payment of customs duties to the rebel authorities. Under such circumstances the rational and necessary presumption is that they yielded to *vis major* and paid under duress, unless the contrary be distinctly shown.

We trust that the manifest justice and reasonableness of this will be borne in mind, in executing the Colombian decree now announced by you, which, regardless of all rational presumption, seems to throw upon the sufferers the burden of proof that positive coercion was resorted to against them.[22]

In subsequent discussion it will be seen that the view expressed here to the effect that the burden of proof is on the restored government to show that duties paid to insurgent authorities were voluntary and not made under compulsion is based on sound principle.

In 1899 an insurrectionary movement broke out at Bluefields, Nicaragua, against the titular government of President Zelaya; and for a time the rebel forces exercised actual control over the place. The insurgents under General Reyes took and held "absolute and uncontested possession of the port and city of Bluefields, of the Government treasury, arms and war munitions, post office, custom-house, army, gunboat, executive mansion, and all public buildings",[23] and from February 3 to February 25, 1899, performed all the functions of government, including the collection of customs duties. During this rather brief period the merchants paid to the insurgent authorities none of the current customs duties in cash, but gave bonds for them, "payable at thirty days' sight, or until such time as a legitimate government, recognized by the foreign powers, is established at

22 The Sec. of State to the Colombian minister, Dec. 11, 1885, *For. Rel.*, 1885, 281.

23 Mr. Merry, American minister, to Mr. Sanson, Foreign Minister of Nicaragua, Sept. 7, 1899, *For. Rel.*, 1900, 807, 808. See also Mr. Merry, American minister, to Mr. Hay, Sec. of State, April 23, 1899, *For. Rel.*, 1899, 569, 570.

this port ".[24] Nevertheless, they did pay in cash for certain customs bonds or notes which had matured and which had been given for duties on goods imported before the civil disturbances in question. These bonds or notes carried a penalty of 5 per cent per month if not paid when due." [25] After the collapse of the revolutionary movement and the restoration of the old government, a peremptory demand was made upon the merchants of Bluefields to pay the dues again or suffer the consequences.[26] In making this demand the Nicaraguan Government seems to have been under the definite impression that the foreign merchants were in sympathy with and actually helped the insurgent movement; [27] that the original payment to the insurgents was voluntary in view of the fact that those merchants who did not pay were not molested; and that the insurgents did not in fact constitute a *de facto* government of the character to which payment of dues could be justified. The American merchants, however, denied any complicity with the revolutionary movement, protested against the demand for a second payment, and appealed to their government for protection. The Government of the United States informed its nationals that since " the payment of duties to an insurgent authority in temporary occupancy of a port is a case of *force majeure*," the Nicaraguan Government was not justified in asking for a second payment; but advised them to make the

24 Note of Foreign Consuls to the Commander of the U. S. S. Marietta, February 22, 1899, *For. Rel.*, 1899, 558-559. See also the Secretary of State to the Secretary of the Navy, March 17, 1899, *For. Rel.*, 1899, 558.

25 Mr. Hay, Sec. of State, to Mr. Merry, Am. minister, July 26, 1899, *For. Rel.*, 1900, 803.

26 Mr. Clancy, Am. consul, to Mr. Merry, Am. minister, March 30, 1899, *For. Rel.*, 1899, 563.

27 Mr. Torres to Mr. Clancy, March 2, 1899, *For. Rel.*, 1899, 564; Mr. Merry to Mr. Hay, April 23, 1899, *For. Rel.*, 1899, 569-571; Mr. Kelting to Mr. Clancy, April 20, 1899, 572-573; Mr. Sanson to Mr. Merry, Aug. 25, 1899, *For. Rel.*, 1900, 806. Contra, Mr. Peterson to Mr. Merry, April 24, 1899, *For. Rel.*, 1899, 574; Mr. Hay to Mr. Merry, July 26, 1899, *For. Rel.*, 1900, 803.

second payment under protest, holding that "payments noted as made 'under protest' might be made the ground of equitable representations to the titular Government should it proceed to recollect duties on resuming control." [28] But the merchants were still inclined to withhold payments for the reason that once second payments were made to the Government of Nicaragua it would be difficult to get the moneys back even if a later inquiry absolved them of complicity with the insurrectionary movement. In this they were supported by the American minister and by the commander of the U. S. S. *Detroit,* then at Bluefields, who cabled a suggestion to the Department of State that second payments be refused, (1) because the revolutionary government was certainly *de facto* and therefore in a position to demand and collect the dues in question, and (2) because such refusal was necessary to the maintenance of the American interests and influence in Nicaragua.[29] The Department of State, however, disregarded this suggestion and followed a more approved course by instructing the American minister as follows:

1. That this Government will not lend its countenance or support as against such second payment to any Americans, if any such there be, who have freely and voluntarily aided or abetted in any manner the said insurrection.

2. But all Americans who made such payment to the insurgent authorities under duress of person or property, or under intimidations amounting to corecion, are entitled, if second payments are demanded by the Nicaraguan Government, to make such payments under protest. Such payment under protest does not prejudice in any manner the legal rights of the Nicaraguan Government nor those of the American merchants. Its effect is merely, notwithstanding such second payments, to reserve to the parties making them their legal rights, and afterwards to demand the refundment of the moneys so paid, if they were illegally exacted. This Govern-

28 Mr. Adee, Second Assistant Sec. of State, to Mr. Clancy, Am. consular agent, March 6, 1899, *For. Rel.*, 1899, 557.

29 Mr. Merry, Am. minister, to Mr. Hay, Sec. of State, April 23, 1899, *For. Rel.*, 1899, 569.

ment will therefore sustain said American citizens in their attitude and claim of the right of protest while making such second payments. If there are any such Americans who have made them and have refrained from protesting against the same because they have been required by the Nicaraguan Government to make them without protest, this Government will, for the purpose of this controversy, treat such second payments as having been actually made under protest, and will consider the ultimate rights of the parties, whatever they may be, as unimpaired by reason of such payments exacted and made without protest.

This Government has not prejudged the rights of the parties, but, pending their consideration and awaiting a full investigation and knowledge of the facts, it withholds its decision until such a time as it can be rendered with due regard to the mutual rights and interests of the parties, to the principle of public law and to the usages of civilized nations. It is actuated by the desire to reach, if possible, a solution of the question consistent at once with the feelings of friendship existing between the two Governments and with the dictates of international justice.[30]

Meanwhile, since the Nicaraguan Government insisted on a second payment without protest, the American minister and the Nicaraguan minister of foreign affairs reached an agreement under which it was arranged that the money demanded by the Government of Nicaragua should be deposited with the British consul pending the final settlement of the controversy.[31] The Nicaraguan Government also agreed to raise the embargo which it had previously placed on certain merchandise in order to enforce its demand for a second payment of the dues already paid to the insurgents. Ultimately the United States approved this arrangement,[32] and the British consul accepted the trust.[33]

30 Mr. Hay, Sec. of State, to Mr. Merry, Am. minister, April 17, 1899, *For. Rel.*, 1899, 566-567.

31 See text of the agreement, *For. Rel.*, 1899, 576.

32 Mr. Hay, Sec. of State, to Mr. Merry, Am. minister, May 6, 1899, *For. Rel.*, 1899, 579.

33 Mr. Bingham, British consul, to Mr. Merry, Am. minister, May 4, 1899, *For. Rel.*, 1899, 581.

The Department of State then undertook to investigate the facts. The evidence submitted to the Department regarding the circumstances of the payment of the dues to the insurgents, consisting in part of the sworn statements of the American merchants, apparently showed (1) "the bona fide neutrality of said merchants preceding and during the revolutionary movement led by General Reyes, and their absolute freedom from complicity in that movement"; (2) the payments actually made to the insurgent authorities were for customs bonds or notes which had matured and which carried a penalty of 5 per cent per month if not paid when due; (3) those customs bonds or notes were in the possession of the same person who had been appointed by the titular government and continued by General Reyes as treasurer at Bluefields, and who demanded their payment; (4) under fear of incurring the penalty and under threats by General Reyes of suspension of importations the merchants were constrained to make said payments involuntarily and at the risk of serious injury and loss if they refused;[34] and (5) during the period of February 3 to 25 the insurgents were in full control and exercise of all the governmental agencies, civil and military, in the district.[35] Under these circumstances, and in the absence of any proof that the original payments were voluntarily made, the Government of the United States expressed the opinion that to exact a second payment

34 "The evidence submitted to the Department of State shows that the customs dues were not voluntarily paid, but were paid under threats, menacing the merchants with the detention of their goods in the custom-house, inflicting serious injury upon their property and business interests and subjecting them to a monthly payment of 5 per cent for delay beyond maturity in the payment of said notes. No evidence has been submitted to this Government that such payments were voluntary. On the other hand, it stands ready to submit proofs to the contrary. The fact that actual violence was not used against those who did not pay is not evidence that those who did pay did so voluntarily." Mr. Hay, Sec. of State, to Mr. Merry, Am. minister, October 2, 1899, *For. Rel.*, 1900, 810.

35 Mr. Hay, Sec. of State, to Mr. Merry, Am. minister, July 26, 1899, *For. Rel.*, 1900, 803-804; Mr. Hay, Sec. of State, to Mr. Merry, Am. minister, October 2, 1899, *For. Rel.*, 1900, 810.

would be "an act of international injustice," and asked the assent of Nicaragua to the return of the money by the British consul to the merchants. The Government of Nicaragua then sought to bring the matter before its judicial tribunals, and to require the merchants involved to establish before those tribunals their "excuse" for their "unwarranted payments" of revenues to the insurgents.[36] The United States, however, objected to this on the ground that the question had become a diplomatic one. It said that it had no objection to an investigation of the matter by the Nicaraguan tribunals and that the Nicaraguan Government had "a right to investigate the facts connected with the Reyes movement and to ascertain whether the merchants participated in and aided the movement"; but it objected to any Nicaraguan court in deciding the question as between the two governments.[37] On this point the Department of State said:

36 The Nicaraguan court at Bluefields did in fact take jurisdiction, and decided that the American merchants must pay the contested duties to the Nicaraguan Government. See text of this decision, *For. Rel.*, 1900, 817-818. However, the Department of State called this "sentence" as "simply null and void and will receive no consideration or respect from the Government of the United States." Mr. Hay, Sec. of State, to Mr. Merry, Am. minister, August 2, 1900, *For. Rel.*, 1900, 820. No attempt was made by the Government of Nicaragua to give effect to this decision.

37 "If the American merchants are summoned as witnesses before Judge Roman they must obey and testify as to the facts. The Nicaraguan Government has a right to investigate the facts connected with the Reyes movement and to ascertain whether the merchants participated in and aided the movement. While the Government of the United States protects its citizens in the engagement of their lawful rights it does not protect them in the prosecution of unlawful acts and enterprises. The Government of the United States is disposed to respect the dignity of the Government of Nicaragua, which maintains that controversies over the payment of customs duties are ordinarily to be determined in the first instance by the local tribunals. The Government of the United States is not inclined to dispute the general principle, but in the present case, having taken diplomatic jurisdiction, it is constrained to adhere to its position." Mr. Hay, Sec. of State, to Mr. Merry, Am. minister, December 15, 1899, *For. Rel.*, 1900, 813-814.

> The Government of the United States does not admit the competency of any Nicaraguan court or tribunal to determine the rights of American citizens in Nicaragua when they have appealed to their Government for protection, and when it has taken up and made their cause its own; and the contention that it has agreed or consented to submit to the assumption and exercise of jurisdiction over such cause by any local Nicaraguan court or tribunal is so extraordinary that it cannot be considered or discussed. If, in the face of said agreement, the Government of Nicaragua persists in its indicated purpose to submit the question at any stage or in any form to its own tribunals for determination as between the two Governments, the Government of the United States will not only ignore the proceedings, but will deem it a sufficient reason for it to proceed to determine the question in the proper way, and to use the necessary measures to enforce its decision.[38]

This statement seems to have terminated the controversy. Although the two governments apparently failed to agree on the important question whether the original payments were made under compulsion to a *de facto* authority, nevertheless, the money deposited with the British consul was ultimately returned to the American merchants with the assent of Nicaragua.[39]

During the two controversies discussed above the Government of the United States uniformly maintained that, in cases where there is no clear evidence of compulsion for payment of duties to insurgents by foreign merchants, "the rational and necessary presumption is that they yielded to *vis major* and paid under duress, unless the contrary be distinctly shown." The burden of proof is on the restored government to show that the payments were voluntary, and moreover, such proof must

38 Mr. Hill, Acting Sec. of State, to Mr. Merry, Am. minister, September 29, 1899, *For. Rel.*, 1900, 809.

39 *For. Rel.*, 1900, 820-824. See also Moore, *Digest*, I, 49-51; VI, 684-688. At one stage of the controversy the United States asked Nicaragua to submit evidence as to the voluntary character of the payments. It said such proof would terminate the controversy; but no proof was submitted.

be based on facts. The mere assertion that such payments were made voluntarily is not sufficient evidence to justify the demand for a second payment of taxes or duties. This seems to be the view sanctioned by international law and applied by international tribunals.[40] In the *De Forge case* [41] the facts revealed that in 1861 certain French citizens shipped brandy to New Orleans, then under the control of the Confederate Government, and prior to the capture of that city by the Federal forces in 1862 a part of the brandy was taken from the custom-house and duties on the brandy so taken were paid to the rebel authorities. It was not shown that the duty in question was paid by the importers under protest or that the collection was actually made by the insurgent authorities under intimidations and sanctions amounting to coercion. Upon the restoration of the authority of the United States, the Federal Government exacted a second payment on the ground that the original payment was an act of aid and comfort to the Confederate Government. However, this position was not sustained by the Commission of 1880 between the United States and France, and the French claim for the return of this second payment was allowed. The Commission held that the payment of customs duties to a revolutionary government in control of a port of entry is not in itself an act in aid of rebellion, and does not constitute unneutral conduct which would bar a claim for damages in international law. In such cases the presumption is that foreign merchants yield to *vis major* and pay under duress, unless the contrary is distinctly shown by the government demanding a second payment. In this instance no proof of the French merchants' guilt was submitted by the Government of the United States. Again in the *Guastini case*,[42] already discussed above, it was specifically stated by the umpire of the Italian-Venezuelan Claims Commission of 1903

40 See the *Guastini case*, Ralston, *Venezuelan Arbitrations of 1903*, 730; the *Santa Clara Estates case*, *ibid.*, 397. *Supra*, pp. 104-106.

41 *De Forge et Fils* (*France*) *v. United States*, French American Claims Commission of 1880, Boutwell's *Report*, 105; Moore, *Int. Arb.*, III, 2781.

42 Ralston, *Ven. Arb. of 1903*, 730; *supra*, p. 104.

that the payment of taxes within insurrectionary lines to a *de facto* authority must be presumed to have been made under compulsion unless the contrary is established.

In order to avoid controversy on the question whether the payment of taxes or duties to an insurgent government was in fact made under compulsion, in recent years foreign states have followed the practice of asking their nationals within insurgent territory to make such payment to the insurgents under protest and to obtain receipts. Wherever possible merchants and taxpayers have been instructed to make their protests a matter of record so that it can be shown that payment was demanded and collection made by the insurgent authorities under duress. This procedure was followed at first by the British Government during the civil conflict in Chile in 1891; and then by the Government of the United States during a succession of revolutions in Mexico from about 1912 to 1917. In 1891, during the civil war between President Balmaceda and the Congressional party, the Balmaceda government claimed the right to exercise authority over ports and places of which the insurgents had obtained *de facto* possession in the course of the revolution. This subjected foreign merchants to double liability, and in consequence various questions arose as to the payment of duties on the exportation of nitrate from the insurgent ports. In view of these facts, certain British subjects who were engaged in the exportation of nitrate sent an inquiry to the British Foreign Office as to whether it was safe to pay to the insurgents in control of the port of Iquique, Chile, the export tax on nitrate. The tax was very heavy in proportion, doubling the cost of nitrate; and it was feared that they might "hereafter be called upon to pay this tax over again if they ship nitrate now when the shipment thereof has been inhibited by the Chilean Government, and when the duties paid thereon would be paid to the insurgents."[43] In reply to this inquiry the Foreign Office stated that it could not "undertake to advise whether it is safe

43 *Blue Book*, Chile, I, 66.

for merchants to pay export duties on nitrate to the insurgent authorities at ports which are in their possession," but said:

Where the insurgent forces are in possession of a port, and refuse to allow nitrate to be shipped unless certain dues are paid, the merchants must decide for themselves what course they will take, taking care, however, that any payments be made, if at all, only on compulsion and under protest. It would of course be preferable that a bond only should be given for the amount, if the insurgent authorities could be induced to accept it.

As to the question of the claim of the Chilean Government to levy over again the duty so exacted, I am to state that Her Majesty's Government do not admit the right of the Chilean Government to exact the duty when there is evidence that it has already been paid on compulsion and under protest to the authorities in actual and complete possession of the port of export. If the claim should be persisted in, a bond might be given for the amount pending settlement of the question between the two Governments.[44]

The important feature here is the definite instruction to the British merchants to pay the export duties in question " only on compulsion and under protest."

Similar instructions as to payment under protest were given by the Government of the United States to its citizens resident in Mexico during the protracted period of civil wars in that country from 1912 to 1917, thus reversing the position previously taken by the Department of State to the effect that in times of armed insurrection " the usual forms of protest are not permitted." In 1912 the American consul in the State of Chihuahua asked for advice from the Department of State in view of the fact that the insurgent government of General Orozco there was demanding the mine taxes due to the Federal Government.[45] The Department sent the following instructions:

44 *Ibid.*, 69.

45 The consul further pointed out that there was a " penalty according to law for non-payment 50 per cent increase first month, 100 second, relinquishment title third. While larger mines can stand double payment in case of failure of rebel movement, it will be burdensome for many small

Department assumes from your telegram . . . that Americans are already paying taxes to insurrectionary authorities. You are instructed that such taxes should be paid under protest. The protest should be made a matter of record in such case as far as possible. Properly authenticated receipts should be secured for all taxes paid. Americans are entitled, however, to pay taxes to persons in de facto authority. . . . Ambassador at Mexico City is being instructed to lay the matter before Mexican Government, calling attention to the exaction of taxes by insurrectionary forces, and stating that this Government will regard payment of such taxes to such persons exercising de facto authority as completely relieving American citizens from further obligation with reference to taxes paid in that way.[46]

After the regular authorities reassumed control in the State of Chihuahua they attempted to collect for a second time these mining taxes already paid to the revolutionary government of General Orozco, which was the *de facto* government at the time of the payment. The Department instructed the American consul there "to advise Americans in his district to decline to pay taxes a second time."[47] Subsequently, the Mexican Government assured the American ambassador in Mexico that it would not attempt a second collection of taxes paid to rebel authorities.[48]

Again, in 1913 a decree was issued by the acting governor of the State of Sonora, in rebellion against the Huerta government, which provided that all taxes previously paid to the federal authorities should be paid to the treasurer of the State of Sonora. More specifically, the decree stipulated that all mining taxes must be paid to the officials of that State, and if not

owners." Mr. Letcher, American consul at Chihuahua, to the Secretary of State, March 23, 1912, *For. Rel.*, 1912, 907.

46 Mr. Wilson, Acting Secretary of State, to Mr. Letcher, American Consul, March 27, 1912, *For. Rel.*, 1912, 907-908.

47 The American Ambassador to the Secretary of State, August 21, 1912, *For. Rel.*, 1912, 910.

48 The American Consul at Chihuahua to the Secretary of State, August 24, 1912, *For. Rel.*, 1912, 910.

so paid the mining properties concerned would be forfeited.[49] Notice of this provision was given by the prefect of each district to owners of mining properties in Sonora. Similar decrees were issued by other Mexican states in rebellion against the Huerta regime.[50] At the same time the Federal authorities continued to exact payment of these taxes, with the result that the taxpayers were confronted with demands from two or more different factions at war with each other. American consuls in these areas and numerous American citizens resident in Mexico applied to the Department of State for advice and instructions.[51] In advising American consuls in Mexico in regard to the exaction by insurrectionary authorities of taxes on mines and other properties owned by American citizens, the Department repeated its instructions of 1912, stated above, according to which (1) American citizens were to pay taxes to persons in *de facto* authority; (2) they were to make payment under protest, "which protest should so far as possible be made a matter of record in each case," and properly authenticated receipts were to be secured for all taxes paid in that way.[52] The Department also stated that taxes so paid would be regarded by the Government of the United States as relieving American citizens from further obligations.[53] These instructions applied to payments of taxes in 1913 and in 1914 to the Carranza

49 For the text of this decree see *For. Rel.*, 1914, 731.

50 *For. Rel.*, 1914, 730.

51 See especially Vice Consul Simpich to the Secretary of State, April 5, 1913, *For. Rel.*, 1914, 730; Vice Consul Bowman to the Secretary of State, April 12, 1913, *For. Rel.*, 1914, 731.

52 Mr. Moore, Acting Secretary of State, to Mr. Simpich, Vice Consul, April 26, 1913, *For. Rel.*, 1914, 732-733.

In one form or another these instructions to the effect that taxes should be paid to insurgents under protest were repeated in the following communications: Mr. Bryan, Sec. of State, to Mr. Miller, Am. Consul, June 15, 1914, *For. Rel.*, 1914, 741; Mr. Bryan, Sec. of State, to Mr. Silliman, Am. Vice Consul, August 22, 1914, *ibid.*, 756; Mr. Bryan, Sec. of State, to the Brazilian Minister to Mexico, August 27, 1914, *ibid.*, 757; Mr. Bryan, Sec. of State, to Mr. Silliman, Am. Vice Consul, September 2, 1914, *ibid.*, 757.

53 *Supra*, p. 108.

faction in revolt against General Huerta who was in control of the federal machinery of government in Mexico. Under practically identical circumstances they were repeated in 1915 and in 1916 when General Villa was in revolt against the Carranza government and was collecting taxes in territories under his control.[54]

During the period in question Huerta and Carranza were in control, respectively, of the federal government in Mexico. There is no evidence that the Huerta government ever attempted to collect for a second time taxes paid to the insurgents representing the Carranza or the Constitutionalist faction. However, it appears that the Carranza Government did make demands for a second payment of taxes paid to the Huerta and Villa factions. Manifestly the demand for taxes paid to Huerta was not seriously meant and was withdrawn without much difficulty.[55] But the demand for taxes paid to Villa seems to have been in earnest. On February 16, 1915, the Treasury Department of the Carranza government issued an order as follows:

There are frequent cases in which Federal tax collectors inquire of this Department whether they should accept as valid the payment of taxes to the pretended authorities who without right

54 See especially the Secretary of State to Consul General Shanklin, March 12, 1915, *For. Rel.*, 1915, 964; the Secretary of State to Consul Guyant, March 23, 1915, *ibid.*, 965; the Secretary of State to Special Agent Silliman, March 28, 1915, *ibid.*, 972; Mr. Osborne, Acting Secretary of State, to Special Agent Silliman, June 30, 1915, *ibid.*, 974; Mr. Carr, Acting Secretary of State, to Mr. Sidney Smith, July 12, 1915, *ibid.*, 974; Mr. Lansing, Sec. of State, to the American National Bank of San Diego, November 30, 1915, *ibid.*, 982; the Secretary of State to Mr. Hoff, November 30, 1915, *ibid.*, 982; the Secretary of State to Consul Simpich, May 19, 1916, *For. Rel.*, 1916, 720-721; the Secretary of State to Special Representative Rodgers, August 12, 1916, *For. Rel.*, 1916, 726.

55 It appears that local authorities of the Carranza government made demands for taxes paid to Huerta, but Carranza himself did not approve this. Mr. Silliman, Am. Vice Consul, to the Secretary of State, August 29, 1914, *For. Rel.*, 1914, 757; the Brazilian Minister to Mexico to the Secretary of State, October 6, 1914, *For. Rel.*, 1914, 758.

had been occupying places that have since returned to the power of the Constitutionalist Army. Once for all, and by order of the First Chief of the Constitutionalist Army, in charge of the Executive Power, be it known by all tax collectors directed by this Department that they must not accept as valid any payment made to pretended authorities not recognized by this Government; and they will proceed to collect the taxes not heretofore collected by our authorities. This order extends to payments hereafter to be made in places now occupied by rebel forces or which they may hereafter occupy.[56]

This was contrary to the principle of international law on the question involved, to the view uniformly expressed by the Government of the United States, and to the instructions sent by that government to its diplomatic and consular agents in Mexico during the period under consideration. The Carranza government was aware of this, and apparently realizing that such an order could not be enforced against the nationals of foreign states, in a subsequent decree it rescinded the order in question and stipulated, *inter alia,* that (1) taxes paid to rebel authorities prior to the date of occupation of each city or village by the Constitutionalist forces are considered paid; but (2) that taxes paid to rebel authorities before they were due or in advance of the date of payment, must be paid again.[57] This second requirement was just, as it is generally recognized that the payment of taxes to insurgents will free taxpayers from further obligation only when it can be shown that such payment

56 *For. Rel.*, 1915, 970.

57 The decree began with the following rather interesting preamble: "That, notwithstanding the fact that taxes paid to the so-called authorities of the Convention and of Villa are void and null and that the Constitutionalist Government could proceed rightly to the repayment of the taxes which were not collected during the time inimical forces to our cause occupied certain cities, nevertheless, as a grace which can only emanate from a legitimate Government as this and in view of the destitute circumstances and of the economic crisis which we are undergoing, through the misbehavior of said inimical forces, I have seen fit to decree as follows." Text of Carranza's decree, *For. Rel.*, 1916, 736. See also Mr. Parker, representing Am. interests, to the Sec. of State, Sept. 22, 1916, *ibid.*, 733.

was due. There is no doubt that this decree met all the expectations of the Government of the United States; solved a difficult international question arising from a unique civil war during which so many insurgent factions collected taxes under compulsion; and terminated all attempts of the Constitutionalist government to collect taxes for a second time, which would have doubtless given rise to future claims against Mexico.

How far the result obtained in Mexico may be said to have been influenced by the fact that American taxpayers in that country could offer proof that they had paid their taxes to insurgent authorities under protest it is difficult to say. It is believed, however, that the practice in recent years of England and the United States in instructing their nationals in Chile and Mexico to pay taxes to insurgents in local control under protest, and to make such protest a matter of record, provides the best protection against a second payment by the titular government. In some cases insurgent authorities may and in some cases they may not permit such protest. But, in order to avoid all controversy with the titular government, it seems to be in the interest of the foreign nationals in a disturbed territory to pay their taxes and duties to the insurgents under protest whenever permissible and thus obtain uncontestable proof that they acted under compulsion and in good faith. It must be pointed out, however, that the making of a protest in such cases is not a requirement of the law of nations. Normally, international tribunals presume that taxpayers and merchants yielded to *vis major* and paid under duress even in the absence of any protest, unless there is evidence to the contrary.

III

The principle that taxes and duties once paid to insurgent authorities are not liable again to be paid when the titular government is restored is, of course, generally recognized in international law and uniformly applied in state practice. Before leaving this subject, however, it is necessary to point out the fact that this principle originally was derived from the law of military occupation and is based on a reasoning by analogy. By the modern law of nations an occupied territory is subject only to be governed by the conqueror during his military possession. The military occupant is merely a temporary authority, who may form a civil government for the conquered country, and may levy taxes and impose duties on imports and tonnage for the support of the civil government thus established and of the army of occupation.[58] Under the general right of control which is granted to a military occupant for the purposes of the war he not only has the right of preventing his enemy from using the resources of the occupied territory; but, since he carries on the functions of government in such territory, he has obviously also the right of appropriating taxes and duties for his own use. In *Dooley v. United States*[59] the Supreme Court explained the basis of such right as follows:

> Under the occupation of the country by the military forces of the United States the authority of the Spanish Government was superseded, but the necessity for a revenue did not cease. The Government must be carried on, and there was no one left to administer its functions but the military forces of the United States. Money is requisite for that purpose, and money could only be raised by order of the military commander. The most natural method was by the continuation of existing duties. In adopting this method, General Miles was fully justified by the laws of war.[60]

58 *United States v. Rice*, 4 Wheaton 246; *Cross v. Harrison*, 16 How. 164; *New Orleans v. Steamship Company*, 20 Wall. 387; *Dooley v. United States*, 182 U. S. 222; *McLeod v. United States*, 229 U. S. 416; *case of McCalmont, Greaves & Co.*, Moore, *Inter. Arbitrations*, III, 2866; Moore, *Digest*, I, 45-51; VII, 269; Hyde, *Int. Law*, II, 368; Magoon's *Report on the Law of Military Occupation*, 227; Richardson's *Messages and Papers of the Presidents*, X, 208, 214; the Hague Regulations of 1907, Relative to the Laws and Customs of War on Land, Section III, where it is stipulated that the occupant should, as far as possible, collect taxes and duties in accordance with the assessment in force; he should defray the expenses of the administration of the occupied territory on the same scale as that before the occupation; he should collect taxes only "under a written order and on the responsibility of the commander-in-chief"; and he should give to the taxpayer a receipt for every payment.

59 182 U. S. 222.

60 *Ibid.*, 230.

But once merchants and taxpayers in territory under military occupation pay their taxes and duties to the occupant, they are free from further obligations. This principle was clearly established in 1819, in the case of the *United States v. Rice,*[61] when the Supreme Court not only held that a military occupant had the right to collect duties but stated as a rule of international law that duties once paid to the government of a military occupation are not liable to be paid for a second time when the enemy is finally expelled or withdraws. It appeared that during the military occupation of Castine, in the State of Maine, from the first day of September, 1814, to February, 1815, the British Government exercised all civil and military authority over the place, established a custom-house, and collected duties on goods imported according to regulations prescribed by itself. After the evacuation of the place by the enemy, and the resumption of authority by the United States, some of the goods thus imported were still found in Castine and the American Government asked for a second payment of duties under its own revenue laws. In rejecting the demand for a second payment, the court said:

> Under these circumstances, we are all of opinion that the claim for duties cannot be sustained. By the conquest and military occupation of Castine, the enemy acquired that firm possession which enables him to exercise the fullest rights of sovereignty over that place. The sovereignty of the United States over the territory was, of course, suspended, and the laws of the United States could no longer be rightfully enforced there or be obligatory upon the inhabitants who remained and submitted to the conquerors. By the surrender the inhabitants passed under a temporary allegiance to the British Government, and were bound by such laws, and such only, as it chose to require and impose. From the nature of the case, no other laws could be obligatory upon them, for where there is no protection or allegiance or sovereignty, there can be no claim to obedience. Castine was, therefore, during this period, so far as respected our revenue laws, to be deemed a foreign port;

61 4 Wheat. 246.

and goods imported into it by the inhabitants were subject to such duties only as the British Government chose to require. Such goods were in no correct sense imported into the United States. The subsequent evacuation by the enemy, and the resumption of authority by the United States, did not, and could not, change the character of the previous transactions. The doctrines respecting the *jus postliminii* are wholly inapplicable to the case. The goods were liable to American duties, when imported, or not at all. That they were not so liable, at the time of the importation, is clear, from what has already been stated; and when, upon the return of peace, the jurisdiction of the United States was reassumed, they were in the same predicament as they would have been if Castine had been a foreign territory, ceded by the treaty to the United States, and the goods had been previously imported there. In the latter case, there would be no pretense to say that American duties could be demanded; and upon principle of public or municipal law, the cases are not distinguishable.[62]

The same principle was applied when similar conditions arose from civil wars. At least as far as the question of collection of taxes and duties are concerned, nations came to realize that there is no fundamental difference between the government of a military occupation and a revolutionary government in control of a part of the national territory. During the American Civil War, which because of its magnitude and its duration served for the first time to clarify some of the very important principles of modern international law bearing on *de facto* governments, the British minister at Washington made an inquiry as to what position the United States proposed to take with regard to the action of the rebel authorities of South Carolina at Charleston in assuming to regulate foreign commerce and to exact duties on imports. In reply, the Department of State at first thought that the payment of duties to a person who was not an officer of the United States and authorized by its laws to receive them would be a mispayment, and that the clearance which might be obtained contrary to those laws could not be

62 *United States v. Rice*, 4 Wheat. 246, 254-255.

regarded as valid by the Federal Government. However, it added that the specific question whether the state of things existing at Charleston would or would not be regarded as a sufficient reason for not exacting the penalties which might be incurred by British subjects, was a question which must be reserved till it arose. It was further said that each case would have its own peculiarities, and no general assurance could be given concerning the intentions of the President. "Any uncertainty on such a subject is in itself an evil which ought to be removed if it could be. But the reliance which your lordship cannot but feel on the justice of this Government will no doubt quiet all apprehension of ultimate wrong to British subjects, if such wrong can possibly be avoided." [63] This was in December, 1860, at just about the beginning of the war. By the time the war was over, all doubt or uncertainty on this subject was gone and there was quite a definite understanding of the law. As a result, no claim for a second payment of taxes and duties exacted by the rebel authorities was ever made by the United States.[64] In fact, many suits which had been brought at the close of the civil war against importers for duties on merchandise paid to insurgent authorities were actually discontinued in view of the well-reasoned decision of the Supreme Court in the *United States v. Rice*.[65] If any doubt still remained on this

63 Moore, *Digest*, VI, 995.

64 The *De Forge* case may be considered as an exception to this statement although that claim was in fact based not on the theory that the United States had a right to a second payment but rather on the theory that that particular payment was made voluntarily in aid of rebellion, *supra*, p. 122.

65 "The principle that duties once paid in a part of the territory of the country in possession of an enemy are not liable again to be paid when the enemy is expelled or withdraws, was solemnly decided by the Supreme Court of the United States in the case of Rice, 4th Wheaton, page 246.

"Since the close of the civil war in this country suits have been brought against importers for duties on merchandise paid to insurgent authorities. Those suits, however, have been discontinued, that proceeding probably having been influenced by the judgment of the Supreme Court adverted to." Mr. Fish, Sec. of State, to Mr. Nelson, minister to Mexico, February 11, 1873, *For. Rel.*, 1873, I, 654; Moore, *Digest*, I, 49.

subject, it was entirely dispelled by a number of decisions subsequently rendered by the same court in certain cases arising from the American Civil War where the rebel governments were classified under the same category with the British military government at Castine and where it was stated that at least certain problems of the two situations were analogous or identical.[66] The collection of taxes and duties by both kinds of *de facto* governments was deemed to be one of these problems.[67]

66 See especially *Thorington v. Smith* (1868), 8 Wall. 1, 8-10; *Williams v. Bruffy* (1877), 96 U. S. 176, 185-186. For a summary of these cases, Moore, *Digest*, I, 41-45, 52-60.

67 In *New Orleans v. Steamship Company*, in making a comparison between acts of an insurgent government and acts of a military occupant, the Supreme Court said: "Although the city of New Orleans was conquered and taken possession of in a civil war waged on the part of the United States to put down an insurrection and restore the supremacy of the National government in the Confederate States, that government had the same power and rights in territory held by conquest as if the territory had belonged to a foreign country and had been subjugated in a foreign war. In such cases the conquering power has a right to displace the pre-existing authority, and to assume to such extent as it may deem proper the exercise by itself of all the powers and functions of government. It may appoint all the necessary officers and clothe them with designated powers, larger or smaller, according to its pleasure. It may prescribe the revenues to be paid, and apply them to its own use or otherwise. It may do anything necessary to strengthen itself and weaken the enemy. There is no limit to the powers that may be exercised in such cases, save those which are found in the laws and usages of war." 20 Wall. 387, 393-394.

CHAPTER V

TORTIOUS ACTS

It is a settled principle of international law that the state is not responsible for injuries to foreign persons, and damages to foreign property inflicted during an insurrection or a civil war by unsuccessful insurgents whose conduct it could not control, and where there is no proven negligence or a want of due diligence on the part of the titular government in preventing the injury or in suppressing the insurrection. This rule is supported by the overwhelming weight of authority, on the part of foreign offices, of arbitral commissions, and of writers.[1] It has been consistently maintained and closely followed by the Department of State in practically all cases involving civil war claims of its citizens against foreign states and even of foreign citizens against the United States, and in exceptional cases the general rule has not been denied but merely limited and jealously qualified.[2] As early as 1836 an American brig was detained apparently by insurgents at Porto Alegre, Brazil, for which the owners wished to prefer a claim against the Government of Brazil. The State Department advised the American chargé that

1 As to the views of writers, see the standard works on international law, especially those cited by Borchard, *Diplomatic Protection*, 229, note 7. The following articles and books may be found of some value: Goebel, in 8 *A. J.* (1914), 802; Arias, in 7 *A. J.* (1913), 724; Calvo, in 1 *R. D. I.* (1869), 417; Anzilotti, in 13 *R. G. D. I. P.* (1906), 305; Pennetti, *Responsabilite internazionale in caso di revolte o di guerre civile*, Napoli, 1899; Wiesse, *Le droit international applique aux guerres civiles*, 1898; Podesta Costa, *Efectos internacionales de la actuacion de los gobiernos de facto*, Buenos Ayres, 1924; Rougier, *Les guerres civiles et le droit des gens*, 1903; Sadoul, *De la guerre civile en droit des gens*, Nancy, 1905; Breton, *Responsabilite des etats en matiere de guerre civile touchant les dommages causes a des ressortissants etrangers*, Nancy, 1906; Strupp, in the Annual Report of the International Law Association, Vol. I.

2 *Infra*, p. 159.

If he [the master of the brig] was detained by the insurgents at Porto Alegre, as he was duly apprised before he left Rio Grande that that place was in their power, it is considered that the Imperial Government cannot be held accountable so long as the insurgent domination lasted.[3]

In 1856 a Mexican warship fired into an American schooner anchored in a Mexican harbor. The Mexican Government stated that at the time the aggression occurred the warship was in a condition of revolt against the authorities of the Republic, and that the Government had issued a circular to the diplomatic corps disavowing any responsibility for any acts the vessel might commit while in a state of mutiny. It appears that the United States was entirely satisfied with these explanations.[4] In 1863 losses were sustained by an American citizen at Puerto Plata during an insurrection against the Spanish authorities in Santo Domingo. The Spanish Government explained that every possible measure had been taken for the protection of foreigners, but that the Spanish troops were obliged by the insurgents to abandon Puerto Plata, and that under the circumstances Spain was not liable for the losses caused by the insurgents. The Department of State seems to have acquiesced in this decision and declined to press a claim preferred against Spain.[5] In 1868 in answer to a letter of an American citizen, making claims against the Government of China for property destroyed in 1861 by rebels against its authority, Secretary of State Seward said:

It is a well established principle of international law maintained by this Government in consideration of claims of its citizens against foreign states and of foreigners against the United States, that no

3 Mr. Forsyth, Sec. of State, to Mr. Hunter, Charge d'affaires, March 13, 1839, Moore, *Digest*, VI, 954. See also Moore, *Int. Arb.*, V, 4615-4617.

4 Mr. Appleton, Acting Sec. of State to Mr. Benjamin, M. C., June 13, 1887, Moore, *Digest*, VI, 955.

5 Mr. Rockpill, Acting Sec. of State, to Mr. Lithgow, Sept. 18, 1896, Moore, *Digest*, VI, 955.

government can be held responsible for the acts of rebellious bodies of men, committed in violation of its authority, where it is itself guilty of no breach of good faith or of no negligence in suppressing insurrection.[6]

The same principle was followed in cases of foreign claims arising from injuries inflicted by the Confederate authorities during the Civil War.[7] When the Prussian Government, for instance, took an exception to a draft of a claims convention which restricted the admission of losses and damages to those caused by persons in the service of the United States and excluded those inflicted by the rebel authorities, the Department of State replied that the general rule that a government is not liable for the tortious acts of unsuccessful insurgents was too well established to admit of discussion.[8] In 1871, in a note to the American minister to Bolivia relating to injuries inflicted upon an American citizen by the orders of a military officer in rebellion against the Government of Bolivia, the Department of State refused to interpose to obtain remuneration from Bolivia, and said:

> It must be anticipated that the Bolivian Government would receive such an application in the same manner as we would receive an application from a foreign power whose subject, while residing in the United States, had been injured by troops acting under the orders of one of the chiefs of the late rebellion. It would of course be repelled; and what we would not ourselves allow, we cannot ask from another government in a parallel cause.[9]

A similar course was followed in regard to losses and damages committed by the insurgents in Cuba in 1875. In refusing to

6 Mr. Seward, Sec. of State, to Mr. Smith, July 9, 1868, Moore, *Digest*, VI, 956.

7 As to the British claims arising from the Civil War, *infra*, p. 149.

8 Mr. Seward, Sec. of State, to Baron Gerolt, Prussian minister, Jan. 9, 1866, Moore, *Digest*, VI, 957.

9 Mr. Davis, Acting Sec. of State, to Mr. Markbreit, minister to Bolivia, July 7, 1871, Moore, *Digest*, VI, 959.

bring claims against the Spanish Government, the Department said that " Spain cannot be held to a greater degree of liability to foreigners for losses incurred by reason of lawlessness in Cuba, than is the United States for similar disorders within its jurisdiction." [10] It was further pointed out that since the Spanish Government was not liable for the tortious acts of the insurgents, and since the insurrection had failed, " there would seem to be no responsible government which would be liable." [11] And again, during the Brazilian insurrection of 1893 the property of an American citizen was destroyed and his business broken up. It appears that his place of business was on an island in the harbor of Rio de Janeiro, directly in range of much of the firing between the opposing forces, and he was apparently unable to show what part of the damage was caused by the Government and what part by the insurgents. Under the circumstances the Department of State could find no valid ground for a claim against Brazil. In directing the American minister to Brazil to drop the matter, the Department said:

> It is a principle of public law too well settled to require the citation of authorities that a sovereign is not responsible for injuries done to alien residents by insurgents whom he cannot control. There is no allegation that the Brazilian Government was able to prevent the acts of the insurgents in this case. The Department cannot therefore present a claim for damages done by them.[12]

The principle was invoked in practically the same form during the Cuban insurrection of 1895 and during the recent revolutionary disturbances in Mexico. In the case of the Cuban insurrection, certain American landowners resident in Cuba made

10 Mr. Bayard, Sec. of State, to Mr. Sutphen, Jan. 6, 1888, Moore, *Digest*, VI, 961, 964.

11 Mr. Hay, Sec. of State, to Mr. Rush, May 18, 1899, Moore, *Digest*, VI, 960.

12 Mr. Olney, Sec. of State, to Mr. Thompson, minister to Brazil, January 29, 1896, Moore, *Digest*, VI, 966. See also Mr. Hay, Sec. of State, to Sir M. Herbert, British Ambassador, Jan. 27, 1903, *For. Rel.*, 1903, 482.

inquiries concerning the protection of their property from seizure or destruction by insurgents. They had learned that the insurgents had forbidden the removal of cattle from the farms, and asked the Department if they had the right to apply to the Spanish authorities for protection of their property, and, in case of refusal, under what circumstances and in what form they could make protest for damages. In answer to this inquiry the Department of State declared that where the Spanish Government was in a position to prevent injury by insurgents, American citizens were doubtless entitled to demand and receive protection, but pointed out that where the insurgents had gone beyond the control of the authorities "it is a generally accepted principle of international law that a sovereign government is not ordinarily responsible to alien residents for injuries that they may receive within its territories from insurgents." [13] In the case of the recent Mexican revolutions, the American Ambassador, in view of a growing number of injuries inflicted upon American citizens and their property, requested the Department of State for definite instructions as to the policy to be followed. The Department stated that the matter of claims against Mexico would be settled later, but said that in any case all claims for damages caused by revolutionists would be subject to the general rule that a government is not ordinarily responsible to alien residents for injuries received within its territory from insurgents whose conduct it could not control.[14] It was pointed out, however, that this rule was subject to important limitations and exceptions and that the Government of the United States could not agree with an

13 Mr. Uhl, Acting Sec. of State, to Mr. Springer, American Vice-Consul-General at Havana, July 1, 1895, *For. Rel.*, 1895, II, 1216; Moore, *Digest*, VI, 966, 967.

14 Mr. Adee, Acting Sec. of State, to Mr. Wilson, American Ambassador, Nov. 7, 1911, *For. Rel.*, 1912, 946; Mr. Wilson, Acting Sec. of State, to Mr. Wilson, American Ambassador, April 8, 1912; *For. Rel.*, 1912, 961; Mr. Wilson, American Ambassador, to Mr. Knox, Sec. of State, January 8, 1913, *For. Rel.*, 1913, 924-925; Mr. Knox, Sec. of State, to Mr. Wilson, American Ambassador, January 25, 1913, *For. Rel.*, 1913, 932-934.

unqualified statement made by the Government of Mexico to the effect that "no state is legally responsible for damages and prejudice which during an insurrection may be suffered by foreigners at the hands of rebels." [15]

The same principle has been maintained also by the British Foreign Office and by practically all other nations.[16] In 1885, a British subject who had been injured by the burning of Colon sought the aid of his government to claim reparation from Colombia for the damages he had suffered. The British minister to Colombia, under instructions from the Foreign Office, replied as follows:

> From the reports obtained by Her Majesty's Government it clearly appears that the destruction of Colon was due solely to the revolutionists, who, declaring themselves against the government, succeeded in obtaining complete possession of the city for a short time, and possessed thereof set it on fire in several places. It appears that when these events took place the Government of Colombia was entirely unable to prevent them, even though it afterwards accidentally succeeded in putting down the rebellion.
>
> Under these circumstances, there is not, in the opinion of Her Majesty's Government, sufficient reason for asserting that the destruction of Colon was directly due to the fault of the Colombian Government, to the extent of justifying a demand for redress in behalf of those English subjects who, like yourself, have unfortunately suffered losses by reason of the fire.
>
> Therefore I have to communicate to you, pursuant to instructions of the prime minister, that, regretting the injuries suffered by you, I am unable to support your claims against the Government of Colombia.[17]

15 Mr. Wilson, American Ambassador, to Mr. Knox, Sec. of State, January 8, 1913, *For. Rel.*, 1913, 924, 925; Mr. Knox, Sec. of State, to Mr. Wilson, American Ambassador, January 25, 1913, *For. Rel.*, 1913, 932.

16 As to the views of a large number of nations in regard to damages caused by insurgents see League of Nations: Conference for the Codification of International Law, Bases of Discussion drawn up by the Preparatory Committee, Vol. III, pp. 108-121.

17 Quoted in the dissenting opinion of Andrade, Venezuelan Commissioner

Again, in 1913, the printed instructions to His Majesty's consular officers provided as follows:

Where claims are made for compensation for damages done by insurgents in armed insurrections against a government which was unable to control them, claimants should be reminded that His Majesty's Government do not regard a government as liable in such cases unless that government were negligent and might have prevented the damage arising or unless they pay compensation to their own citizens or subjects or to other foreigners in similar cases, or unless the rebellion has been successful and the insurgent party has been installed in power.[18]

The practice of other European states as to the practically uniform acceptance of the general rule is evidenced by numerous treaties between those states and certain Latin-American republics.[19] One of the provisions, which is common to all

in the case of the *Venezuelan Steam Transportation Company* (*U. S.*) *v. Venezuela*, Moore, *Int. Arb.*, II, 1659, 1728.

18 Mr. Wilson, American Ambassador to Mexico, to Mr. Stronge, British minister, Jan. 27, 1913, *For. Rel.*, 1913, 937. See also Mr. Stronge, British minister to Mexico, to Mr. Wilson, American Ambassador, Jan. 28, 1913, *For. Rel.*, 1913, 938.

During the civil disturbances in Mexico the British Foreign Office followed the view that "His Majesty's Government do not regard a government as liable for compensation for damages done by insurgents in armed insurrection unless the rebellion has been successful." The British minister to the American Ambassador, Jan. 28, 1913, *For. Rel.*, 1913, 938.

As to the British practice see also Peruvian S. S. *Huascar case*, 1877, 68 *British and Foreign State Papers*, 745.

19 Treaties confirming the general rule of nonliability for tortious acts of uncontrollable insurgents have been concluded between France and Mexico in 1886, art. 11, 77 *British and Foreign State Papers*, 1090; France and Colombia in 1893, 84 St. Pap. 137, and *For. Rel.*, 1894, 200; Germany and Mexico in 1882, art. 18, Martens' *Recueil des treates*, vol. 59, 476; Germany and Columbia in 1892, art. 20, 84 *State Papers*, 144; Italy and Mexico in 1889, art. 16, Martens, Vol. 68, 711, 771; Italy and Colombia in 1892, art. 21, Martens, Vol. 72, 313; Italy and Venezuela in 1861, art. 4, 54 *State Papers*, 330; Belgium and Mexico in 1895, art. 15, Martens, Vol. 73, 73; Belgium and Venezuela in 1884, art. 18, 75 *State Papers*, 39; Spain and Venezuela in 1861, 53 *State Papers*, 1050; Spain and Equador in 1888, art. 3,

the treaties cited, of the treaty of 1886 between France and Mexico, stipulates as follows:

> It is agreed further between the contracting parties, that their respective governments, save in cases where there is a want of vigilance on the part of the authorities of the country or their agents, will not hold each other reciprocally liable for the injuries, oppressions, or exactions which the citizens of one may experience in the territory of the other in time of insurrection or civil war, through the insurrectionists . . . who refuse obedience to the government.[20]

79 *State Papers*, 632, and Olivart's *Tratados de Espana*, Vol. 9, 27; Spain and Honduras in 1894, art. 4, Olivart, Vol. 11, 156; Spain and Colombia in 1894, art. 4, Olivart, Vol. 11, 64; Spain and Peru in 1897, art. 4, Olivart, Vol. 12, 348; Sweden and Mexico in 1885, art. 21, Martens, Vol. 63, 690.

See Borchard, *Diplomatic Protection*, 244; Moore, *Int. Arb.*, II, 1727; and the *Aroa Mines Case*, British-Venezuelan Claims Commission of 1903, Ralston, *Venezuelan Arbitrations of 1903*, 384-385.

Mr. Andrade, Venezuelan Commissioner, in commenting on the European practice as to the nonliability of the State for injuries inflicted by uncontrollable insurgents in his dissenting opinion in the *Venezuelan Steam Transportation Company Case*, said: "France, after the revolution of July 1830; the uprising of Lyons in 1834; the revolution of the month of February of 1848; the insurrection of Commune in Paris in 1871; and the events of Port Said in 1881; Belgium, on the occasion of the disturbances which took place there about the month of April 1834; . . . categorically rejected the principle of *obligatory indemnity by the state* in the circumstances cited. Whenever they have accorded pecuniary assistance to the victims of insurrections of that nature, they have expressly declared that they did so through spontaneous liberality, not through *legal obligation*; in the sense of *compassion for personal misfortune and not as a legal right or for indemnity*; that acts of reparation in such cases are not founded on legal obligation; that such events come under the category of those inevitable acts to which all inhabitants of a country are exposed as they are to the effects of plague, and they cannot compromise the responsibility of the state; and that aliens establishing themselves on national territory to engage in business, *ipso facto* submit themselves to local law and courts." Moore, *Int. Arb.*, II, 1659, 1728.

20 Article II, sec. 2, of the treaty of 1886 between France and Mexico, 77 *State Papers*, 1090. See also Moore, *Int. Arb.*, II, 1727.

In certain of the treaties cited, the provision for non-liability for acts of uncontrollable insurgents is not reciprocal, but is made expressly in favor of the Latin-American nations. It is stated, for instance, that "the German

This principle has been also uniformly applied to a variety of claims by an impressive number of international arbitral commissions in cases where by the protocol their jurisdiction was not specifically limited.[21] For example, the United States and Mexican Claims Commission of 1849 disallowed a claim for pillage of goods of an American citizen by unsuccessful revolutionary forces in Mexico.[22] The United States and Mexican Claims Commission of 1868 rejected and dismissed, on the one hand, a claim against the United States for the destruction by the Confederate forces of cotton belonging to a Mexican citizen;[23] and, on the other hand, claims against Mexico for damages such as imprisonment[24] and injury[25] to persons of American nationality, and destruction[26] and confiscation[27] of American property caused by the Zuloaga, Miramon, and Maximilian governments and other rebel forces. The American and British Claims Commission of 1871 disallowed claims arising from the destruction of British property by the authorities of the Confederate States.[28] The United States and Spanish Claims Commission of 1871 absolved Spain from any liability for damages caused as a result of an attack

Government will not attempt to hold the Colombian Government responsible," etc. See art. 20 of the treaty of 1892 between Germany and Colombia, 84 *State Papers*, 144; and art. 21 of the treaty of 1892 between Italy and Colombia, Martens, vol. 72, 313.

21 For cases decided under protocols expressly or allegedly admitting responsibility, see *infra*, p. 211.

22 *Pope case*, Moore, *International Arbitrations*, III, 2972.

23 *Prats case*, Moore, *Int. Arb.*, III, 2886.

24 *Walsh case*, Moore, *Int. Arb.*, III, 2978.

25 *Burn case*, *Frazier Case*, and *Blumenkron Case*, Moore, *Int. Arb.*, III, 2978.

26 *McKenny Case*, Moore, *Int. Arb.*, III, 2881; *Vesseron Case*, *ibid.*, 2975; *Cummings Case*, *ibid.*, 2976; *Crother Case*, *ibid.*, 2977; *Wyman Case*, *ibid.*, 2978; *Silva Case*, *ibid.*, 2979.

27 *Jansen Case*, Moore, *Int. Arb.*, III, 2902; *Baxter Case*, *ibid.*, 2934.

28 *Hanna Case*, Moore, *Int. Arb.*, III, 2982; *Laurie Case*, *ibid.*, 2987 and *Stewart Case*, *ibid.*, 2989.

on an American plantation and for destruction of other property by Cuban insurgents in 1870.[29] During the Venezuelan Arbitrations of 1903, the umpires of practically all the various Commissions assembled in Caracas were of the opinion that under international law there existed no responsibility on the part of the Venezuelan Government for the tortious acts of unsuccessful revolutionists,[30] such as forced loans and requisitions,[31] seizure of property,[32] and damages to and destruction

29 *McGrady Case*, Moore, *Int. Arb.*, III, 2981; *Zandiver Case*, *ibid.*, 2982.

30 The Venezuelan Arbitrations of 1903 comprised of the following Commissions: American-Venezuelan Commission, Bainbridge, Umpire; British-Venezuelan Commission, Plumley, Umpire; Italian-Venezuelan Commission, Ralston, Umpire; Netherlands-Venezuelan Commission, Plumley, Umpire; French-Venezuelan Commission; Spanish-Venezuelan Commission, Gutierrez-Otero, Umpire; German-Venezuelan Commission, Duffield, Umpire. See Ralston, *Venezuelan Arbitrations of 1903, passim.*

Practically all of the umpires of these Commissions expressly stated that under international law no claims for damages arising from acts of unsuccessful insurgents could be allowed; but some of them allowed such damages under a construction of the protocols under which they acted. In the *Guastini Case*, Ralston, Umpire of the Italian-Venezuelan Commission, commented on the fact that the umpires were uniformly in favor of the general rule and said: "Such is the view of the umpires of the English and Netherlands Commission, of the German Commission, and, as it appears, of the Spanish Commission. Furthermore, it is the opinion of the umpires above referred to (save that of the Spanish Commission, possibly) that such claims are inequitable. It is true that the umpire of the German Commission, influenced by a construction of his protocol which this umpire cannot conscientiously follow, has allowed (but within strict limits) certain claims of the character in question. It is also true that the umpire of the Spanish Commission, notwithstanding his apparent belief as to their illegality, has granted claims of this nature, considering the objection raised thereto by Venezuela as 'technical' and therefore opposed to the protocol. This view the present umpire is unable to accept, believing as he does that an obligation going to the foundation of the right to recover for claims of this nature. Nothing is said above about the decision of the umpire of the French Commission, as . . . the reasons for his decision were not given and the particular facts are unknown." Ralston, *Ven. Arb. of 1903*, 730, 748.

31 *Sambiaggio Case*, Italian-Venezuelan Commission, Ralston, *Venezuelan Arbitrations of 1903*, 666, 679; *Guastini Case*, Italian-Venezuelan Commission,

of property.[33] During the Arbitration between the United States and Great Britain of 1910, a claim for losses and damages sustained by an American religious society during a native rebellion in the British protectorate of Sierra Leone in 1898 was disallowed.[34] And, lastly, the General Claims Commission of 1923, between the United States and Mexico, rejected and disallowed a claim by the American Government to obtain compensation for cattle said to have been taken from the ranch of an American citizen in Mexico by the unsuccessful revolutionary forces of General de la Huerta in 1924.[35]

In subsequent discussion we will have an opportunity to take into consideration the reasons advanced and the conclusions reached in some of the most important cases decided by these commissions.

II

Two reasons have been advanced for the practically uniform acceptance and application by international arbitral tribunals and by foreign offices of the principle stated above. First, it is said that the state is not liable because unsuccessful insurgents are not the government or the "authorities" or the agents of the state. Second, that liability does not attach because, while an armed insurrection lasts, the insurgents are *ipso facto* considered to have gone beyond government control.

The fact that, under international law, unsuccessful insurgents are not regarded as the government or authorities of the

ibid., 730; *Acquatella Case*. Opinion of Commissioner Paul, French-Venezuelan Commission, *ibid.*, 486.

32 *Aroa Mines Case*, British-Venezuelan Commission, Ralston, *Ven. Arb. of 1903*, 344, 350; *Santa Clara Estates Case, ibid.*, 397; *Von Dissel & Co. Case, ibid.*, 565.

33 *Salas Case*, Netherlands-Venezuelan Commission, Ralston, *Ven. Arb. of 1903*, 903.

34 *Home Missionary Society case*, American Agent's Report, 425; Moore, *Int. Arb.*, III, 2991-2992; Moore, *Digest*, VI, 956.

35 *Solis Case, Opinions*, 1929, 48. See also *Coleman Case, ibid.*, 56.

state has already been discussed elsewhere.[36] Here we may consider certain decisions of the United States and Mexican Claims Commission of 1868 in cases arising from injuries by unsuccessful insurgents and directly dealing with the point in question. The language of the claims convention of 1868 between the United States and Mexico confined indemnity to injuries arising from acts of "authorities of the Mexican Republic" or "authorities of the United States", as the case may be. The Commission was, therefore, required to decide whether unsuccessful insurgents were the authorities of the state or not. In the *Prats Case* [37] the United States was charged with responsibility for the destruction by the Confederate forces of a number of bales of cotton partly owned by a Mexican citizen. Mexico alleged that the rebel authorities inflicting the injurious act were in fact "authorities of the United States"; the American Government denied this. The Commission decided the case against Mexico and dismissed the claim. It pointed out that the rebel armed forces who destroyed the cotton in question were "neither *de facto* nor *de jure* authorities of the United States, nor any of the States of the Union",[38] but that the Confederate Government was in fact a rebel government which had neither authority nor capacity which could be recognized as legitimate as far as its relations with foreign governments were concerned. It was said further that those who acted as the authorities of the so-called Southern Confederacy had been declared rebels and traitors by the Federal Government, and, whatever the constitutional propriety or legitimacy of that declaration, foreign nations were obligated

36 *Supra*, Ch. I.

37 Moore, *International Arbitrations*, III, 2886-2900.

38 *Prats case*, Opinion of Mr. Palacio, Mexican Commissioner, Moore, *Int. Arb.*, III, 2892-2893. Mr. Wadsworth, American commissioner, said: "The Confederate armed forces were in no sense 'authorities of the United States' within the meaning of the convention under which we are assembled." *Ibid.*, 2886.

In this, and many other cases, the American and Mexican Commissioners rendered separate but concurring opinions.

to accept it and to regard the rebels as utterly lacking in power to act in the name of the United States. The Commission came to the conclusion that since the rebel States were thus in fact and in law deprived of their participation in the affairs of the nation, it followed that acts of a tortious nature inflicted by their agents could not involve the responsibility of the United States.[39] In the *McKenny case*,[40] decided by the same Commission, the Government of the United States supported a claim of an American citizen against Mexico for the destruction of property by the unsuccessful insurgent party of Zuloaga and Miramon in 1859. The claimant undertook to show that Zuloaga and Miramon were, in succession, the heads of a *de facto* government of Mexico, to which the persons who committed the injurious act adhered. The Commission had already decided in a previous case[41] that the faction under Zuloaga and Miramon never attained power in Mexico and never became the government. In the instant case it continued, therefore, to adhere to the view previously expressed by it as to the legal standing of the leaders of the opposition to the constitutional government under Juarez and as to the absence of any liability on the part of Mexico for their acts. In holding that the Zuloaga and Miramon authorities were not the government of Mexico, it further said

> that the great mass of the people of Mexico continued to adhere to and obey the government of President Juarez from the start, and continued to resist the attempt to set up another government instead thereof under Zuloaga and his successors, finally suppressing all such attempts and quenching them at last in the blood of Maximilian and Miramon.[42]

39 *Prats Case*, Opinion of Palacio, Mexican Commissioner, Moore, *Int. Arb.*, III, 2892-2893.

40 Moore, *Int. Arb.*, III, 2881.

41 *Cucullu Case*, Moore, *Int. Arb.*, III, 2873-2881. See *supra*, Ch. I.

42 *McKenny Case*, United States and Mexican Claims Commission of 1868, Moore, *Int. Arb.*, III, 2881, 2885.

In the *Jansen Case* [43] a claim was again presented to the United States and Mexican Claims Commission of 1868 for the confiscation of an American bark and her cargo by the authorities of the Maximilian government in Mexico in 1866. The Mexican Government moved to dismiss the claim on the ground that the injury complained of was not committed by the authorities of the Mexican Republic. This motion was sustained and the case was dismissed. In holding that the Maximilian government was not and never did become the government of Mexico, it said:

> . . . the so-called empire was not a government *de facto*; because, lacking the element of popular support or of habitual obedience from the mass of the people, it rested alone on the assistance of foreign force, which contemplated and extended only a temporary interference, and because another government disputing successfully its pretensions, bore rule in Mexico as a fact, in possession of much the largest part of the territory, and sustained by the mass of the people.[44]

Accordingly, a number of other American claims arising from injury to persons and damages to property inflicted by unsuccessful insurgents and temporary *de facto* governments in local control in Mexico were dismissed and disallowed by the same Commission expressly on the ground that such insurgents and local *de facto* authorities did not in fact become the government of Mexico.[45]

43 Moore, *Int. Arb.*, III, 2902.

44 *Jansen Case*, Moore, *Int. Arb.*, III, 2902, 2930.

In the *Baxter Case* the same Commission referred to its decision in the *Jansen Case* and said: "Having settled that the Maximilian regime in Mexico did not constitute a government *de facto* . . . we have no other choice left but to dismiss this claim." Moore, *Int. Arb.*, III, 2934.

45 See especially the *Schultz Case*, Moore, *Int. Arb.*, III, 2973; the *Walsh Case*, *ibid.*, 2978; the *Wyman Case*, *ibid.*, 2978; and the *Silva Case*, *ibid.*, 2979.

See also the *Sambiaggio Case*, where the umpire of the Italian-Venezuelan Commission of 1903 held: "Revolutionists are not the agents of government, and a natural responsibility does not exist." Ralston, *Ven. Arb. of 1903*, 666, 680.

Doubtless the second reason, that is, the lack of control by the parent government, is just as important for a proper understanding of the general rule that the state is not responsible for the tortious acts of unsuccessful insurgents. In the ***Prats Case***[46] the United States and Mexican Claims Commission of 1868 said:

> The principle of non-responsibility for acts of rebel enemies in time of civil war rests upon the ground that the latter have withdrawn themselves by force of arms from the control and jurisdiction of the sovereign, putting it out of his power, so long as they make their resistance effectual, to extend his protection within the hostile territory to either strangers or his own subjects, between whom, in this respect, no inequality of rights can justly be asserted.[47]

In the *Hanna case*,[48] decided by the American and British Claims Commission of 1871, the United States was charged with liability for the destruction by orders of the authorities of the Confederate States and of the rebel State of Louisiana of cotton belonging to a British subject, for the purpose of preventing such cotton from falling into the hands of the Federal forces. The United States denied liability on the ground, *inter alia*, that the damage was done by rebels who were in fact beyond its control. The case was decided on this point alone, and in dismissing the claim the Commission said:

> The claim is made for the loss sustained by the destruction of cotton belonging to the claimant by men who are described by the claimant as rebels in arms against the Government of the United States.
>
> The commissioners are of opinion that the United States cannot be held liable for injuries caused by the acts of rebels over whom they could exercise no control, and which acts they had no power to prevent.

46 Moore, *Int. Arb.*, III, 2886.

47 *Prats Case*, Moore, *Int. Arb.*, III, 2886, 2889-2890.

48 Moore, *Int. Arb.*, III, 2982.

Upon this ground, and without giving any opinion upon the other points raised in the case, which will be considered hereafter in other cases, the claim of John Holmes Hanna is therefore dismissed.[49]

In the *Salas Case*,[50] decided by the Netherlands-Venezuelan Commission of 1903, the umpire denied liability and disallowed the claim for damages to the buildings and other property of a subject of Netherlands living in Venezuela expressly on the ground that the injuries in question were received from unsuccessful insurgents whom the Venezuelan Government was unable to control. It appears that in 1902 the revolutionary forces besieged and attacked the City of Barquisimeto, and as a result of this attack the Government troops were driven out of the city and the revolutionary forces occupied the place for some time thereafter. While the attack was successful and the revolutionary party for the time being became the dominant force in that immediate vicinity, and inflicted the destruction and damages which gave rise to the claim, the revolution itself was nevertheless unsuccessful. The umpire, after noting the fact that no allegation was made that the injury was received to the buildings or property from the Government troops and no negligence on the part of the government was alleged or proved, said:

There can be no question that the injuries were received from the hands of revolutionary soldiers, who for the time being and within that city were beyond the control of the government. The

49 *Hanna Case*, Moore, *Int. Arb.*, III, 2982, 2985.

This was among the earliest of the decisions of the American and British Claims Commission of 1871, and it appears that in consequence of it a large number of claims of similar character awaiting presentation were never presented to the Commission. In respect of this class of claims the Commission laid down the general proposition as declaratory of international law that "no government is responsible for injuries done to the inhabitants of the country, whether citizens or foreigners, by rebels or by alien enemies exercising in the particular locality or for the time being superior force against such government." Moore, *Int. Arb.*, I, 684.

50 Ralston, *Ven. Arb. of 1903*, 903.

Government in fact was defeated and was driven out of the city, so that in no way can it be held that they could have prevented these acts, and they cannot be charged with neglect of duty in not having done what they could not do.[51]

And, lastly, in the *Sambiaggio Case*,[52] a claim for forced loans and requisitions exacted from an Italian citizen by the armed forces of an unsuccessful revolution in Venezuela was rejected and dismissed by the umpire of the Italian-Venezuelan Commission of 1903 on the ground, *inter alia*, that the insurgents were beyond governmental control. He noted that there existed open and determined war for the overthrow of the government, and said:

Governments are responsibile, as a general principle, for the acts of those they control. But the very existence of a flagrant revolution presupposes that a certain set of men have gone temporarily or permanently beyond the power of the authorities . . . We find ourselves therefore obliged to conclude, from the standpoint of general principle, that . . . the Government should not be held responsible for the acts of revolutionists because—

1. Revolutionists are not the agents of government, and a natural responsibility does not exist.
2. Their acts are committed to destroy the government, and no one should be held responsible for the acts of an enemy attempting his life.
3. The revolutionists were beyond governmental control, and the Government cannot be held responsible for injuries committed by those who have escaped its restraint.[53]

Thus, the cases cited establish beyond any doubt that inability to control absolves a state from responsibility for tortious acts of unsuccessful insurgents. But the question still remains as to what constitutes inability to control. Doubtless one of the tests in proving that insurgents have gone beyond the con-

51 *Salas Case*, Ralston, *Venezuelan Arbitrations of 1903*, 903-904.

52 Ralston, *Ven. Arb. of 1903*, 666.

53 *Ibid.*, 666, 680.

trol of the titular government is recognition of belligerency either by the parent state or by the claimant government or even by third powers.[54] Recognition of the belligerency of the insurgents by the parent government is presumed to release the state from responsibility for all acts of the insurgents subsequent to recognition, and foreign states will find it difficult to prove such responsibility. Recognition by a foreign state operates as an estoppel as to that state and its subjects, since such an act indicates that so far as the recognizing power is concerned the insurgents have gone beyond the control of the parent government.[55] In a conversation with Earl Russell dealing with the British recognition of Confederate belligerency, Mr. Adams observed on June 12, 1861, that

> . . . at any rate, there was one compensation, the act had released the Government of the United States from responsibility for any misdeeds of the rebels towards Great Britain. If any of their people should capture or maltreat a British vessel on the ocean, the reclamation must be made only upon those who had authorized the wrong. The United States would not be liable.[56]

And again, on January 12, 1864, in a note to the American minister to France, Secretary of State Seward said:

> France, by recognizing the insurgents as belligerents, may be expected to have accepted all the responsibility of that measure,

54 *Prats Case*, United States and Mexican Claims Commission of 1868, Moore, *Int. Arb.*, III, 2886, 2888 *et seq.*; *Hanna Case*, American and British Claims Commission of 1871, Moore, *Int. Arb.*, III, 2982.

55 In a separate opinion in the *Hanna Case*, where the United States denied liability on the ground, *inter alia*, that the British Government had recognized the belligerency of the Confederate States, Mr. Frazier, American Commissioner, said: "Her Britannic Majesty had recognized the so-called Confederate States as a belligerent and the contest of arms then prevailing as a public war. After such recognition by the sovereign, the subject of such sovereign cannot, in his character as such subject, aver that the fact was not so. The act of his government in that regard is conclusive upon him." Moore, *Int. Arb.*, III, 2986.

56 Mr. Adams, American Minister to England, to Mr. Seward, Sec. of State, June 14, 1861, *Dip. Cor.*, 1861, 87, 89; Moore, *Digest*, I, 185; VI, 956.

and to be content to regard her subjects domiciled in belligerent territory as identified with belligerents themselves.[57]

The result is the same, of course, when the claimant state recognizes merely the existence of a status of insurgency, since such an act or conduct ordinarily implies the admission that at the time of the commission of wrongful acts the government of the disturbed state "lacked the power of prevention or suppression." [58] During the Cuban insurrection of 1895 the President of the United States issued a proclamation stating that Cuba was "the seat of civil disturbances, accompanied by armed resistance to the authority of the established Government of Spain," and admonishing all persons within the territorial jurisdiction of the United States to observe the neutrality laws and to abstain from taking part in the disturbances against the Spanish Government.[59] In his annual message of December 2, 1895, he described this "greatly disturbed" condition of things in Cuba as an "insurrection," a "flagrant condition of hostilities," and a "sanguinary and fiercely conducted war" between armed insurgents and the Spanish forces.[60] The Supreme Court pointed out that this was in fact a recognition of a status of insurgency of the rebels in Cuba and "sharply illustrated"

57 Mr. Seward, Sec. of State, to Mr. Dayton, American Minister to France, Jan. 12, 1864, *Dip. Cor.*, 1864, III, 17; Moore, *Digest*, VI, 957. See also the note of the Secretary of State to the Spanish Minister, June 28, 1886, *For. Rel.*, 1887, 1007; Moore, *Digest*, VI, 964.

58 Hyde, *International Law*, I, 541.

59 29 Stat. 871. See also the proclamation of July 27, 1896, 29 Stat. 881.

60 Richardson's *Messages and Papers of the Presidents*, Vol. 9, 626, 636.

See also President Celeveland's annual message of December 7, 1896, where he stated that "the insurrection in Cuba still continues with all its perplexities," and reviewed the situation at length. Referring to the inability of the Spanish authorities to maintain control, except in large towns and their immediate suburbs, he said: "It is reported, indeed, on reliable authority that, at the demand of the commander-in-chief of the insurgent army, the putative Cuban government has now given up all attempt to exercise its functions, leaving that government confessedly (what there is the best reason for supposing it always to have been in fact) a government merely on paper." Moore, *Digest*, I, 198.

The distinction between recognition of belligerency and recognition of a condition of political revolt, between recognition of the existence of war in the material sense and of war in a legal sense. . . . For here the political department has not recognized the existence of a *de facto* belligerent power engaged in hostility with Spain, but has recognized the existence of insurrectionary warfare prevailing before, at the time and since this forfeiture is alleged to have been incurred. . . . We are thus judicially informed of the existence of an actual conflict of arms in resistance of the authority of a government with which the United States are on terms of peace and amity, although acknowledgment of the insurgents as belligerents by the political department has not taken place; and it cannot be doubted that, this being so, the act in question [the neutrality statute] is applicable.[61]

Thus, the recognition of a state of insurgency implied that at least in so far as the Government of the United States was concerned " the insurgents were not *de facto* under the control of Spain," and the Spanish Government therefore could not be held liable for the wrongful acts of such insurgents.[62]

However, neither recognition of belligerency nor recognition of a status of insurgency is really essential to establish a proof of lack of governmental control over insurgents. The existence of armed insurrection or a *de facto* civil war means the absence of the territorial jurisdiction of the titular government and an absence of allegiance on the part of the people in revolt. Such a state of war is, therefore, sufficient evidence that the rebellion has in fact gone beyond the control of the authorities of the disturbed state.[63] And since protection depends on governmental control, it follows that when there exists " open, flagrant, bloody, and determined war " for the purpose of destroying the existing government and substituting in its place

61 *The Three Friends* (1897), 166, U. S. 63-64, 65-66.

62 Benton, *International Law and Diplomacy of the Spanish-American War*, 34-37.

63 *Sambiaggio Case*, Ralston, *Ven. Arb. of 1903*, 680; *Acquatello Case*, *ibid.*, 486.

"another of different personnel or controlled by different principles,"[64] there is nothing much that the government can do for the protection of foreign persons and property at the hands of revolutionists within the insurrectionary line. Above all, it is this fact of the existence of civil war in the material sense that releases the state from responsibility for insurgent acts regardless of the question of recognition of either insurgency or belligerency. Apparently this point was not clear at one time, and on two occasions at least the Department of State of the United States and the Mexican Government attempted a distinction between the effect of recognition and of non-recognition of belligerency of insurgents. In 1873 Secretary of State Fish contended that Mexico was liable for forced loans exacted from two American citizens by unsuccessful insurgents whose belligerency had not been recognized either by Mexico or by any foreign power. He maintained that the liability of a government to protect aliens from violence on the part of insurgents "may be regarded as continuing at least until the government of a neutral country, whose citizens may be aggrieved in the course of the hostilities, shall recognize the insurgents as entitled to belligerent rights. There was no such recognition by this Government at the time when the claimants adverted to sustained the injuries of which they complain."[65] In answer to a Mexican note pointing out the fact that after the Civil War the United States had refused liability for wrongful acts of the Confederate authorities, it was said that the cases were different.

64 *Sambiaggio Case*, Ralston, *Ven. Arb. of 1903*, 666, 679.

65 Mr. Fish, Sec. of State, to Mr. Foster, American Minister to Mexico, Aug. 15, 1873. Moore, *Digest*, VI, 974. Mr. Fish held liability for acts of unrecognized insurgents to be the general rule subject to the following exceptions: "Perhaps the rule should not always apply to persons domiciled in a country, and rarely to such as may visit a region notoriously in a state of civil war, or even to such part of a country as may virtually be dominated by savage tribes."

It is true that the government has not confessed its liability for the injuries to foreigners by persons claiming authority in the South during the rebellion. The reason for this is believed to be as strong as that for the accountability of Mexico in the other case. Belligerent rights had tacitly at least been granted to the insurgents not only by this government but by those of the principal European nations. This is a concession which may be allowed to carry with it an acknowledgment that the party, in whose favor it may be made, is both competent and willing to do justice to the citizens or subjects of the grantor, and indeed may of itself be allowed to exempt the other party from such accountability. This Department is not aware that the Mexican Government ever acknowledged the belligerent rights of the insurgents in New Leon. It is believed to be certain that they were never acknowledged by any foreign government.[66]

In a subsequent communication this particular ground of Mexican liability appears to have been reaffirmed but not especially pressed, and the argument was apparently shifted to the question of Mexican liability for the acts in question under the provisions of the treaty of 1831, which was said to exempt citizens of contracting parties from forced loans presumably even at the hands of insurgents.[67] It does not appear that the controversy went beyond this point, and apparently the claim was dropped in view of the Mexican contention that during the insurrection in question it had done its best towards protecting the inhabitants in the disaffected region generally from the violence of the insurgents. Curiously enough, at about the same time the Mexican Government itself was attempting to hold the United States liable for the wrongful acts of the Confederate authorities by advancing before the United States and Mexican Claims Commission of 1868 arguments in every respect similar to those of Secretary of State Fish in the pre-

66 Mr. Fish, Sec. of State, to Mr. Foster, American Minister to Mexico, Dec. 16, 1873. Moore, *Digest*, I, 975, 976. See also Moore, *Digest*, VI, 980-981.

67 Mr. Cadwalader, Acting Sec. of State, to Mr. Foster, American Minister to Mexico, Sept. 22, 1874. Moore, *Digest*, VI, 978. *Infra*, p. 192.

ceding case. In the course of its arguments in the *Prats Case*,[68] the Mexican Government made a distinction between the effect of recognition and of non-recognition of insurgent belligerency and contended that because it had refused to recognize Confederate belligerency it was therefore entitled to claim and obtain remuneration for injuries inflicted by the Confederate authorities. It was further said that England, for instance, had no such right because it recognized the Confederate States as a belligerent. The Commission, however, rejected this view of the consequences of the refusal by Mexico to recognize the rebels as a belligerent power and said:

Non-liability on the part of the United States for injuries by the Confederate enemy within the territories of that government to aliens did not result from the recognition of the belligerency of the rebel enemy by the strangers' sovereign. It resulted from the fact of belligerency itself, and whether recognized or not by other governments. But the proclaimed recognition of the fact by a government is conclusive evidence of the fact, and, so to speak, an *estoppel* as to that government . . . had Great Britain never recognized the Confederates as belligerents at all, the consequences of the state of war as a fact to Great Britain, as to all other neutral powers, would have been the same: such as the liability of their vessels on the high seas to search and seizure as prize by the armed cruisers of the United States, and the capture for attempts to violate the blockade. These rights the United States exercised against Mexico and all other nations, and did it in virtue of the fact of war, and not because of the recognition of the belligerency of the insurgents by those powers or any of them. Mexico conceded to the United States the exercise of these rights of war against her, and is equally estopped now with other nations to deny the *fact* or to ignore the changes which the war introduced into the relations between the two governments. . . .

So far, therefore, as the responsibility of the United States to Mexico in this case is concerned, it is in nowise increased or diminished by the failure of the latter to accord belligerent rights to the Confederates.[69]

68 Moore, *Int. Arb.*, III, 2886.

69 *Prats Case*, Moore, *Int. Arb.*, III, 2886, 2888-2889.

A similar conclusion was reached by the Spanish Treaty Claims Commission of 1901, which after examining the question of responsibility of Spain for injurious acts of Cuban revolutionists from 1895 to 1898, said:

> Although the late insurrection in Cuba assumed great magnitude and lasted for more than three years, yet belligerent rights were never granted to the insurgents by Spain or the United States so as to create a state of war in the international sense, which exempted the parent government from liability to foreigners for the acts of the insurgents.
>
> But where an armed insurrection has gone beyond the control of the parent government the general rule is that such government is not responsible for damages done to foreigners by the insurgents.
>
> This Commission will take judicial notice that the insurrection in Cuba, which resulted in intervention by the United States, and in war between Spain and the United States, passed from the first beyond the control of Spain, and so continued until such intervention and war took place.[70]

It is clear from the foregoing that the existence of war in the material sense is to be taken as the real point of departure as to when insurgents may be said to have gone beyond governmental control. When such a state of war exists between armed insurgents and the forces of the government, the duty of the state to give protection must be measured in accordance with it and its responsibility must be determined without losing sight of that important fact. And this because

> Under such a state of things it is not in the power of the nation to prevent or to avoid the injuries caused or intended to be caused by the rebels, either to the foreign residents or to the native citizens of the country; and as nobody can be bound to do the impossible, from that very moment the responsibility ceases to exist. There is no responsibility without *fault* (culpa), and it is too well known that there is no *fault* (culpa) in having failed to

70 Fuller's *Report*, 299. See also the final report of the Commission, Sen. Doc. 550, 61st Cong., 2nd Sess., pp. 4, 7.

do what was impossible. The *fault* is essentially dependent upon the will, but as the will completely disappears before the force, whose action cannot be resisted, it is a self-evident result that all the acts done by such force, without the possibility of being resisted by another equal or more powerful force, can neither involve a fault nor an injury nor a responsibility.[71]

III

The general rule that the state is not liable for damages caused to foreign persons and property by wrongful acts of unsuccessful insurgents "has been generally limited and jealously qualified." [72] The uniform practice of foreign offices and of international courts of arbitration has been not to state it "in broad and unqualified terms" but to surround it "with a statement of any generally accepted limitations and exceptions." [73] Practically any unqualified statement of the rule will result in disagreement and controversy among nations, as illustrated by the following incident. On December 2, 1912, in answer to a claim presented by the American Embassy for the value of merchandise alleged to have been destroyed by revolutionary forces, the Mexican Foreign Office disclaimed liability on the ground that

it is a universally recognized principle of international law, which has always been observed by your excellency's government as well as by that of Mexico, that no state is legally responsible for damages and prejudices which during an insurrection or civil war may be suffered by foreigners at the hands of rebels, as under such

71 *Prats Case*, Moore, *Int. Arb.*, III, 2895-2897.

72 Mr. Olney, Sec. of State, to Mr. Terrell, Am. Minister to Turkey, October 17 and October 28, 1896, *For. Rel.*, 1896, 892-893; Moore, *Digest*, VI, 965-966. Mr. Olney referred to the general rule also as "the limited and jealously qualified rule of international law relative to the irresponsibility of a government for the acts of uncontrollable insurgents."

73 Mr. Knox, Sec. of State, to Mr. Wilson, Am. Ambassador to Mexico, Jan. 25, 1913, *For. Rel.*, 1913, 932-933.

circumstances they should suffer the same consequences as the natives.[74]

In reply, the Department of State instructed the American Minister to inform the Mexican Foreign Office that "the Government of the United States cannot admit the existence of any such unqualified rule as that stated by the Mexican Government."[75] In a subsequent note the Department explained these instructions as follows:

> In its note regarding the Sherron case the Mexican Government stated very broadly and incompletely the principle of international law with reference to a government's liability for damages suffered by foreigners in times of insurrection, without admitting any exceptions to the rule. It was to the failure of the Mexican note to acknowledge any exceptions to the broad rule of international law therein set forth that the Department instructed you to demur. . . . If the principle is stated correctly in the Mexican note, Mexican federal troops might stand by and witness wanton destruction of foreign life and property at the hands of rebels whose actions they might easily control, without the Mexican Government's incurring any liability in the premise.[76]

The question, however, as to what constitute proper exceptions, which, when established by the particular facts and circumstances of any case, would suspend the general rule and fix the legal liability, presents a major difficulty. In the *Sambiaggio Case*, Ralston, umpire, admitted that under certain exceptional circumstances the state may be held liable and stated these exceptions as follows:

74 Mr. Lascurain, Minister for Foreign Affairs, to Mr. Wilson, American Ambassador, Dec. 2, 1912, *For. Rel.*, 1912, 984.

75 Mr. Knox, Sec. of State to the American Charge, Dec. 19, 1912, *For. Rel.*, 1912, 984.

76 Mr. Knox, Sec. of State to Mr. Wilson, American Ambassador to Mexico, Jan. 25, 1913, *For. Rel.*, 1913, 932, 933. See also Mr. Wilson, Am. Ambassador, to Mr. Knox, Sec. of State, Jan. 8, 1913, *For. Rel.*, 1913, 924, 925.

> . . . where a state has fallen into anarchy, or the administration of law has been nerveless or inefficient, or the government has failed to grant to a foreigner the protection afforded citizens, or measures within the power of the government have not been taken to protect those under its jurisdiction from the acts of revolutionists.[77]

So also Hyde says that

> If the government which is successful in its work of repression [of insurgents] is burdened with responsibility, it must be because (a) it "has failed to use promptly and with appropriate force its constituted authority" to oppose the revolutionists; or (b) because it has condoned by some process their internationally illegal acts; or (c) because it has entered into a relationship whereby it has become the legal successor to those whose conduct it previously opposed.[78]

These two statements taken together give a fairly accurate idea of the scope of exceptions to the general rule frequently mentioned in diplomatic correspondence and in decisions of international courts of arbitration specifically dealing with the question under consideration. They are, however, by no means all-inclusive, and in the following discussion an attempt will be made to make the list of exceptions as complete as the records permit. A careful survey of available material shows that in the past the following exceptions have been urged: (1) negligence or fault or lack of due diligence on the part of the government to suppress insurrection, to prevent injury, or to punish offenders; (2) responsibility under "special protection" clause of a preexisting treaty; (3) responsibility for confiscated property used by insurgents for a public purpose; (4) responsibility for granting amnesty; (5) responsibility under agreement between the government and insurgents; (6) responsibility under protocol of arbitration.

77 Sambiaggio Case, Ralston, *Ven. Arb. of 1903*, 666, 679-680.

78 Hyde, *International Law*, I, 540.

1. *Negligence.*—According to international law "the foreign state whose nationals are subjected to improper treatment by insurgents may, during the course of the conflict, justly urge the government to bend every effort to accord adequate protection; and vigorous protest will be forthcoming if that government fails to render such protection as it is known to possess the ability to afford."[79] If there is any reason to believe that the government of the disturbed state was negligent in the due performance of its duty of protection, claims may be preferred against it after the suppression of the revolt, and in fact such claims for indemnity have been very often referred to international courts of arbitration, charging the government with fault, negligence, and lack of due diligence in preventing injury or suppressing insurrection or punishing wrongdoers.[80] In such cases the question has been raised as to what constitutes negligence or what is the degree of diligence required for the due performance of the duty of protection in case of civil war. In the *Prats Case*,[81] the United States and Mexican Claims Commission of 1868 attempted to answer this question. It came to the conclusion that during a civil conflict it is not, as a rule, in the power of the government to prevent or to avoid injuries caused by the rebels; that "the only means the legitimate authorities possess to preserve order and maintain

79 Hyde, *Int. Law*, I, 540-541. During the Cuban insurrection of 1895-1898 the Department of State urged Spain "to exercise due diligence for protection" of American persons and property: Mr. Uhl, Acting Sec. of State, to Mr. Springer, Am. Vice-Consul, July 1, 1895, *For. Rel.*, 1895, II, 1216, Moore, *Digest*, VI, 966; Mr. Olney, Sec. of State, to Mr. Taylor, Minister to Spain, Dec. 15, 1896, *For. Rel.*, 1896, 704, Moore, *Digest*, VI, 968; Mr. Olney, Sec. of State, to Messrs. Lauman & Kemp, Jan. 13, 1896, Moore, *Digest*, VI, 967; Mr. Sherman, Sec. of State, to Mr. Dupuy de Lome, Spanish Minister, July 6, 1897, *For. Rel.*, 1897, 516, Moore, *Digest*, VI, 969; Mr. Adee, Acting Sec. of State, to same, July 29, 1897, *For. Rel.*, 1897, 519, Moore, *Digest*, VI, 970.

80 See especially *Prats Case*, Moore, *Int. Arb.*, III, 2886; *Baldwin's Case*, *ibid.*, 2899; *Cummings Case*, *ibid.*, 2976; *Santa Clara Estates Company Case*, Ralston, *Ven. Arb.*, 397.

81 Moore, *Int. Arb.*, III, 2886.

the empire of law consist in raising the military forces required to subdue the rebels"; and that the extent of the duty of protection is commensurate with the extent of means for performing it, and if the state employs all the means within its reach, that is, if it uses all its armed forces and its resources to suppress the revolution and to cause the war to be as short and exempt from disasters as possible, it fulfills its duty and cannot be blamed for omission or negligence, and consequently cannot have any responsibility.[82] In this particular case the issue involved the destruction by the Confederate forces within the insurrectionary lines of a number of bales of cotton partly owned by a Mexican citizen. Mexico alleged, *inter alia,* that the United States was liable for neglect of duty imposed by the law of nations or stipulated by treaty. The Commission held that the immense magnitude of its efforts in suppressing the rebellion showed that the United States had in fact fulfilled its duty nobly and worthily, and that further than that

> . . . The United States . . . government was under no obligation, by treaty or the law of nations, to protect the property of aliens situate inside the enemy country against the enemy. The international duty of the United States or its engagements by treaty to extend protection to aliens, transient or dwelling, in its territories, ceased inside the territory held by the insurgents from the time such territory was withdrawn by war from the control of that government, and until her authority and jurisdiction were again established over it.[83]

In the *Santa Clara Estates Company Case*[84] the issue of negligence turned wholly on the question of time required to subdue a rebellion. This was a claim for losses arising from the taking of live stock for the use of the unsuccessful Matos revolution in Venezuela in 1902. The British Government alleged that the fact that the insurgents were allowed for so

82 *Prats Case*, Moore, *Int. Arb.*, III, 2893-2897.

83 *Ibid.*, 2889-2890.

84 Ralston, *Venezuelan Arbitrations of 1903*, 397.

long to maintain an independent government was due to the negligence of the titular government; and that there is a limit which must be reached within which the government must either reduce the revolutionists to subjection, or declare the independence of the revolted territory and thereby permit foreign governments to take the protection of their subjects into their own hands, or accept liability to pay compensation for the damages suffered at the hands of the revolutionary authorities because of apparent and actual negligence and inactivity. In this case, said the British Government, the first step, that of reduction to subjection, was not taken within a reasonable time; that a whole year was beyond that proper limit of time during which the Venezuelan Government was justified in tolerating an independent government of the insurgents, for one determined battle would have been enough to dispose of the whole trouble; and that since the government had not reduced the rebels to subjection within a reasonable time, nor permitted their independence, it must therefore take liability for wrongful acts. The umpire of the British-Venezuelan Commission of 1903 pointed out the extent and the seriousness of the Matos revolution and held that there was no undue delay on the part of the Venezuelan Government in the restoration of its power in the district occupied by the insurgents. The revolution, it was said, remained out of control for such a long time not through the weakness, inefficiency, or passivity of the government, but rather through the insurgents' own inherent strength in men, materials, and money, and in certain other assisting circumstances. He further said:

> . . . it is the opinion of the umpire that more dependence should be placed upon the actual diligence applied by the titular government to regain its lost territory and to suppress the revolutionary efforts than upon the mere question of time taken to accomplish that end; and the umpire recalls that Great Britain contended for seven years against the revolt of the thirteen American colonies before it consented to separation; that the United States of America fought the secession of the Confederate States for more than four years

before it regained its revolted territory and had subjected the rebellious citizens to its control. And neither Great Britain nor the United States, notwithstanding the length of time intervening between the revolt and the termination of the same, admitted or discharged any liability to foreign governments for the acts of the revolutionaries in question. Other pertinent illustrations might be drawn from history more remote and more recent wherein a similar rule of non-liability under circumstances where the length of time elapsing between the revolt and subjection by the titular government or success on the part of the revolutionary forces was greater than in the present case.[85]

In the *Home Missionary Society Case*,[86] the issue of negligence turned upon the question of degree of diligence required to give protection within vast unsettled regions subject to revolutionary disturbances. More specifically, Great Britain was accused of negligence for losses and damages sustained by an American religious body during the native rebellion in 1898 in the British protectorate of Sierra Leonne. It was contended by the United States that the revolt was the result of the imposition and attempted collection of a so-called "hut tax"; that it was known to the British authorities that this tax was the object of native resentment; that in the face of the danger the British Government failed to take proper steps for the protection of life and property; that the loss of life and damage to property were the result of negligence and failure of duty; and that the British Government was therefore liable to pay compensation. The British-American arbitral tribunal of 1910 dismissed the claim on the ground that negligence could not be alleged in view of the unexpected character of the uprising and the lack of capacity on the part of British authorities to give protection in the vast unsettled regions in question. It was further said that whatever warning the British authorities may have had with regard to possible disturbances, it was

85 *Santa Clara Estates Company Case*, Ralston, *Ven. Arb. of 1903*, 397, 398.

86 Arbitration between the United States and Great Britain of 1910, American Agent's *Report*, 425.

not such as to lead to apprehension of a revolt such as occurred; that there was no lack of promptitude or courage on the part of the British troops, but that on the contrary evidence proved that "under peculiar difficulty and trying conditions they did their duty with loyalty and daring" in affording on a few hours' notice whatever protection they could to the buildings and properties in isolated and distant villages of a vast region. The tribunal held, therefore, that in this case the charge of liability for damages caused by insurgents could not be sustained in view of the fact that Great Britain was guilty of no breach of good faith or of no negligence in suppressing insurrection.[87]

Doubtless the capacity of the government to give protection depends not only upon the seriousness of the rebellion but also upon the character of the particular region under revolt. In centers of population the degree of diligence to afford immediate and adequate protection is greater than in sparsely populated regions. Long before the decision in the preceding case this point was made clear by the Department of State when in 1887 it refused to press the claim of one Negrete, an American citizen, against Spain for damages caused by insurgents in Cuba. On that occasion the Department said:

> The measure of diligence to be exercised by a government in the repression of disorder is not that of an insurer, but such as prudent governments are, under the circumstances of the case, accustomed to exercise . . . the diligence good governments are *accustomed* to exercise under the circumstances must be exercised in each case; and every government is liable to foreign powers for injuries to them or their subjects from lack of such customary diligence in the preservation of order.
>
> What then is the custom which thus becomes the guide? . . . custom depends on conditions; so that the degree of diligence customary and reasonable in a newly and sparsely settled region

87 *Home Missionary Society Case*, Arbitration between the United States and Great Britain of 1910, American Agent's *Report*, 425. See also Moore, *Int. Arb.*, III, 2991; Moore, *Digest*, VI, 956.

of country where the police force is weak and scattered, where armed forces cannot be maintained and where custom throws on the individual, in a large degree, not merely the preservation of order but the vindication of supposed rights, is very different from the degree of diligence customary in a center of population under a well-organized police, and in which armed forces could be promptly summoned in support of the law. There are eras of revolt against which no government could protect itself except by maintaining a standing army which would not only be a menace to free institutions but would impose on the community burdens which in themselves might be the cause of revolts far more serious than those it was intended to prevent. Such a period marked the beginning of the late civil war in the United States, when this Government found itself without the means of immediately suppressing the insurrection in which the property and persons of foreigners as well as of citizens were involved. When foreign governments complained of the injuries their subjects had thus sustained, they were informed "this insurrection is one of those calamities against which no prudent government could guard, except by measures more determined than the evil they are intended to remedy." [88]

As a rule, even if states were actually negligent either in suppressing a revolution or in preventing injuries at the hands

88 Mr. Bayard, Sec. of State, to Mr. Sutphen, Jan. 6, 1888, Moore, *Digest*, VI, 961, 962-963.

In 1885 insurgent forces succeeded in obtaining complete control of the city of Colon in the State of Panama, Colombia, and set it on fire in several places. Certain foreign subjects whose property had been destroyed by the fire wished to make a claim against Colombia on the ground that the injury was due to the fault of the authorities. They alleged that the president of the State of Panama withdrew all military forces of the government from Colon in the middle of March, 1885, together with the entire police force, thus inviting the lawless and evil-minded people to commit the depredations complained of. The Government of the United States apparently declined to prefer claims against Colombia. Moore, *Digest*, VI, 961. The British Government took a similar attitude, since the English merchants at Bogota were informed that Her Majesty's Government, after consulting the law officers of the crown, had decided that there was no "sufficient ground for contending that the destruction of Colon was directly due to any default on the part of the Colombian Government as to justify a demand for compensation." Moore, *Digest*, VI, 961.

of insurgents in the course of the civil conflict, "that fact would be extremely difficult to prove, and if the claims rested upon this ground alone few of them could be prosecuted to payment," [89] as it has been seen in the foregoing cases. In at least two cases on record claims for negligence in suppressing insurrection or in preventing injury have been allowed; but even in those cases there were involved issues other than that of negligence, and it is therefore practically impossible to say what degree of importance should be attached to the last issue. The first case is that of *Baldwin's Tehuantepec Claims,*[90] decided by the United States and Mexican Claims Commission of 1839. It appears that in 1833 a body of men organized a central junta or revolutionary government in Tehuantepec, Mexico, and exercised jurisdiction over an important part of the republic; they had a military force on foot which sustained their authority; they instituted courts which exercised undisputed power; and they collected taxes. From June to December, 1833, the Government of Mexico made no effort to suppress the insurrection, and when the insurgents did finally put down their arms it was by means of an amnesty and not through forces employed by the government for that purpose. During that period one Baldwin, an American citizen resident in Mexico, was stripped of his property and was arrested and thrown into prison by the insurgents. The United States charged liability on the ground, *inter alia*, that Mexico was negligent in not using force to suppress the insurgents for many months. Mexico admitted that it used no force, but said that instead of suppressing rebellion by force it had been the policy of "the directors of that Republic, without ceasing to oppose themselves to factions, to avail themselves of every occasion that presents itself to terminate their wars through the medium of conviction, or of pardon extended to the mutinous." [91] The

89 Borchard, *Diplomatic Protection*, 243.

90 Moore, *Int. Arb.*, III, 2859.

91 *Ibid.*, 2859, 2865.

Commission allowed the claim without, however, stating the particular reason for its decision from among a number of reasons advanced by the Government of the United States, such as failure to suppress insurrection, failure to punish offenders, and the granting of amnesty.[92] The second case is that of the American steamer *Montijo* [93] which was seized in the State of Panama, Colombia, in 1871 by insurgents who were ultimately unsuccessful. It does not appear that the Colombian authorities used armed forces to suppress the insurrection, and apparently an end was put to the incident by means of an amnesty. Aside from the question of negligence, in this case also were involved a number of other issues, such as failure to punish wrongdoers, the granting of amnesty, and failure to keep an agreement made with insurgents by the authorities to pay compensation for their injurious acts.[94] As to the specific issue of negligence the umpire said:

> It was, in the opinion of the undersigned, the clear duty of President of Panama, acting as the constitutional agent of the Government of the Union, to recover the *Montijo* from the revolutionists and return her to her owner. It is true that he had not the means of doing so, there being at hand no naval or military force of Colombia sufficient for such a purpose; but this absence of power does not remove the obligation.[95]

92 As to the question of amnesty see, *infra*, p. 198.

In the *Cummings Case*, decided by the United States and Mexican Commission of 1868, Mr. Wadsworth, American Commissioner held "the Mexican Government responsible for the violent destruction of property at Matamoras by Carvajal . . . because that government has never made any reasonable efforts to suppress the disorders which have been so frequent, almost continuous, in that city, and conducted by high military chiefs holding high rank and authority in the Mexican service," although for the time being insurgent. Moore, *Int. Arb.*, III, 2976-2977. The umpire, however, held Mexico not liable because Carvajal was an insurgent chief.

93 Moore, *Int. Arb.*, II, 1421; Moore, *Digest*, VI, 973-974; *For. Rel.*, 1871, 230; *For. Rel.*, 1872, 146.

94 As to amnesty and agreement with insurgents see, *infra*, p. 198 and 208.

95 *Montijo Case*, Moore, *Int. Arb.*, II, 1421, 1444.

Accordingly, the claim was allowed on the ground, *inter alia,* of neglect of duty for suppressing insurrection or preventing injury. Apparently the umpire regarded this as the " stronger reason " for holding Colombia liable in this case, although the influence of the other issues upon the final decision appears to have been just as important.

Sometimes states have been charged with negligence for failure to punish unsuccessful insurgents who inflicted injuries upon foreign persons and property. Here a distinction should be made between (1) failure to punish offenders who either did not rise to the dignity of insurgents or who were once insurgents but had become mere armed bands carrying on lawless acts although acting with a political object, and (2) failure to punish those who did rise to the dignity of insurgents and were actually carrying on acts of war against the government in the sense of international law. Doubtless a neglect of duty to prosecute offenders falling in the first category would give rise to liability. It was so held in the *De Brissot Case;* [96] and it was one of the principal grounds of state liability in the *Bovallins and Hedlund Case* [97] and in the *Montijo Case.*[98] The same principle was applied during the recent Mexican arbitrations by the Special Claims Commission of 1923 between the United States and Mexico and by the British-Mexican Claims Commission of 1926. Under both the American and British protocols of arbitration Mexico accepted liability for wrongful acts, *inter alia,* of " bandits " and " brigands " and of other armed bands carrying on lawless acts while pursuing a political object, " provided that in each case it be established that the

96 Moore, *Int. Arb.*, III, 2949. This case was decided by the United States and Venezuelan Claims Commission of 1885. The Venezuelan Commissioner attempted to show that the wrongdoers were in fact insurgents for whose acts liability could not attach under international law. The majority of the Commission did not agree with this, holding that the offenders were armed bands of a lawless nature, even though acting for a political object.

97 Ralston, *Ven. Arb. of 1903*, 952. *Infra*, p. 202, note 175.

98 Moore, *Int. Arb.*, II, 1421. *Infra*, pp. 200 and 208.

competent authorities omitted to take reasonable measures . . . to punish those responsible." [99] Accordingly, Mexican liability was held to depend on proof to establish the fact whether action was or was not taken by competent authorities to prosecute or punish offenders of the kind under consideration. In the *Santa Isabel Case*,[100] which is doubtless the most important case of these Mexican arbitrations involving the particular point under consideration, the American-Mexican Special Claims Commission held that the Villistas ceased to possess the dignity of insurgents at about the end of 1915, and from 1916 to 1920 they were mere bandits or armed bands of a lawless nature, though admittedly still acting for a political object. This was a claim for the murder of certain American citizens by a band of Villistas on January 10, 1916. The American Commissioner maintained that the Villistas in 1916 were not bandits but revolutionary forces who were ultimately unsuccessful and for whose acts Mexico had voluntarily accepted liability under another clause of the protocol.[101] The majority

99 Article 3, section 5, of the convention of 1923 between the United States and Mexico, and of the convention of 1926 between Great Britain and Mexico. See also, *Opinions*, the Special Claims Commission of 1923, United States and Mexico, 1931, *passim*; *Decisions and Opinions*, the British-Mexican Claims Commission of 1925 and 1930, 1931 and 1933, *passim*; and *Opinions*, the French-Mexican Claims Commission of 1924, 1932, *passim*. The conventions creating all these three commissions were similar.

100 Special Claims Commission of 1923, United States and Mexico, *Opinions*, 1931, 1. *Infra*, p. 206.

101 Another and perhaps the most important argument advanced by the United States in this case, which has no definite bearing here, was that the Mexican government shortly before the events in question had practically invited the victims to go back to their mining works, with a definite promise of protection which amounted to a guaranty of safety against armed bands. Before the Commission the Mexican Agent argued that no such promise had been given by the Government itself; that what is called an official promise of protection is nothing more than a statement to that effect made by General Obregon, Chief of the Army, at a banquet; and that, at any rate, the Mexican Government was not bound by what Obregon had promised under those circumstances. The Commission did not attach great importance to this aspect of the case.

of the Commission held, however, that at this time the Villistas had ceased to possess the dignity of insurgents and were mere bandits;[102] and that Mexico was not liable in this particular case because the murderers were pursued and executed by the authorities. It was further said that it is true that Villa was not captured, but Villa was not present at the event, and the Government of Mexico never ceased to pursue him. In support of its view that the Villistas were bandits, the Commission pointed out that at this time the official reports of the American consuls and special agents in Mexico described Villa and his followers as bandits; that on March 26, 1916, President Wilson stated that the American military expedition to Mexico was ordered "for the sole purpose of capturing the bandit Villa"; that the Department of State and the Senate made statements to the same effect; and that a few days after the crime was committed at Santa Isabel, Carranza himself issued a decree outlawing Villa and his followers as bandits. By that decree, said the Commission, "it may be seen that Villa was then nothing else but a bandit, and that the *Santa Isabel Case* was an act of banditry pure and simple."[103]

102 Before the Commission the Mexican Agent divided the revolutionary careers of Villa and Zapata into three periods. First, from the beginning to about September, 1914 Villistas and Zapatistas formed part of the Constitutionalist army, and Mexico was therefore liable for their acts in this period. Second, from September, 1914 to about the end of 1915 they were insurgents fighting against the Constitutionalists, and under the protocol Mexico voluntarily accepted liability for their acts during this period. Third, from 1916, when they ceased to possess the dignity of insurgents, to 1920 they were bandits for whose acts Mexico was liable only if negligence could be shown. The Commission, in effect, approved this view of the matter.

The same division was attempted by the Mexican Agent before the British-Mexican Claims Commission of 1926 and before the French-Mexican Claims Commission of 1924. In subsequent discussion it will be seen that these commissions did not entirely agree with Mexico and held Villa and his followers to be insurgents during the third period.

103 *Santa Isabel Case*, Special Claims Commission of 1923, United States and Mexico, *Opinions*, 1931, I, 7-8. For other issues involved in this case, see *infra*, p. 206.

As to failure to punish armed insurgents falling within the second category, that is, persons who have attained the dignity of insurgents and carry on regular war for a political object, the question of negligence is not so simple. In order to fix liability, here again a distinction should be made between two categories of insurgent acts; (1) acts of a political or military character, done in pursuance or in aid of political aims, and (2) acts of brigandage or criminal acts in the ordinary sense. It is generally accepted that insurgents cannot be "held accountable to private suitors in the local courts for the commission of acts of a belligerent character incidental to the conflict. On the other hand, . . . the commission of internationally illegal acts, shown to be of a private rather than a public character, and not fairly to be regarded as incidental to the conflict in the course of which they were committed" [104] might render the insurgent wrongdoers liable. By applying this criterion, it is clear that the duty of a government to prosecute former insurgents for acts of an injurious nature is thus limited. A state cannot be held liable for insurgent acts falling in the first category; but liability will attach for insurgent acts of brigandage falling in the second category if it can be clearly established that there was a failure on the part of either the insurgent government or the titular government to punish wrongdoers. This distinction between the two categories of insurgent acts was made clear during the recent Mexican arbitrations by the British-Mexican Claims Commission of 1926 in a number of cases.[105] In the *Buena Tierra Mining Company Case*,[106] the British Government charged Mexico with liability

104 Hyde, *Int. Law*, I, 542-543.

105 Although these cases were decided under admission of liability in the protocol, such admission by Mexico did not in fact go beyond the general rule of international law. Mexico accepted liability for wrongful acts of insurgents in case negligence could be established. See Article 3, section 5, of the convention.

106 British-Mexican Claims Commission of 1926 and 1930, *Decisions and Opinions*, 1933, 259.

for loss of property confiscated or taken by revolutionaries of General Villa's faction during the period from November 1913 to September 1919. The losses complained of included, *inter alia*, coal requisitioned by the so-called government of Villa in January and February 1915; horses taken by Villistas in November 1915; an iron case destroyed in the claimant company's mine by Villistas in December 1915; gold, alfalfa, candles, gasolene, and grease taken by the same forces in 1915 and 1916; and in January 1919 Villa himself visited the claimant company's minefield, ordered a safe to be broken up and took possession of a sum of Mexican gold. In addition, Villistas assaulted a train in September, 1919, and robbed a sum of gold belonging to the claimant company. With the exception of this last item, which was regarded as an act of brigandage for which Mexico could be held liable only in case of negligence to punish offenders, the Commission considered these acts as acts incidental to the civil conflict and falling within the first category for which, it was said, Mexico could not be held liable. This view was stated as follows:

> In the opinion of the Commission, these acts, with possibly the exception of the train assault and gold taking in September, 1919, were *prima facie* of a political or military character, done in pursuance or in aid of political aims, and they can find no evidence sufficient to establish that the acts were pure brigandage. . . . The seizure or confiscation of coal, gasolene, and other materials, and even in some instances of cash by forced loans or otherwise fall under this description, and having regard to this factor and to the general circumstance in Mexico, the Commission do not feel that they can necessarily class all such acts as brigandage or criminal acts in the ordinary sense. The Commission desire, however, to make clear that they are not speaking here of acts such as wanton murder or other crimes committed with no possible legitimate excuse or reason of military necessity. Proceeding on the lines indicated above they find that the confiscations and takings in this case . . . with the possible exception of that on the 13th September, 1919, belonged to the category of military or political

acts as before described, and they give the Mexican Government the benefit of the doubt as regards the event of the 13th September, 1919. But in any case as regards this act, it has not been proved that there was any negligence on the part of the authorities, nor that the occurrence was of notoriety, nor that it was brought to the notice of the authorities, or that they were informed thereof in due time, so as to fix responsibility on them for non-punishment. . . . Therefore for all the above reasons the Commission hold that the Government of Mexico is absolved from financial liability for all these acts.[107]

By far the greater number of claims dealt not with insurgent acts of the kind incidental to the conflict for which Mexico was thus absolved from liability, but with acts of brigandage committed by "insurrectionary forces" or unsuccessful rebels for which Mexico would be held liable in case "it be established that the competent authorities omitted to take reasonable measures . . . to punish those responsible." [108] The Commission, therefore, undertook to ascertain whether there was or was not failure on the part of the Mexican authorities to punish insurgents for acts of brigandage. In the case of the *Mexico City Bombardment Claims*,[109] the British Government charged Mexico with liability for failure to punish insurgents who looted or destroyed the personal property of certain British subjects. It appears that during a period known as "the tragic ten days" in February 1913 revolutionary troops belonging to the forces of General Felix Diaz, then in arms

107 British-Mexican Claims Commission of 1926 and 1930, *Decisions and Opinions*, 1933, 259, 263-265.

The distinction between insurgent acts of "a political or a military nature, or directed towards political or military aims" and insurgent "acts of brigandage" was also made by the same Commission in the *Patton Case*, *ibid.*, 215, 218, and in the *Henderson Case*, *ibid.*, 307 involving acts of Zapatistas in 1915.

108 Article 3, section 5, of the convention of 1926 between Great Britain and Mexico.

109 British-Mexican Claims Commission of 1926, *Decisions and Opinions*, 1931, 100.

against the administration of President Madero, occupied the Y. M. C. A. building in Mexico City and ordered the claimants to leave without delay. When they returned to their rooms after hostilities had ceased, they found that their personal property had been either destroyed or looted by the revolutionaries. At first the British Agent raised the question that, in view of the fact that in this particular battle General Huerta who succeeded in establishing a government and General Felix Diaz made common cause in overthrowing President Madero, the Felicistas should be regarded as successful revolutionists for whose acts Mexico was liable. The majority of the Commission, however, did not admit "such a close cooperation and community of aim between General Felix Diaz and General Victoriano Huerta as to identify them both together as one revolutionary force, which, after the overthrow of President Madero, set up a Government *de facto*." In their opinion, the Felicistas were mere rebels or unsuccessful insurgents for whose acts Mexico could be held liable only in case, according to the protocol, "it be established that the competent authorities omitted to take reasonable measures to suppress the insurrections, risings, riots or acts of brigandage in question or to punish those responsible for the same; or that it be established in like manner that the authorities were blamable in any other way."[110] The Commission then proceeded to decide whether Mexico was liable in view of the facts in this particular case. It came to the conclusion that there had been a neglect of duty on the part of the authorities to punish the armed insurgents who looted the building and appropriated the personal property of the claimants. The claims were therefore allowed for the following reasons:

In a great many cases it will be extremely difficult to establish beyond any doubt the omission or the absence of suppressive or punitive measures. The Commission realizes that the evidence of

110 Article 3, section 5, of the conventions of 1926 between Great Britain and Mexico.

negative facts can hardly ever be given in an absolutely convincing manner. But a strong *prima facie* evidence can be assumed to exist in these cases in which *first* the British Agent will be able to make it acceptable that the facts were known to the competent authorities, either because they were of public notoriety or because they were brought to their knowledge in due time, and *second* the Mexican Agent does not show any evidence as to the action taken by the authorities.

In the claims here dealt with both conditions seem to be fulfilled. The occupying and the looting of the building must have been known to the authorities obliged to watch over and to protect life and property; and, furthermore, the British Agent showed notes of sufficient authenticity, written in the British Legation in margin of the affidavits of the claimants, which notes satisfy the majority of the Commission that the events have been duly and without delay intimated to the public authorities.

On the other hand there is no evidence at all that the soldiers, who looted the Hostel, have been prosecuted.[111]

Accordingly, the Commission decided the case in favor of the claimants. It allowed compensation to those of the claimants in this case who were able to submit proof showing the amount of the loss for which compensation was claimed, but refused to grant compensation to those who were unable to submit such proof.

The principle of this case was applied to a number of subsequent claims. In cases where, on the one hand, the British Agent submitted proof that the acts in question were either of public notoriety or that the authorities were informed of them in due time, and where, on the other hand, the Mexican Agent submitted no proof that the authorities had taken action to punish the insurgent wrongdoers, Mexico was held liable. In the *Case of Bowerman and Burberry's*,[112] a claim was made for the loss of a trunk, and a quantity of sample garments con-

111 *Mexico City Bombardment Claims*, British-Mexican Claims Commission of 1926, *Decisions and Opinions*, 1931, 100, 104.

112 British-Mexican Claims Commission of 1926, *Decisions and Opinions*, 1931, 141.

tained therein, which was destroyed *en route* from Tampico to Vera Cruz by rebels or insurrectionary forces who assaulted and burned the train in 1919. It appears that the claimant left Mexico almost immediately after the loss, and did not call the attention of the authorities to the matter at the time. The Commission, however, held Mexico liable and the Mexican authorities blamable on the ground that "an assault on, and the burning of, a train on the line from Mexico City to Vera Cruz was an occurrence of such importance that it cannot be supposed that the authorities were unaware of it, and the Mexican Agent has not shown that they took any action whatever in the matter." In the *Santa Gertrudis Jute Mill Company Case*,[113] the claim was for the loss of three cars of jute which were burnt at the Paso del Macho station in 1917 when it was attacked, taken and set fire to by rebel forces under General Aguilar. General Aguilar and his followers were described as permanent rebels who did not fight for any revolutionary program but who acted against every organized system of government, ready to side with any force opposed to it. Apparently no proof was submitted that the claimant company had informed the authorities of this loss, but the Commission held Mexico responsible on the ground that

the attack on an important station of one of the main railroads of the country, and the destroying by fire of several wagons, are facts, which must have been of public notoriety and were sure to come at once to the knowledge of the authorities. The railway between the capital and Vera Cruz is of such a vital importance to Mexico that it was to be expected that measures should have been taken to prevent acts of this kind. That they could occur is always a strong presumption of the absence of sufficient watchfulness. . . . As the authors were known at the time of the facts, a prosecution would have been possible, but there had not been produced any evidence showing that action was taken, and the fact that a few years later General Aguilar was still in command of armed men and able to place them under General Obregon's banner

113 *Ibid.*, 147.

shows that he was not interfered with and retained complete liberty of movement.[114]

In the *Case of John Gill*,[115] the claim was for the loss of personal property taken or destroyed by revolutionary forces opposing the Madero Government. The loss occurred in Sultepec on September 1, 1912, when the rebels attacked a power plant where he was employed and near where he resided. The whole matter, including the losses, were reported to the British Legation in Mexico City, which in turn informed the President of the Republic and the Minister for Foreign Affairs. These Mexican authorities "stated that they were touched by the account", but declined to consider the question of compensation for the reason that "the precedent might have grave consequences." The Commission held Mexico liable on the ground that "the Mexican Agent has not shown a single proof that any action to inquire, suppress or prosecute was taken, although Sultepec is within easy distance of the Capital." In the *Case of William McNeill*,[116] the claim was for "physical, moral and intellectual damages" caused by arrest and imprisonment by revolutionary forces at Bacis, in the State of Durango, in April 1913. The Claimant was the General Manager of the Bacis Gold and Silver Mining Company, a British concern. Revolutionary forces visited the mining area and demanded from the Company a sum of money. He was arrested and imprisoned for refusing this demand, but finally had to deliver five bars of silver and a promissory note for a sum of money in order to get free. It appears that the local Jefe Politico intervened to the extent of returning the five bars of silver and the promissory note to the company in exchange for a cash payment.

114 British-Mexican Claims Commission of 1926, *Decisions and Opinions*, 1931, 147, 151.

115 British-Mexican Claims Commission of 1926, revised in 1930, *Decisions and Opinions*, 1933, 85.

116 British-Mexican Claims Commission of 1926 and 1930, *Decisions and Opinions*, 1933, 96.

Mexico was held liable on the ground that this action of the Jefe Politico indicated that the authorities were informed of what happened; that "apart from this it seems next to impossible that such a sensational act as the imprisonment of the General Manager of one of the principal concerns of the State could not have come to the knowledge of those whose function it was to watch over and to protect life and property"; and that "not the slightest indication has been given that they took any action."[117] And finally, in the *Case of Mrs. Edith Henry*,[118] a claim was made for the murder of the claimant's husband and for loss of personal property at the hands of a band of Zapatistas at Zacualpan in January 1916. There was a question whether Generals Villa and Zapata and their followers should be considered as bandits or insurgents during this period, that is, after September 1915 when General Carranza succeeded in establishing a *de facto* government. The Commission held that they were insurrectionary forces, capable of performing acts incidental to the civil conflict on the one hand and acts of brigandage on the other hand.[119] It then undertook to decide whether Mexico was liable for the particular acts of brigandage in this case. It appears that in due time representations were made to the Constitutionalist authorities in Mexico in respect of this murder, but apparently no action was taken and no punishment inflicted upon the guilty parties. In view of this fact, the Commission held that the claimant was entitled to compensation for the murder of her husband.

The principle of liability for failure to punish insurgent wrongdoers for acts of brigandage, as formulated in the above cases, was said to be subject to certain limitations. The Commission stated some of these limitations as follows:

117 British-Mexican Claims Commission of 1926 and 1930, *Decisions and Opinions*, 1933, 96, 100.

118 *Ibid.*, pp. 165 and 299.

119 This decision that Villistas and Zapatistas were rebels and not bandits in this period is opposed to the view of the United States-Mexican Special Claims Commission of 1923 in the *Santa Isabel Case*. *Supra*, p. 171.

> The majority fully realises that there may be a number of cases, in which absence of action is not due to negligence or omission but to the impossibility of taking immediate and decisive measures, in which every Government may temporarily find themselves, when confronted with a situation of a very sudden nature. They are also aware that authorities cannot be blamed for omission or negligence, when the action taken by them has not resulted in the *entire* suppression of the insurrections, rising, riots or acts of brigandage, or has not led to the punishment of *all* the individuals responsible. In those cases no responsibility will be admitted.[120]

The Commission also refused to hold Mexico liable in cases where the authorities had no knowledge of the insurgent acts complained of, either because such acts were not of public notoriety or because the authorities were not informed of them in due time by the claimants. For instance, in the *Case of Mrs. Christina Patton,*[121] the claimant had suffered losses when her house in a Mexican city was attacked and looted in March 1915 by armed Zapatistas. At that time there was no established government in Mexico, since Carranza on the one hand and Zapata and Villa on the other hand were still fighting for supremacy. The Commission stated that in view of the fact "that the Police continued to function, that it continued to regulate traffic in the capital, to investigate crimes and to arrest criminals, as also that the Courts continued to administer justice . . . that public authorities that were obliged to watch over and protect life and property continued to exist, although it is not denied that the performance of those duties will often have been very difficult in those disturbed times of civil war," it would be willing to render a judgment in favor of the claimant if negligence or omission on the part of this "permanent organization of the public service" [122] was proved. It discov-

120 *Case of John Gill*, British-Mexican Claims Commission of 1926 and 1930, *Decisions and Opinions*, 1933, 85, 88-89.

121 British-Mexican Claims Commission of 1926 and 1930, *Decisions and Opinions*, 1933, 215.

122 *Case of Mrs. Christina Patton*, British-Mexican Claims Commission

ered, however, that no such proof had been shown; that the event could not be considered as being of public notoriety and that nothing had been produced to prove that the competent authorities were informed or that either the claimant or any of the British representatives approached the police, or any other authority, with an account of the occurrences. The claim was, therefore, disallowed and dismissed.

In addition, the principle of liability for negligence may be said to be subject to other limitations such as continued domicile by a foreigner in the territory in insurrection, visiting and trading with a region notoriously in a state of civil war, and participation in the rebellion on the part of a foreigner.[123] Under such circumstances it is assumed, as a rule, that a foreigner voluntarily exposes himself to danger and assumes the risk, thus relieving the government from its duty of protection and therefore of liability. In 1873 Secretary of State Fish stated that "if a country receives strangers within its limits, it thereby incurs a liability to protect them from violence . . . on the part of insurgents," he nevertheless added that "perhaps the rule should not always apply to persons domiciled in a country, and rarely to such as may visit a region notoriously in a state of civil war." [124] In 1887 Secretary of State Bayard

of 1926 and 1930, *Decisions and Opinions*, 1933, 215, 218.

In this respect, the Commission stated that "even when a country passes through a period of anarchy, even when an established and recognized Government is not in existence, the permanent machinery of the public service continues its activity. The Commission shares the view expressed in this regard by the General Claims Commission between Mexico and the United States" to the effect that the greater part of governmental machinery in every modern country is not affected by revolutionary changes in the higher administrative offices. *Hopkins Case*, General Claims Commission of 1923, United States and Mexico, *Opinions*, 1927, 42, 44-45. *Supra*, p. 84.

123 Borchard, *Diplomatic Protection*, 235.

124 Mr. Fish, Sec. of State, to Mr. Foster, Am. Minister to Mexico, Aug. 15, 1873, Moore, *Digest*, VI, 974.

In a note of November 16, 1865, Secretary of State Seward disavowed liability for injuries to foreigners domiciled "in a country in a state of civil war." He said: "By voluntarily remaining in a country in a state of civil

declined to press the claim of one Negrete, an American citizen, against Spain for damages caused by insurgents in Cuba on the ground that the claimant had voluntarily gone to regions under insurgent control where it was impossible for the Spanish Government to protect him or his property. He stated that in times of civil conflict " it is the duty of foreigners to withdraw from such risks and if they do not, or if they voluntarily expose themselves to such risk, they must take the consequences," and said:

It is a matter of notoriety that when Mr. Negrete visited Cuba, and there purchased an estate, that island was in a state of insurrection. I have no information as to the price he paid for the property nor from whom he bought it, nor the conditions of the sale; nor what influence the existence of the insurrection had upon the price. It is, however, notorious that estates in the district exposed to insurrection were from that cause and naturally greatly depreciated in value. So far as the information before me goes, Mr. Negrete voluntarily incurred the risks incidental to his purchase . . . and therefore has no right to call on his Government to demand from Spain indemnity for his losses so incurred.[125]

Similarly, foreign subjects who participate in an insurrection *ipso facto* forfeit their standing as claimants against the titular government for injuries inflicted either by the insurgents or even by the authorities of the state.[126] Aliens giving aid and

war they [foreigners] must be held to have been willing to accept the risks as well as the advantage of that domicile. The same rule seems to be applicable to the property of neutrals, whether that of individuals or of governments, in a belligerent country. It must be held to be liable to the fortunes of war." Wharton, *Int. Law Digest*, II, 577. See also Mr. Bayard, Sec. of State, to Mr. O'Connor, Oct. 29, 1885, *ibid.*, II, 581; the claim of *Rosa Gelbtrunk*, Arbitration between the United States and Salvador, *For. Rel.*, 1902, 876-878.

125 Mr. Bayard, Sec. of State, to Mr. Sutphen, Jan. 6, 1888, Moore, *Digest*, VI, 961, 964.

126 As to the effect of such participation on citizenship and on the right to national protection see *Young Case*, Moore, *Int. Arb.*, III, 2752; *Clark Case, ibid.*, 2729; *cases of Wyeth and Speakman, ibid.*, 2777; *Case of Cannon and Groce*, 4 *A. J.* (1910) 674.

comfort to the Confederate authorities in the United States were held to have forfeited their neutrality and were excluded from the right to compensation before the domestic and international commissions sitting after the Civil War. In the case of *Whitty*[127] a British subject who had joined the Confederate army in 1861, but had left it because of ill-health, brought a claim against the United States for the destruction and appropriation of rum and molasses in Louisiana by the Federal forces in 1864. The United States and British Claims Commission of 1871 held that "the claimant having been actively engaged in the late rebellion against the United States, has no standing before this commission for the prosecution of a claim like this, and the claim is therefore disallowed."[128] It appears that a similar rule was applied by the Spanish Treaty Claims Commission[129] and by domestic commissions in Colombia and other Latin-American republics.[130]

When the question of neglect of duty or failure to suppress insurrection, to prevent injury, and to punish insurgent wrongdoers is raised in a case, the burden of proof is on the claimant government to establish such negligence. International courts of arbitration have almost uniformly enforced this rule, notwithstanding the great difficulty of proving governmental negligence in this respect. In the *Aroa Mines Case*[131] it was held that "the want of due diligence must be made a part of the claimant's case and be established by competent evidence." In the *Henriquez Case*[132] and in the *Salas Case*[133] it was said that the issue that the respondent government was "negligent in a given case must be alleged and proved." And again, in

127 Moore, *Int. Arb.*, III, 2820.

128 *Ibid.*, 2820, 2823.

129 *Cases of Caldwell* (No. 283) *and Jova* (No. 122), Crandall, 4 *A. J.* (1910), 822.

130 Borchard, *Diplomatic Protection*, 237-238.

131 Ralston, *Venezuelan Arbitrations of 1903*, 344, 384.

132 *Ibid.*, 896, 899.

133 *Ibid.*, 903.

1888, the Department of State declared that "the mere fact that an insurrection occurred is not proof of negligence, and indeed, the fact that an insurrection maintains itself for any considerable length of time is *prima facie* proof of *vis major* which throws upon the party alleging particular negligence the burden of proving it." [134] It is also clear that two elements enter into such proof. In the first place, it must be shown that the respondent government had the power or the capacity to take action at the time of the act complained of; and, in the second place, it must be established that there was a neglect or failure to take such action. This point was made clear by the Department of State in 1895, when speaking of insurgent acts in Cuba it advised certain American citizens that "in the event . . . of injury, a claim would necessarily have to be founded upon averment and reasonable proof that the responsible officers of the Spanish Government, being in a position to prevent such injury, have failed to use due diligence to do so." [135] This point was the sole question in the *Revesno Case*,[136] where it was held by the umpire that proof of failure to take action was not sufficient but that it must also be shown by the claimant government that at the time of the injury the respondent government was in a position to take action to suppress insurrection, to prevent injury, or to punish insurgent wrongdoers. In this case the Italian Government contended that since the taking of property of certain Italian subjects was done by the Matos revolutionists under the command of General Rolando in 1902 and 1903, and since the events took place from a distance not greater than 30 miles from Caracas, the Venezuelan Government could have prevented them by the exercise of proper diligence. The umpire said:

134 Mr. Bayard, Sec. of State, to Mr. Sutphen, Jan. 6, 1888, Moore, *Digest*, VI, 961, 964.

135 Mr. Uhl, Acting Sec. of State, to Mr. Springer, United States Vice-Consul-General at Havana, July 1, 1895, *For. Rel.*, 1895, II, 1216; Moore, *Digest*, VI, 966-967.

136 Ralston, *Ven. Arb. of 1903*, 753.

A study of these cases will show that the burden of proving want of diligence rests upon the claimants. In the "expedient" now under consideration not a word of affirmative proof is furnished to show negligence on the part of the Government. The umpire is aware of the fact that for several months the revolutionists remained within a short distance of Caracas without being dislodged by the Government, or perhaps without serious attempt being made to dislodge them. But he is also aware that during that time war was being actively prosecuted over large areas of the country, while the external relations of Venezuela were in a state of danger. He is unable, and if furnished with data would doubt his right, to judge as to the military or political considerations which made military activity or concentration more necessary in one portion of the country than another.

Furthermore, he knows nothing of the relative strength of the forces of General Rolando and of the Government in this neighborhood or their advantages of location. He only knows that when the tension was apparently released elsewhere the forces of General Rolando were attacked and ultimately defeated . . .

In view of the foregoing an order dismissing said cases will be signed.[137]

And, finally, in the case of claims arising from the Cuban insurrection of 1895, the Spanish Treaty Claims Commission made it clear to the claimants "that in order to recover for damages done by insurgents it was necessary for them to allege and prove that at the time and place when and where the injury was done the Spanish authorities could, by due diligence, and should have prevented such injury." [138]

However, during the recent Mexican arbitrations the usual rule that the claimant government must prove the respondent

137 *Revesno Case*, Italian-Venezuelan Claims Commission of 1903, Ralston, *Ven. Arb. of 1903*, 753.

138 Fuller's *Report*, 25; Rule 4 of the Principles of Allowance, Final Report of the Commission, 1910, Sen. Doc. 550, 61st Cong. 2nd Sess., p. 6; Hyde, *Int. Law*, I, 540-541; Borchard, *Diplomatic Protection*, 233. See also the rule of the Nicaraguan Mixed Claims Commission of 1911; and the treaty of 1892 between Italy and Colombia which provides for "proven want of due diligence."

government's ability as well as its failure to take action was, on the whole, subjected to a fundamental change. In the *Parker Case*[139] the General Claims Commission of 1923 between the United States and Mexico denied "the existence in international procedure of rules governing the burden of proof borrowed from municipal procedure", and expressly decided that

> however appropriate may be the technical rule of evidence obtaining in the jurisdiction of either the United States or Mexico as applied to the conduct of trials in their municipal courts, they have no place in regulating the admissibility of and in the weighing of evidence before this international tribunal . . . municipal restrictive rules of adjective law or of evidence cannot be here introduced and given effect by clothing them in such phrases as "universal principles of law", or "the general theory of law", and the like.
>
> . . . it is the duty of the respective Agencies to cooperate in searching out and presenting to this tribunal all facts throwing any light on the merits of the claim presented. The Commission denies the "right" of the respondent merely to wait in silence in cases where it is reasonable that it should speak . . . While ordinarily it is incumbent upon the party who alleges a fact to introduce evidence to establish it, yet before this Commission this rule does not relieve the respondent from its obligation to lay before the Commission all evidence within its possession to establish the truth, whatever it may be.
>
> For the future guidance of the Agents of both Governments, it is proper to here point out that the parties before this Commission are sovereign Nations who are in honor bound to make full disclosures of the facts in each case so far as such facts are within their knowledge, or can reasonably be ascertained by them. The Commission, therefore, will confidently rely upon each Agent to lay before it all of the facts that can reasonably be ascertained by him concerning each case no matter what their effect may be. In any case where evidence which would probably influence its decision is peculiarly within the knowledge of the claimant or of

139 *Opinions*, 1927, 35, 38-40. See also the *Archuleta Case*, *ibid.*, 1929, 73, 76.

the respondent Government, the failure to produce it, unexplained, may be taken into account by the Commission in reaching a decision.[140]

The Commission further rejected "the contention that evidence put forward by the claimant and not rebutted by the respondent must necessarily be considered as conclusive," but held that "when the claimant has established a *prima facie* case and the respondent has offered no evidence in rebuttal the latter may not insist that the former pile up evidence to establish its obligations beyond reasonable doubt without pointing out some reason for doubting."

The above view as to the burden of proof, however much it may be deemed to differ from the usual rule, was fully accepted by the British-Mexican Claims Commission of 1926.[141] In a number of cases involving the question of negligence or due diligence on the part of Mexico to punish insurgent wrongdoers, the Commission ruled that the Mexican Government must contribute to evidence and submit proof of its diligence. It referred "to the difficulty of imposing on the British Government the duty of proving a negative fact such as an omis-

140 *Parker Case*, General Claims Commission of 1923, United States and Mexico, *Opinions*, 1927, 35, 38-40.

In rejecting the view that there was a settled rule in international arbitral law and judicial procedure as to the burden of proof being on the respondent government, the Commission said: "The absence of international rules relative to a division of the burden of proof between the parties is especially obvious in international arbitrations between governments in their own right, as in those cases the distinction between a plaintiff and a respondent often is unknown, and both parties often have to file their pleadings at the same time. Neither the Hague convention of 1907 for the pacific settlement of international disputes, to which the United States and Mexico are both parties, nor the statute and rules of the Permanent Court of International Justice at the Hague contain any provision as to a burden of proof. On the contrary, article 75 of the said Hague convention of 1907 affirms the tenet adopted here by providing that 'The parties undertake to supply the tribunal, as fully as they consider possible, with all the information required for deciding the case!'" *Ibid.*, 35, 40.

141 The same view was also adopted by the French-Mexican Claims Commission of 1924 in the *Pinson Case, Opinions*, 1932, 1, *passim*.

sion on the part of the Mexican Government to take reasonable measures," and held that "the Commission is at liberty to assume that strong *prima facie* evidence exists of a fault on the part of the authorities" whenever the British Agent proves that the authorities were aware of an event causing loss or damage and the Mexican Agent fails to show that any action was taken in the matter. This rule was formulated as follows:

> In a great many cases it will be extremely difficult to establish beyond any doubt the omission or the absence of suppressive or punitive measures. The Commission realizes that the evidence of negative facts can hardly ever be given in an absolutely convincing manner. But a strong *prima facie* evidence can be assumed to exist in those cases in which *first* the British Agent will be able to make it acceptable that the facts were known to the competent authorities, either because they were of public notoriety or because they were brought to their knowledge in due time, and *second* the Mexican Agent does not show any evidence as to action taken by the authorities.[142]

The Commission further said that the reason for requiring the Mexican Agent to submit evidence as to action taken by the authorities was because "evidence to that effect, would, when existent be at the disposal of said Agent, to whom the Archives of the Republic, of the various States and of the Municipalities are available for this purpose." [143]

In a number of dissenting opinions in the cases already discussed, the Mexican Commissioner pointed out that under the

142 The case of the *Mexico City Bombardment Claims*, British-Mexican Claims Commission of 1926, *Decisions and Opinions*, 1931, 100, 104. *Supra*, p. 175.

See also the case of *Bowerman and Burberrys, ibid.*, 141, 143; *Santa Gertrudis Jute Mill Company* case, *ibid.*, 147, 151; the case of *Mr. Joseph Taylor, ibid.*, 297; the case of *John Gill, Decisions and Opinions*, 1933, 85, 88-89; the case of *William McNeill, ibid.*, 96; the case of *Mrs. Edith Henry, ibid.*, 165 and 299; the case of *Mrs. Christina Patton, ibid.*, 215; and the case of *The Buena Tierra Mining Company, ibid.*, 259.

143 The *case of John Gill*, British-Mexican Claims Commission of 1926 and 1930, *Decisions and Opinions*, 1933, 85, 88-89.

protocol of arbitration the burden of proof was on the British Government "to demonstrate the fact of negligence on the part of the Mexican authorities in suppressing the insurrections or in punishing the guilty parties";[144] that by its action the Commission was in fact inverting the usual rule of evidence and shifting the burden of proof on the respondent Mexican Government; and that such action amounted to a violation of the protocol and of the usual rule of evidence uniformly enforced by other international commissions. He further said:

> The Mexican Government is not bound to prove that it acted diligently. The law presumes that the Government has to act diligently, not only to protect other persons' interests, but also to safeguard its own existence . . . the Convention imposed the burden of proof of negligence on the demandant Government. If this be difficult it only means that it is also difficult to give judgment against Mexico for mutinies or upheavals, or for acts committed by insurrectionary forces . . . there is no reason why it should be inverted, and thus impose the burden of proof on the Government against whom claim is made.[145]

On the theory that the burden of proof was on the claimant British Government, the Government of Mexico refused to submit evidence to establish the fact that it had fulfilled its duty of diligence in suppressing insurrection or punishing insurgent wrongdoers. The Commission, therefore, proceeded to decide these cases solely on proof by the claimant government to the effect as to whether the Mexican authorities were aware of the events causing losses or damages to the British subjects or to their property. The British Government was not required to submit proof of negligence or of failure of the Mexican

144 Article 3, section 5, of the British-Mexican Convention of 1926 held Mexico liable "provided that in each case it be established that the competent authorities" failed to take action or were negligent.

145 *Santa Gertrudis Jute Mill Company case*, British-Mexican Claims Commission of 1926, *Decisions and Opinions*, 1931, 147, 153.

authorities to take action. As a result, the decisions rendered in some of these cases do not appear to be quite satisfactory, since Mexico was held liable for injurious acts of unsuccessful insurgents whom it could not control or against whom the authorities were unable to take action. In the case of the *Mexico City Bombardment Claims*,[146] for instance, the losses were incurred by armed insurgents under General Felix Diaz in 1913 over whom the newly established Huerta government admittedly had no control and against whom neither General Huerta nor the Mexico City police were able to take any punitive action. To a lesser extent, this same observation applies to the cases of *John Gill*,[147] *William McNeill*,[148] and perhaps others. If the Commission had in mind punishment of the insurgent wrongdoers in these cases after a responsible government was established in Mexico, it is believed that even in such a case punishment of such persons would have been impossible. It should be remembered that a responsible government was not actually established in Mexico for many years after some of these events took place. It certainly would have been impossible for the Carranza government in 1916 to find and punish an insurgent wrongdoer, perhaps a resident of a remote State, who took the personal property of the Englishman in Mexico City in 1913 while fighting under General Felix Diaz. These considerations should have been urged on the Commission by Mexico, and to this extent therefore Mexico's refusal to cooperate was a mistake. In fact there is no reason why an international commission should not require a respondent government to show whether action was taken in a given case. But no less a mistake was the failure of the Commission to inquire into the possibility of taking action against armed insurgents. In cases where the Mexican authorities, either the

146 British-Mexican Claims Commission of 1926, *Decisions and Opinions*, 1931, 100. *Supra*, p. 175.

147 *Ibid.*, *Decisions and Opinions*, 1933, 85. *Supra*, p. 179.

148 *Ibid.*, 96. *Supra*, p. 179.

Federal and State governments or the local police, were in no position to take action, it was obviously meaningless to inquire, as the Commission did, whether they did take action. And the question whether the competent authorities were able to take action or not, was one which could be determined by the Commission itself on the basis of the facts in each case.

2. *Responsibility under "special protection" clause of a preexisting treaty.* On occasion it has been contended that a state is exceptionally liable for wrongful acts of unsuccessful insurgents in cases where there exists a " special protection " clause in a preexisting treaty between the claimant and respondent states. In such cases it has been apparently assumed that such a treaty provision serves as a contractual guaranty against injury, thereby affording better protection to the nationals of the states involved than could be obtained under customary international law. While under international law a state may not incur liability for injuries inflicted by unsuccessful insurgents, under the " special protection " clause such liability will nevertheless attach because, it is said, even the inability on the part of the government to prevent or put down a rebellion can not excuse the nonfulfillment of a treaty obligation. In 1834 the Department of State said that the United States could not accept the mere " revolutionary state " of a part of Mexico as a defense to a claim for injuries inflicted on American citizens in violation of treaty engagements.[149] In 1873 Secretary of State Fish held that under the special protection provision of the treaty between the United States and Mexico, the latter country was liable for forced loans exacted from two American citizens by insurgents.[150] At about the same time he ad-

149 Mr. McLane, Sec. of State, to Mr. Butler, Am. Minister to Mexico, June 20, 1834, Moore, *Digest*, VI, 972; Wharton, *Int. Law Digest*, II, 576.

150 Mr. Fish, Sec. of State, to Mr. Foster, Am. Minister to Mexico, Aug. 15, 1873, Moore, *Digest*, VI, 974; Mr. Cadwalader, Acting Sec. of State, to Mr. Foster, Sept. 22, 1874, Moore, *Digest*, VI, 978. But see Mr. Evarts, Sec. of State, to Mr. Scott, Am. Consul at Chihuahua, April 17, 1877, Moore, *Digest*, VI, 917.

vanced a similar argument against Colombia, charging that country with liability under the treaty of 1846 for the seizure of the American steamer *Montijo* by insurgents.[151] In 1888 the Department of State contended that under the "full and perfect protection" clause of the treaty of 1870 Peru was liable for failure to protect an American citizen against imprisonment and illegal treatment by insurgents.[152] The same contention has been raised before international commissions. During the American-Mexican arbitrations of 1839, the United States Commissioners argued that under the "special protection" clause of the treaty of 1831 Mexico was liable for permitting insurgents to seize and confiscate the property of an American citizen and imprison him in violation of her treaty obligations.[153] It was further said that Mexico's "inability to keep down rebellion in her territory, while it might be her misfortune, could not excuse the nonfulfillment of her contract." During the American-Mexican arbitrations of 1868, the tables were turned, and this time Mexico charged the United States with neglect of duty to give "special protection" under the treaty of 1831 to Mexican citizens and their property in the course of the Civil War and to prevent injury at the hands of the Confederate authorities.[154] And, lastly, during the British-American arbitrations of 1871, the British Government charged the United States with liability for failure to prevent violation by the rebel states of the treaties of 1794, 1815, and 1827, which stipulated for the protection of the British subjects and their property from injury or damage. In view of the fact that losses were incurred by the British subjects at the hands of the Confederate States, it was said that the United States

151 Moore, *Digest*, VI, 973-974; Moore, *Int. Arb.*, II, 1421; *For. Rel.*, 1871, 230; *For. Rel.*, 1872, 146.

152 Mr. Buck, Am. Minister to Peru, to Mr. Alzamora, Minister of Foreign Relations, 1888, *For. Rel.*, 1888, II, 1372; Moore, *Digest*, VI, 986.

153 *Baldwin's Case*, Moore, *Int. Arb.*, III, 2859, 2862. Also *Divine Case*, *ibid.*, 2980.

154 *Prats Case*, Moore, *Int. Arb.*, III, 2886, 2887-2838.

"having finally maintained its authority over those States, its liability to Great Britain for violation of these treaties by those respective States remained precisely as if there had been no insurrection or civil war." [155]

However, with the exception of one case, the argument as to liability on the exceptional ground of special protection provision of a treaty was not reflected in the final decisions of these commissions either because they were not impressed by such argument or because they had better grounds on which to base their decisions. The one case in which the matter was discussed in the final decision is that of *Prats*,[156] decided by the United States and Mexican Claims Commission of 1868. In referring to the Mexican argument in that case that the "special protection" provision of the treaty of 1831 rendered the United States exceptionally liable because "each government has thereby contracted to guarantee the safety" of the persons and property of the citizens of the other, the Commission said:

> The argument for claimant treats this stipulation for special protection as a guaranty of security under all circumstances; but we do not take that view of it. The most literal interpretation of special protection cannot make an insurance.
>
> The whole article defines the character of this protection and shows that the government merely designed to place aliens, transient or dwelling within their territory, on an equality with citizens in this respect. Herein consists this special protection. Indeed, it stipulates no more than every just government must undertake in behalf of its own citizens within its own jurisdiction. We do not think by this article either of the governments has agreed to afford any more or further protection to strangers within its borders than is justly due to its own citizens, or meant to establish any inequality between subjects and strangers either in the matter of protection or in the mode or measure of redress for injuries to persons or property. Each government *has* given special protection

155 *Hanna Case*, Moore, *Int. Arb.*, III, 2982, 2983-2984.

156 Moore, *Int. Arb.*, III, 2886.

to all having a right to invoke it whenever it does all in its power to enforce *its* laws, redress and punish violence, and put down by force of arms armed revolt.

In these particulars, for aught that here appears, the United States is blameless so far as claimant is concerned. He makes no charge against the United States for failure to enforce her laws before they were overthrown at New Orleans by war; and after the war broke out it will be difficult to deny the magnitude of the sustained exertions of the United States or the sacrifice incurred by that government to suppress and put down the violence of the insurgents.[157]

It thus appears that the duty of protection under the special protection clause of a preexisting treaty may be no more than the degree of protection afforded under international law, and is subject to the same limitations in case of civil war. Now, what is the degree of protection under international law? On November 16, 1865, Secretary of State Seward answered this question as follows:

It is believed to be a received principle of public law that the subjects of foreign powers domiciled in a country in a state of war are not entitled to greater privileges or immunities than the other inhabitants of the insurrectionary district. If for a supposed purpose of the war one of the belligerents thinks proper to destroy neutral property, the other cannot legally be regarded as accountable therefor. By voluntarily remaining in a country in a state of civil war they must be held to have been willing to accept the risks as well as the advantages of that domicile. The same rule seems to be applicable to the property of neutrals, whether that of individuals or of governments, in a belligerent country. It must be held to be liable to the fortunes of war.[158]

157 *Prats Case*, Moore, *Int. Arb.*, III, 2886, 2888.

158 Wharton, *Int. Law Digest*, II, 577. In 1854 Secretary of State Marcy said: "The undersigned is not aware that the principle that foreigners domiciled in a belligerent country must share with citizens of the country in the fortunes of war has ever been seriously controverted or departed from in practice." To the same effect see also Mr. Bayard, Sec. of State, to Mr. O'Connor, Oct. 29, 1885. Wharton, *Int. Law Digest*, II, 581.

During the arbitration between the United States and Salvador in 1902, the umpire disallowed the claim of an American citizen for looting and destruction of his property by insurgents in Salvador in 1898 on the ground that under international law foreigners were entitled to no better treatment than nationals in such cases. He said:

> A citizen or subject of one nation who, in the pursuit of commercial enterprise, carries on trade within the territory and under the protection of the sovereignty of a nation other than his own is to be considered as having cast in his lot with the subjects or citizens of the State in which he resides and carries on business. Whilst on the one hand he enjoys the protection of that State, so far as the police regulations and other advantages are concerned, on the other hand he becomes liable to the political vicissitudes of the country in which he thus has a commercial domicile in the same manner as the subjects or citizens of that State are liable to the same. The State to which he owes natural allegiance has no right to claim for him as against the nation in which he is resident any other or different treatment in case of loss by war—either foreign or civil—revolution, insurrection, or other internal disturbance caused by organized military forces or by soldiers, than that which the latter country metes out to its own subjects or citizens.
>
> This I conceive to be now the well-established doctrine of international law. The authorities on which it has been so established consist of the writing of publicists and diplomats, the decisions of arbitrators—especially those of mixed commissions—and the text of writers on international law.[159]

From the foregoing it is clear that in cases of this kind foreigners have "exactly the same claims for indemnity against the government concerned, as citizens of that country have, and no other or greater rights to indemnity." [160] As a rule, a government does not hold itself accountable for wrongful acts

159 Claim of *Rosa Gelbtrunk*, *For. Rel.*, 1902, 876, 877-878.

160 Mr. Seward, Sec. of State, to Baron Gerolt, Prussian Minister, Jan. 9, 1866, Moore, *Digest*, VI, 957.

of unsuccessful insurgents, but if it indemnifies citizens, it must also indemnify foreigners. It was for this reason that when an American citizen, who had suffered at the hands of insurgents in Haiti, stated that his partner, a Haitian citizen, was to be remunerated for his losses, the American Minister at Port au Prince was instructed by the Department of State to use his good offices to obtain for the American citizen a share of the indemnity.[161]

If this is true, it follows that a claim by a foreign state for exceptional treatment under the special protection clause of a preexisting treaty to indemnify its nationals for injuries inflicted by unsuccessful insurgents is not justified by international law, unless it can be shown that in this respect international law was modified by such treaty provision. But it has never been successfully maintained that the special protection stipulation of a treaty constitutes a modification of international law as to claims arising from acts of unsuccessful insurgents. The phrase "special protection," as it is ordinarily used in international treaties, is not a comparative term denoting more or better protection for foreigners than is given to citizens. As the United States and Mexican Claims Commission of 1868 pointed out in the *Prats Case*, the most literal interpretation of "special protection" does not go beyond the duty on the part of one contracting party to place the nationals of the other on an equality with citizens in this respect.

3. *Responsibility for confiscated property used for public purposes.*—In the *British Shareholders of the Mariposa Company Case*,[162] the facts disclosed, *inter alia*, that on August 18, 1915, the commanding officer of the Villista troops at Muzquiz, in the State of Coahuila, Mexico, ordered twenty head of cattle from the claimant company's ranch in order to supply

161 Mr. Evarts, Sec. of State, to Mr. Longston, American Minister to Haiti, Moore, *Digest*, VI, 960.

162 British-Mexican Claims Commission of 1926, *Decisions and Opinions*, 1933, 304.

meat to the population of the town. At that time there was no established federal government in Mexico, since the government of Huerta had been overthrown and Villa and Zapata on the one hand and Carranza on the other hand were still fighting for control. Under these circumstances, the British-Mexican Claims Commission of 1926 held that

> as regards the Villistas, the Commission have taken into account the fact that, in so far as the taking of the cattle is concerned . . . it was to a large extent confiscated in order to supply the population of the town of Muzquiz with meat. It seems a postulate of equity, to award compensation for cattle thus exacted.[163]

4. *Responsibility under amnesty.*—Does amnesty constitute an exceptional ground of state liability for wrongful acts of unsuccessful insurgents? In the earlier decisions of international courts of arbitration there exists a difference of opinion on this subject. On the one hand, in the *Divine Case*,[164] the umpire of the American-Mexican Claims Commission of 1868 held, without any qualifications or limitations, that the granting of amnesty to insurgents does not render the state liable for their acts. The claim in this case was for the burning of a house and its contents by Mexican revolutionists in 1851. It appears that the insurgent General Carvajal beseiged and finally assaulted the city of Matamoras, and in the course of the assault the house in question was destroyed. The United States urged liability on the ground that the insurgent leader, having been defeated, "was pardoned under a general amnesty and restored to his civil rights, was afterward commissioned a brigadier-general and made civil and military governor of Tamaulipas and other States, was sent in 1864 to the United States as a commissioner with extraordinary powers, and was appointed and continued to be a major-general in the Mexican

163 British-Mexican Claims Commission of 1926, *Decisions and Opinions*, 1933, 304, 306. As to liability of the state for insurgent loans used for public purposes, see *supra*, p. 20.

164 Moore, *Int. Arb.*, III, 2980.

army." The umpire, after stating that as a general rule a state is not liable for tortious acts of unsuccessful insurgents, dismissed the claim against Mexico and said:

> It is urged that the Mexican Government granted amnesty to Carvajal and, therefore, made itself responsible for his acts. Other governments, including that of the United States, have pardoned rebels, but they have not on this account engaged to reimburse to private individuals the losses caused by those rebels.[165]

On the other hand, in a number of cases it has been either argued by the claimants or held by the commissions involved that the grantor of an amnesty *ipso facto*, and apparently without any qualifications or limitations, assumes liability for wrongful acts of unsuccessful insurgents thus pardoned. In the *Baldwin Case*,[166] involving injuries to an American citizen and confiscation of his property by a revolutionary junta in Mexico in 1833, the United States claimed liability on the ground, *inter alia*, that as the result of an amnesty "the present authorities of Mexico have never treated the members of this junta as lawless insurgents deserving punishment, but on the contrary have commended their conduct on this occasion and bestowed on some of them high official station"; that "after the authority of the junta was ended, some of its members continued in office, and that their acts under the intrusive government were approved, commended, and actually continued by their legitimate successors"; and that these consequences of the amnesty left to the injured party no remedy at all, since the leaders of the junta who were given or left in high positions used their power to thwart his attempt to secure redress in local courts.[167] Mexico admitted that "it made the revolutionary junta of Tehuantepec submit and cease from their political errors by means of an amnesty"; that "as the

165 *Divine Case*, Moore, *Int. Arb.*, III, 2980, 2981.

166 Moore, *Int. Arb.*, III, 2859. *Supra*, p. 168.

167 Moore, *Int., Arb.*, III, 2859, 2861-2866.

effect of all amnesties is to restore the individuals whom it embraces to their anterior rights and privileges, those to whom Baldwin refers retained their rights to situations and places of honor or profit"; but said that the amnesty in this case was granted "without prejudice to the rights of a third party."[168] The umpire of the United States and Mexican Commission of 1839 allowed the claim without, however, stating the grounds for his decision. Since there were other issues involved, it is difficult to say to what extent the question of amnesty influenced the final decision in this case. In the *Montijo Case*[169] the United States made a claim for the capture of an American steamer by insurgents in revolt against the State of Panama, Colombia, in 1871. It appears that, instead of using force against the insurgents and recovering the steamer for the owners, the president of the State of Panama came to terms with the insurgent leaders and concluded "a treaty of peace" by which a complete amnesty was granted. The umpire allowed the claim on the ground, *inter alia*, that amnesty incurred liability. He said:

> . . . the grantor of an amnesty assumes as his own the liabilities previously incurred by the objects of his pardon toward persons or things over which the grantor has no control. In the present case it will scarcely be contended that the captors of the *Montijo* had any right, beyond that emanating from a revolutionary movement, to take the vessel from the dominion of her owners. . . . If, therefore, the captors had no right before the amnesty to take the *Montijo*, it is evident that the President of Panama could not by the terms of that document confer it on them. They, therefore, are liable to the owners for the expenses incurred and damages occasioned. If no amnesty had ever been granted, and had Herrera, Diaz, and their associates been honestly and effectively proceeded against in the courts of the republic . . . the aspect of the case would have entirely changed. . . . But the amnesty deprived the Messrs. Schuber of the power of trying the question. Therefore

168 *Ibid.*, 2859, 2865.

169 *Ibid.*, II, 1421. *Supra*, p. 169.

the President of Panama, having no right to dispose of interests which were not his property and which, on the contrary, he was bound by a public treaty to protect, assumed the responsibility to the owners of those interests of persons by whom they had been injured. It is an old saying that one must be just before one is generous.[170]

Accordingly, and in view of the failure on the part of Panama to make compensation, he held Colombia liable because "it is the natural heir (if the expression may be permitted) of the liabilities of the State of Panama."[171] In the *Wenzel Case*,[172] involving injuries to property inflicted by unsuccessful insurgents under General Hernandez in 1899 and in 1900, Germany urged liability on the ground that Venezuela had granted a general amnesty[173] to those who had participated in the Hernandez revolution and that General Hernandez himself was given a diplomatic assignment as Venezuelan minister to the United States. The umpire pointed out that the precedents of former arbitral Commissions seemed to be in favor of liability under similar circumstances, and said:

170 Moore, *Int. Arb.*, II, 1421, 1438-1439.

171 In this case Colombia raised the question that the liability was that of the State of Panama which under the federal constitution was an "independent" state. The Commission held that for purposes of international claims the federal government of Colombia was the only one which could be recognized. *Ibid.*, 1439-1442. For other cases where the question of federal form of government has been raised to escape liability for insurgent acts see, *De Brissot Case*, Moore, *Int. Arb.*, III, 2949; and *Wyman's Case*, *ibid.*, 2978. In the *Hanna Case*, on the other hand, Great Britain raised the same question to establish liability of the United States. *Ibid.*

172 Ralston, *Venezuelan Arbitration of 1903*, 590.

173 President Castro's decree of amnesty of 1902 states, *inter alia*: "I open the doors of all the prisons of the Republic to the political prisoners who are still confined therein. I likewise open the doors of the country to Venezuelans who for the same reasons are in foreign lands, and I restore to the enjoyment of the constitutional guaranties property of all revolutionists which was embargoed for reasons of public order." *Wenzel Case*, *ibid.*, 590, 593.

> In the opinion of the umpire a general pardon of past offenses by a government is an amnesty, which is commonly defined to be an act of oblivion. Its effect is that the crimes and offenses named in the act are obliterated, and they can never again be charged against the guilty parties. Where no offenses are named in the act the amnesty is general.[174]

However, he held that in this particular case the amnesty, though a general one which absolved " from all punishment in the courts or by the authorities of Venezuela all political prisoners in Venezuela and all political offenders in other countries for any act committed by them while in rebellion," did not make the state liable for damages and injuries inflicted by the persons pardoned because it was granted by the Chief Executive of Venezuela in violation of the constitution which " confers no power upon the Executive to grant amnesties, but in express terms gives the legislative branch of the government that power." [175]

Both of the views stated above as to the effect of amnesty upon state liability are, of course, unsatisfactory. In recent years, therefore, there has taken place a greater recognition of the fact that the effect of amnesty upon the liability of the grantor state for acts of unsucessful insurgents depends wholly upon the nature and the scope of the pardon given and its relations to different categories of insurgent acts in question. As

174 *Wenzel case*, Ralston, *Ven. Arb. of 1903*, 590, 593-594.

175 Article 54, section 21, of the Venezuelan Constitution of 1901 provided: "The Congress of the United States of Venezuela shall have the following powers . . . to grant amnesties." *Ibid.*, 594.

In the *Bovallins and Hedlund case*, involving a claim for loss of cash and personal effects and for imprisonment of Swedish and Norwegian citizens in Venezuela, the umpire of the Swedish-Venezuelan Claims Commission of 1903 held that Venezuela was liable for conferring various public offices upon the leaders of the unsuccessful revolution, thereby tacitly approving their conduct, instead of punishing them for wrongs inflicted. Ralston, *Ven. Arb. of 1903*, 952.

See also the case of *Cotesworth & Powell*, for a discussion of the effect of amnesty upon state liability in case of successful revolution. Moore, *Int. Arb.*, II, 2050, *Miller case, ibid.*, III, 2974.

already stated, insurgents are capable of performing different categories of acts, such as (1) insurrectionary acts of a political or military nature and acts incidental to the civil conflict and committed for a public rather than a private end, and (2) acts of brigandage and criminal offenses committed for a private rather than a public end. Now, the important question is whether a given amnesty covers both or only one of these two main categories of insurgent acts. The better opinion is that if an amnesty covers only the first category of acts, no liability can attach, if it also covers the second category of acts, liability must attach because the injured parties are thereby prevented from securing redress in local courts. Speaking of the effect of a grant of amnesty in this respect, Hyde observes:

> The purpose of such a grant is to pardon the commission of acts incidental to revolution and directed against the grantor, and also to render the actors harmless from prosecution. It may naturally embrace internationally illegal acts incidental to the conflict and committed for a public rather than a private end and against whomsoever directed.
>
> The pardon of insurgents on account of acts of revolution does not necessarily condone the method by which they were accomplished; nor does it necessarily deprive the alien victim, if there be one, of any valuable right, inasmuch as the actors could not, even in the absence of a grant of amnesty, be held accountable to private suitors in the local courts for the commission of acts of a belligerent character incidental to the conflict.
>
> On the other hand, if the amnesty should embrace the commission of internationally illegal acts, shown to be of a private rather than a public character, and not fairly to be regarded as incidental to the conflict in the course of which they were committed, condonation would be apparent. In such case the State, by shielding the actors from prosecution, might be said to approve of the wrong done, and by failing to prosecute the actors, would itself become neglectful of a duty of jurisdiction. From such condonation responsibility would arise.[176]

176 Hyde, *Int. Law.*, I, 542-543.

This view was adopted during the recent Mexican arbitrations by the American-Mexican and British-Mexican Claims Commissions. In the cases of *West*[177] and *Snapp*[178] the United States charged Mexico with liability for the murder of two American citizens by the rebel leader Rosales and his followers in 1922 on the ground that instead of punishing the murderers the Mexican Government had granted an amnesty which included this particular crime. The facts disclosed that on December 30, 1922, the Mexican Government had issued an act of amnesty as follows:

> Amnesty is hereby granted to those guilty of rebellion and sedition and any act committed in connection therewith up to the date of the publication of the present act and beginning with the year of 1920.[179]

In answer to an inquiry whether any steps were being taken for the apprehension and punishment of the murderers, the Mexican Government interpreted this amnesty act so as to cover the murder of West and Snapp. The General Claims Commission of 1923 took judicial notice of this fact and held Mexico liable on the ground that by granting amnesty to the murderers the Mexican Government "has voluntarily deprived itself of the possibility of prosecuting and punishing them." It said:

> There would seem no doubt but that granting amnesty for a crime has the same effect, under international law, as not punishing such a crime, not executing the penalty, or pardoning the offense.[180]

In the *Buena Tierra Mining Company case*,[181] decided by the British-Mexican Claims Commission of 1926, a claim was

177 General Claims Commission of 1923, United States and Mexico, *Opinions*, 1927, 404.

178 *Ibid.*, 407.

179 *West case*, General Claims Commission of 1923, United States and Mexico, *Opinions*, 1927, 404, 405.

180 *Ibid.*, 404, 405.

181 British-Mexican Claims Commission of 1926, *Decisions and Opinions*, 1933, 259.

made for the loss of property confiscated or taken by revolutionaries of Villa's faction during the period from November 1913 to September 1919. In December 1915 the government of Carranza issued a general amnesty decree and a large number of Villistas took advantage of it and retired to private life. On July 28, 1920, the Provisional Government of Mexico under de la Huerta entered into an agreement with Villa which provided that (1) "General Villa shall lay down his arms and retire to private life," swearing "on his word of honour that he will not take up arms against the Constitutional Government or his fellow countrymen"; (2) the government agreed to give him a large estate in the State of Durango where he was to reside, and an escort of fifty trusted men chosen by Villa and who were to be paid by the War and Navy Department but who could not be withdrawn or "divested from its sole object of watching over the personal needs of General Villa"; and (3) the government undertook to give a year's pay to "persons at present forming part of General Villa's forces," to provide tillable lands for those who wished to retire to private life, and to admit into the national army those who desired to continue the career of arms.[182] The British Agent argued that the effect of this agreement and the general amnesty of 1915 was to render Mexico financially liable for non-punishment of Villa and the Villistas for the wrongful acts giving rise to the present claim. The Mexican Agent, on the other hand, maintained that the amnesty of 1915 and the agreement of 1920 should be regarded as pardoning only the political acts of the Villistas and not their criminal acts. As to acts falling under this last description, it was said that Mexico could be held liable only if negligence or blame were proved against it. The Commission agreed as to the division of Villa's acts into (1) insurrectionary acts and (2) acts of brigandage, and pro-

182 For the text of the agreement of 1920 with Villa see, British-Mexican Claims Commission of 1926, *Decisions and Opinions*, 1933, 259, 263-264; Special Claims Commission of 1923; United States and Mexico, *Opinions*, 1931, 21-22.

ceeded to investigate the nature of the particular acts giving rise to the claim in this case. It pointed out that some of them, such as the taking of coal, gasoline, and other materials, were incidental to the civil conflict and therefore classified them as insurrectionary acts. As to this class of acts, the Commission held that " the Villa Agreement was an act of political expediency, on the basis of the Villistas being regarded as belligerents, and does not in itself involve the Mexican Government in financial liability for acts done by Villistas of a political or military nature in pursuance and in aid of their political aims." The presumption here is, of course, that such acts must be regarded as proper objects of amnesty. One of the acts complained of in this case was a train assault and robbery by Villistas in 1919, and the Commission classified this as an act of brigandage. It intimated that liability would attach for this particular act if it could be shown that the agreement of 1920 covered also acts of brigandage such as robbery, wanton murder or other crimes " committed with no possible legitimate excuse or reason of military necessity." It was pointed out that the claimant had failed to bring the train robbery incident of 1919 to the knowledge of the Mexican authorities in order to test the scope of the agreement of 1920, and therefore it could not be said that the agreement in question was intended to cover that particular offense or crimes of a similar character. Accordingly, the claim was disallowed and dismissed.[183] In the case of the *Santa Isabel Claims*,[184] decided by the United States and Mexican Special Claims Commission of 1923, the American Agent argued, *inter alia*, that the agreement of 1920 was an act of lenity toward Villa and his followers and therefore rendered Mexico liable for the murder of certain American citizens by Villistas in 1916. The Commission held that the agreement in question had no such effect, and that " it can-

183 *Buena Tierra Mining Company case*, British-Mexican Claims Commission of 1926, *Decisions and Opinions*, 1933, 259, 264-265. *Supra*, p. 173.

184 *Opinions*, 1931, 1. See also, *supra*, p. 171.

not be looked upon as an act of lenity in connection with the events of Santa Isabel." It was pointed out that the Villistas who committed the Santa Isabel murders were pursued and executed by the Mexican Government; that "it has not once been alleged that Villa was among the assailants of the train or that he ordered the attack" and the murders; and that since Villa was not personally implicated, it could not be maintained therefore that the agreement of 1920, which was chiefly political in its character and in its effect, was to be regarded as an act of lenity in connection with that particular offense.[185] No question was raised as to whether the chief of an insurgent movement is responsible for the criminal acts of his forces. If Villa was responsible for the criminal acts of his subordinate officer who ordered the Santa Isabel murders, the presumption is that the agreement of 1920 was in effect a general amnesty or a pardon or an act of lenity of a character which would render Mexico liable. In one sense the Commission attempted to answer this question by stating that one Pablo Lopez, who ordered the Santa Isabel murders, was "known as a Villista officer *in the past*" and that at the time of the crime in question he and his band were bandits and not insurgents.[186] The claims were dismissed chiefly on the ground that Mexico had fulfilled its international duty by pursuing and executing the actual murderers in this case.

From the foregoing discussion it follows, on the one hand, that liability will not be incurred by the state if the scope of an amnesty is limited to insurrectionary acts or acts incidental to the conflict, presumably because such acts are to be regarded as proper objects of amnesty; but, on the other hand, liability will attach if the scope of an amnesty is broad enough to pardon insurgent acts of brigandage and common law crimes, because in such case the state voluntarily deprives itself of the

185 *Santa Isabel Claims*, United States and Mexican Special Claims Commission of 1923, *Opinions*, 1931, I, 11-12.

186 As to the question whether murderers in this case were bandits or insurgents, *supra*, p. 171.

possibility of prosecuting and punishing the insurgent offenders and because claimants are thereby prevented from securing redress in local courts. Under the description of insurrectionary acts fall all political and military acts of insurgents against the state, provided they are not in violation of international law;[187] acts in pursuance and in aid of rebellion, such as seizure of a vesel for belligerent purposes[188] or taking of property for the use of insurgent forces[189] or forced loans;[190] acts incidental to the conflict, such as destruction of property in the track of war;[191] and all other insurgent acts done under high command for a public rather than a private end. Under the description of acts of brigandage fall murder in the sense of criminal law;[192] imprisonment and torture of persons for a private end;[193] looting of property and robbery;[194] destruction of property not incidental to the conflict;[195] and other acts of a similar character.

5. *Responsibility under agreement with insurgents.*—In the *Montijo Case*,[196] involving the seizure of an American steamer

187 At the conclusion of the Boer War clause 4 of the Terms of Surrender of the Boer Forces in the field excluded from the amnesty "certain acts, contrary to usages of war, which have been notified by the Commander-in-Chief to the Boer Generals, and which shall be tried by court-martial immediately after the close of hostilities." Parliamentary Papers, South Africa, 1902, Cd. 1096, quoted in Oppenheim, *Int. Law*, 2 ed. II, 334; Hyde, *Int. Law*, I, 542.

188 *Montijo case*, Moore, *Int. Arb.*, II, 1421-1447. *Supra*, p. 169.

189 *Buena Tierra Mining Company case*, British-Mexican Claims Commission of 1926, *Decisions and Opinions*, 1933, 259. *Supra*, p. 173.

190 See, however, Mr. Fish, Sec. of State, to Mr. Foster, Am. Minister to Mexico, July 15, 1875, where liability for forced loans was claimed as result of amnesty granted by Mexico to insurgents. Moore, *Digest*, VI, 980.

191 *Divine case*, Moore, *Int. Arb.*, III, 2980. *Supra*, p. 198.

192 Cases of *West* and *Snapp*, General Claims Commission of 1923, United States and Mexico, *Opinions*, 1927, 404-408. *Supra*, p. 204.

193 *Baldwin case*, Moore, *Int. Arb.*, III, 2859. *Supra*, p. 168.

194 *Ibid.*, 2859; *Buena Tierra Mining Company case*, *op. cit.*, 259.

195 *Wenzel case*, Ralston, *Ven. Arb. of 1903*, 590. *Supra*, p. 201.

196 Moore, *Int. Arb.*, II, 1421. *Supra*, p. 169.

by insurgents in Colombia in 1871, the president of the State of Panama, which was then a part of Colombia, came to terms with the leaders of the revolution and made a treaty of peace by which, *inter alia*, "the government assumed as its own the expense of the steamers and other vehicles which the revolution has had to make use of up to that date." This agreement of the government of the State of Panama with the insurgent chiefs to compensate the owners of the vessel was not kept. The umpire made an award in favor of the American owners of the *Montijo* on the ground, *inter alia*, that the agreement in question was binding on the State of Panama, and, in case of default, on Colombia as "the natural heir (if the expression may be permitted) of the liabilities of the State of Panama." He said:

> . . . the treaty of peace . . . contains in its seventh article a distinct engagement that the government of Panama will pay for the use of the *Montijo*. The undersigned considers this fact so important and conclusive that he contents himself with putting it on record without further comment. Why the engagement was not carried out the undersigned can not say. That arbitrators were appointed to fix the amount, and that they came to a decision respecting it is on record. But their sentence was apparently not ratified; at any rate, it was not carried out. The State of Panama therefore remains to this day responsible, both by implication and by express engagement, for the acts of the revolutionists in this matter.[197]

A similar result would be obtained "should the *de jure* government enter into an agreement with the revolutionists to cooperate in establishing a new government as the representa-

197 *Ibid.*, 1421, 1439. In this respect see also Miller's case where Lieber, umpire of the United States and Mexican Claims Commission of 1868, held Mexico liable for a forced loan on the ground, *inter alia*, that the leader of the unsuccessful revolution "was received some time after by the government, which, as it might be urged, thus adopted his obligations." Moore, *Int. Arb.*, III, 2974. In the *Bovallins and Hedlund Cases* the umpire held that by appointing the principal leaders of an unsuccessful revolution to official positions the Venezuelan Government thereby tacitly approved their conduct. Ralston, *Ven. Arb. of 1903*, 952.

tive of the two opposing forces," since in such a case "it might be urged by a foreign claimant State, that that government as the resultant of both parties, would be the legal successor of each, and hence responsible for the illegal acts attributable to the authorities of each." [198] This was the view taken by the Department of State in the case of the claim of one MacCord, an American citizen, who had been thrown into prison and had sustained ill-treatment there at the hands of the revolutionary forces of General Caceres in 1885. It appears that the Iglesias Government of Peru, instead of using force against the insurgents, came to terms with General Caceres and by mutual agreement a new provisional government was established in December 1885. On June 3, 1886, General Caceres was installed as the constitutional president of Peru, succeeding the provisional government. The Government of the United States contended that Peru was liable in view of the attitude adopted toward the insurgents:

> By the act of December 2, 1885, signed by Generals Caceres and Iglesias, the contending governments were by mutual agreement merged into the provisional government then established, of which the existing government was the successor. The present constitutional government, therefore, existed by consent of the people of Peru, as the duly elected successor of the Iglesias and Caceres governments, and should therefore be responsible for the acts of the officials of both.[199]

Subsequently Peru agreed to pay an indemnity on account of the claim in question, and by a protocol signed at Washington

198 Hyde, *Int. Law*, I, 543.

199 Mr. Buck, American Minister to Peru, to Mr. Alzamora, Peruvian Minister of Foreign Relations, Sept. 3, 1886, *For. Rel.*, 1888, II, 1372; Moore, *Digest*, VI, 987.

For other questions involved in this case see Mr. Rives, Acting Sec. of State, to Mr. Buck, Min. to Peru, June 23, 1888; *For. Rel.*, 1888, II, 1369; Mr. Alzamora, Min. of *For. Rel.*, to Mr. Buck, Min. to Peru, Aug. 28, 1888, *For. Rel.*, 1888, II, 1372; Same to Same, Nov. 6, 1888, Sen. Ex. Doc. 4, 53rd Cong., 3rd Sess. 23, Moore, *Digest*, VI, 988; Mr. Buck, Min. to Peru, to Mr. Alzamora, Min. of For. Rel., Sept. 3, 1888, *For. Rel.*, 1888, II, 1372, Moore, *Digest*, VI, 986.

in 1898 the two governments referred to the Chief Justice of the Supreme Court of Canada "the question of amount" of the indemnity to be paid.[200]

6. *Responsibility under protocols of arbitration.*—In exceptional cases governments have on occasion assumed liability for wrongful acts of unsuccessful insurgents by agreement with claimant states and under protocols of arbitration. Admissions of liability in such cases may be divided into three classes. Under the first class fall cases where liability for a particular claim is accepted by the respondent state and expressly stated in the protocol and the commission is required to decide only the question of the amount of indemnity. In the *Easton Case*[201] the Government of the United States presented to the Peruvian Government a claim for property losses and personal injuries inflicted upon an American citizen by unsuccesful insurgents in 1854. After a somewhat protracted diplomatic discussion of the case, the Peruvian Government finally admitted liability and in due course the question of amount of indemnity was referred to the United States and Peruvian Claims Commission of 1863 for determination. As stated above, a similar

200 Mr. Olney, Sec. of State, to Mr. McKenzie, Min. to Peru, June 27, 1896, Sen. Doc. 7, 55th Cong., 1st Sess. 4-7, Moore, *Digest*, VI, 989; President McKinley's annual message, Dec. 5, 1898, *For. Rel.*, 1898, LXXX, Moore, *Digest*, VI, 990.

Peru also paid a claim for seizure and destruction of property in 1885 of an American citizen by the insurgent forces of General Caceres. *For. Rel.*, 1901, 427-430, Moore, *Digest*, VI, 990-991.

"In his message to Congress, Aug. 27, 1913, concerning relations with Mexico, President Wilson stated that he had instructed Mr. Lind, his personal representative, to urge the agreement of all parties in Mexico to abide by the results of a contemplated election and to co-operate in the most loyal way in organizing and supporting the administration to be chosen. (*A. J.*, VII, Supp., 279.) It is believed that if the revolutionary forces had agreed with the provisional government of that country in the way suggested, the resultant government might have been regarded as the successor of the several factions, and responsible for the internationally illegal acts of each." Hyde, *Int. Law*, I, 543.

201 Moore, *Int. Arb.*, II, 1629.

procedure was followed by these two governments in the *MacCord Case*[202] in 1898.

Under the second class fall cases where liability for acts of unsuccessful insurgents is accepted in principle by the respondent government and so stated in the protocol, but where the commission is required to determine the nature of each claim in view of such admission as well as to decide the amount of indemnity. The several protocols of the recent Mexican arbitrations stipulated, *inter alia*, that the respective commissions shall undertake to examine with care, and to judge with impartiality, in accordance with the principles of justice and equity, all claims presented, since it is the desire of Mexico *ex gratia* fully to compensate the injured parties, and not that her responsibility should be established in conformity with the general principles of International Law; and it is sufficient therefore that it be established that the alleged damage actually took place, and was due to any of the causes enumerated in Article 3 of this Convention, for Mexico to feel moved *ex gratia* to afford such compensation.[203]

And Article 3 provided that the losses and damages must have been caused during the period from November 20, 1910, to May 31, 1920, by any one of the following forces:

1. By the forces of a Government *de jure* or *de facto*;
2. By revolutionary forces, which after the triumph of their cause, have established Governments *de jure* or *de facto*, or by revolutionary forces opposed to them;

202 *Supra*, p. 210. In this connection see also the admission of liability by Peru for damages caused by the sacking of Callao in 1865 by the revolutionary forces of Colonel Prado, the award having been made by a mixed commission appointed by the diplomatic corps resident in Lima, and the minister for foreign affairs of Peru, Mr. Brent, Charge at Lima, to Mr. Fish, Sec. of State, March 14, 1871, Moore, *Digest*, VI, 973; by Colombia for seizure of certain steamers by insurgents in 1875, Mr. Scruggs, Min. to Colombia, to Mr. Fish, Sec. of State, May 18, 1876, Moore, *Digest*, VI, 981; and by Egypt in 1882, 73 Br. & For. State Papers, 236, Moore, *Digest*, VI, 984.

203 Article 2 of the Special Claims Convention of 1923 between the United States and Mexico; of the Claims Convention of 1926 between Great Britain and Mexico; and of Claims Convention of 1924 between France and Mexico.

3. By forces arising from the disjunction of those mentioned in the next preceding paragraph up to the time when a *de jure* government had been established, after a particular revolution;
4. By forces arising from the disbandment of the Federal Army;
5. By mutinies or risings or by insurrectionary forces other than those referred to under sub-division 2, 3 and 4 of this Article, or by brigands, provided that in each case it be established that the competent authorities omitted to take reasonable measures to suppress the insurrections, risings, riots or acts of brigandage in question, or to punish those responsible for the same; or that it be established in like manner that the authorities were blamable in any other way.[204]

Briefly, these forces may be classified as (1) successful insurgents and federal forces on the one hand, with which this study is not concerned, and (2) unsuccessful insurgents on the other hand. Unsuccessful insurgents, in turn, may be divided into two groups, as provided by section 2 and section 5 respectively. According to section 5, Mexico accepted liability for acts done " by mutinies or risings or by insurrectionary forces . . . provided that in each case it be established that the competent authorities omitted to take reasonable measures to suppress . . . or to punish those responsible . . . or that it be established in like manner that the authorities were blamable in any other way." Apparently this was intended to cover acts of most of unsuccessful insurgents or "insurrectionary forces" in Mexico during the period from 1910 to 1920, such as General Felix Diaz in 1913, and the Villistas and Zapatistas during the period from January 1916 to 1920. To this extent Mexico's admission of liability in the protocol does not in fact go beyond the ordinary rule of international law, since in any case a state is liable for acts of unsuccessful insurgent or " insurrectionary forces " if negligence can be shown.

204 Article 3 of the several Mexican claims conventions, *ibid.* During the revision of the British-Mexican Convention in 1930 the second part of section 2 and all of section 3 of this article were omitted; so also claims for Huerta's acts.

According to section 2, however, Mexico exceptionally and unconditionally accepted liability for losses and damages caused by another group of unsuccessful insurgents, that is, " by revolutionary forces, which, after the triumph of their cause, have established Governments *de jure* or *de facto*, or by revolutionary forces opposed to them." [205] The phrase " by revolutionary forces opposed to them " was apparently intended by the contracting parties and was interpreted by the American, English and French Commissions of the Mexican arbitrations to include more specifically insurgent forces under Villa and Zapata during the period from September 1914 to December 1915, when after the overthrow of Huerta in August 1914 they separated from Carranza because of dissensions and ceased to be part of the Constitutionalist army. In that period there was no central government in Mexico, and Villa and Zapata were " revolutionary forces " opposed to the revolutionary forces of General Carranza who finally triumphed and established a government *de facto* and *de jure*.[206] For acts done by these two rebel leaders during the period under consideration, Mexico accepted full and unconditional liability in the protocol. Accordingly, in the *Pinson Case* [207] the French-Mexican Claims Commission of 1924 held that by her own admission in section 2 of Article 3 of the Convention, Mexico was liable for losses and damages inflicted upon a French citizen by Zapatistas in February 1915. In the *Caire Case* [208] the same commission held Mexico similarly liable for the murder of a French citizen

205 Article 3, section 2, of the Mexican Claims Conventions.

206 In the *Russell Case*, United States and Mexican Special Claims Commission of 1923, *Opinions*, 1931, p. 44, the American Agent argued that Mexico was liable by her own admission in section 2 of article 3 of the protocol for the killing of an American in 1912 by Orozquistas on the ground that General Orozco was then in revolt against and opposed to Madero who established a government de facto or de jure. The majority of the Commission held that acts of Orozquistas were not covered by the Convention and did not therefore come under the Mexican admission.

207 French-Mexican Claims Commission of 1924, *Opinions*, 1932, I, 101-132.

208 *Ibid.*, 207.

by forces of General Villa in December 1914. In the case of the *Santa Isabel Claims*,[209] involving the murder of certain American citizens by Villistas in January 1916, the United States and Mexican Special Claims Commission of 1923 agreed that Mexico was liable for acts of Villistas by her own admission in the protocol, but limited such admission of liability as to time. It held that under the protocol Mexico had accepted liability for acts of Villistas only for the period from about August 1914 to about December 1915, when Villistas were in fact revolutionary forces; but that such admission of liability did not cover acts done during the period after January 1916, when Villistas were held to be bandits and not revolutionary forces in the sense of the Mexican admission. In view of the fact that the Santa Isabel murders took place on January 10, 1916, the Commission therefore absolved Mexico from liability on the ground that the case did not come under the Mexican admission in the protocol and that otherwise Mexico had fulfilled its international duty by capturing and executing the wrongdoers.[210] The British-Mexican Claims Commission of 1926, on the other hand, had no opportunity to decide cases concerning this matter prior to the revision in 1930 of the Convention of 1926, when the Mexican admission of liability for acts of Villistas and Zapatistas in section 2 of article 3 was eliminated.[211] In view of this fact, the Commission held that under the revised Convention Mexican liability for acts of unsuccessful insurgents depended solely upon proof to establish negligence.[212]

209 Special Claims Commission of 1923, United States and Mexico, *Opinions*, 1931, 1.

210 For other issues involved in the *Santa Isabel Claims case*, see, *supra*, p. 171.

211 British-Mexican Claims Convention of 1930, *Decisions and Opinions*, 1933, 1.

212 See the *Patton Case, Decisions and Opinions*, British-Mexican Claims Commission of 1926, 1933, 215; the *cases of Mallard, Grave and Jones*, *ibid.*, 250-257.

Under the third class fall cases where admission of liability in the protocol by the respondent government for wrongful acts of unsuccessful insurgents is not perhaps so clear, and the commission is therefore required to interpret the protocol in regard to the question as to whether such admission does or does not exist. The German, English, and Italian protocols of the Venezuelan arbitrations of 1903 provided, *inter alia*, that

> The Venezuelan Government admit their liability in cases where the claim is for injury to or a wrongful seizure of property and consequently the Commission will not have to decide the question of liability, but only whether the injury to or the seizure of property were wrongful acts and what amount of compensation is due.[213]

Before the Commissions the Venezuelan Government maintained that this admission of liability should be interpreted to include only injuries to and wrongful seizures of property by the government troops or government officials, but that it was not intended to and "does not include wrongful seizures of or injuries to property by revolutionists." Germany, Italy, and England, on the other hand, contended that it was intended to and should include injuries to and seizures of property by insurgents as well as by the government forces. As a result the Commissions were required to decide the scope of Venezuela's admission of liability. The umpire of the German Commission held that the admission in question included injuries to and seizures of property by revolutionists; but the umpires of the English and Italian Commissions took the contrary view. In the *Kummerow Case*[214] involving confiscation of property by unsuccessful insurgents, the umpire of the German-Venezuelan Commission agreed that under international

213 Article 3 of the German-Venezuelan Protocol of February 13, 1903, Ralston, *Venezuelan Arbitrations of 1903*, 511; of the British-Venezuelan Protocol of Feb. 13, 1903, *ibid.*, 292; and Article 4 of Italian-Venezuelan Protocol, Feb. 13, 1903, *ibid.*, 643.

214 Ralston, *Venezuelan Arbitrations of 1903*, 526.

law Venezuela could not be held liable for damages caused by unsuccessful insurgents in the absence of proof of negligence, but held that the admission of liability in the protocol "extends to claims of German subjects for wrongful seizures of or injuries to property resulting from the present Venezuelan civil war, whether they are the result of acts of governmental troops or of Government officials or of revolutionists." [215] In support of this interpretation, he referred to the fact that on December 9, 1902, the allied powers established a blockade of the ports of Venezuela and seized certain of her war vessels; that one of the German demands for terminating the blockade and for returning the vessels was the admission of liability by Venezuela for injuries to and wrongful seizures of German property "originating from the Venezuelan civil war of 1898 to 1900"; and that this admission was exacted prior to the protocol of arbitration, which limited the Commission to a determination of injuries and seizures and the amount of compensation. It was further stated that at first Venezuela had been unwilling to admit liability for insurgent acts "because of her statute which she then insisted and still insists declared the correct international-law rule of liability," but that "from the necessity of the situation" she "receded from her position and admitted her liability." [216] He said:

Now, Venezuela having by her admission regained control of her ports and her war vessels, contends that she admitted liability

215 Ralston, *Venezuelan Arbitrations of 1903*, 526, 559.

216 *Ibid.*, 526, 555. In connection with this question of admission of liability under duress see also the demand upon and the admission by Mexico of liability for a sum of money taken from the English legation in 1860 by order of General Miramon. 52 *British and Foreign State Papers* (1861), 237; Moore, *Int. Arb.*, III, 2906. During the Miramon revolution and the intervention of 1862, Mexico was apparently willing to make similar concessions to France by making some equitable adjustment of the Jecker bonds, which were issued to finance its enemies. In commenting on this phase of the question of liability for acts of unsuccessful insurgents, Lieber, umpire of the United States and Mexican Claims Commission of 1868, said: "Nations as strong even as Great Britain sometimes assume a liability, rather than risk the consequences." *Cucullu Case*, Moore, *Int. Arb.*, III, 2879.

only in cases where she was legally liable. Certainly, this position cannot be maintained. She was always liable for claims for which she was legally liable. Hence she admitted nothing. And yet we have seen of what momentous consequence this admission was to her. It is perfectly plain that Germany would never have released the ships and ports from which they were in position to make payment of the claims of their subjects if Venezuela had then interpreted her admission as she now seeks to do, or if Germany had had any conception that such interpretation would be sought to be given to words admitting liability generally.[217]

The umpires of the Italian and the British Commissions held, on the contrary, that Venezuela's admission of liability was solely for acts of violence on the part of the Venezuelan Government and its forces, and that it was not intended to cover acts of insurgents.[218] In support of this view it was pointed out that the protocols of arbitration between Venezuela and the so-called "three war powers", that is, Germany, England, and Italy, "does not directly recognize any obligation on the part of Venezuela to pay for injuries inflicted by revolutionary troops"; that if the contracting parties had intended that the Venezuelan admission should also cover acts of insurgents, such "agreement would naturally have found direct expression in the protocol itself and would not have been left to doubtful interpretation";[219] and that the admission in question does not recognize such liability even by implication, because a careful examination of all the correspondence and conferences leading to the signing of the protocols fails to

217 *Kummerow Case*, Ralston, *Ven. Arb. of 1903*, 526, 556.

This decision was affirmed by the same umpire in the *Redler Case*, *ibid.*, 560; *Fulda Case*, *ibid.*, 561; *Valentiner Case*, *ibid.*, 565; *Mohle Case*, 574; and the *Great Venezuelan Railroad Case*, *ibid.*, 639.

The umpire confined his decision strictly to the specific insurrection covered by the admission, that is, the Venezuelan Civil War of 1898 to 1900. See the Von Dissel Case, *ibid.*, 565, 573.

218 See the *Sambiaggio Case*, Ralston, *Ven. Arb. of 1903*, 666, 687-689; the *Aroa Mines Case*, *ibid.*, 344, 350.

219 *Sambiaggio Case*, *ibid.*, 666. 689.

show "a sentence, a word, or a syllable suggestive of a claim by either of these three powers that Venezuela should respond in damages or be held to indemnities because of the acts of insurgents." [220]

220 *Aroa Mines Case*, Ralston, *Ven. Arb. of 1903*, 344, 373.

The Venezuelan Arbitrations of 1903 operated under two sets of protocols, one between Venezuela and the war powers, that is, Germany, England, and Italy, who established a blockade of Venezuelan ports in 1902; and the other between Venezuela and the peace powers, that is, the United States, France, Spain, Belgium, Netherlands, and Sweden and Norway, who did not participate in the blockade. The protocols of the latter powers did not contain the admission stated above. Nevertheless, the umpires of the Spanish and the French Commissions allowed claims for acts of unsuccessful insurgents against Venezuela for a different reason. The protocols of the peace powers, including the French and the Spanish, provided that "the commissioners, or, in case of their disagreement, the umpire, shall decide all claims upon a basis of absolute equity, without regard to objections of a technical nature, or of the provisions of local legislation." The umpire of the Spanish Commission made a distinction between a tribunal which is called upon to decide cases according to the accepted principles of international law, and a tribunal which must decide on a basis of absolute equity. He held that a commission of the second type must render judgment in accordance with the conscience of the arbitrators, and thought it equitable to allow claims for insurgent acts against Venezuela. When the Venezuelan Government pointed out that no such liability exists under international law, the umpire held that the general principle of international law if invoked before a court of absolute equity, such as the Spanish Commission in this case, becomes a technical objection which is expressly barred by the terms of the protocol. *Padron Case, ibid.*, 923; *Mena Case, ibid.*, 931. The umpire of the French Commission gave no reason for his decision in holding Venezuela liable for acts of unsuccessful insurgents; but in view of the similarity of the French and Spanish protocols, it is presumed that he agreed with the reasoning of the umpire of the Spanish Commission. *Acquatella Case, ibid.*, 487.

BIBLIOGRAPHY

(List of Principal Sources)

American Journal of International Law, cited as *A. J.*

American Agent's *Report*, Arbitration between United States and Great Britain of 1910.

Borchard, E. M., *Diplomatic Protection of Citizens Abroad*, New York, 1915.

Boutwell's *Report*, French-American Claims Commission of 1880.

British and Foreign State Papers.

British-Mexican Claims Commission of 1926, *Decisions and Opinions*, 1931-1933.

British Parliamentary Papers.

Foreign Relations of the United States, 1870–.

French-Mexican Claims Commission of 1924, *Opinions*, 1932.

General Claims Commission of 1923, United States and Mexico, *Opinions*, 1927, 1929, and 1931.

Hale's *Report*, British-American Claims Commission of 1871.

Hyde, Charles Cheney, *International Law*, 2 vols., Boston, 1922.

Magoon's *Report on the Law of Military Occupation*, Washington, 1902.

Martens' *Recueil des traités*, Leipzig.

Moore, J. B., *Digest of International Law*, 8 vols., Washington, 1906.

——, *International Arbitrations*, 6 vols., Washington, 1898.

Ralston, J. H., *Venezuelan Arbitrations of 1903*, Washington, 1904.

Revue Générale de Droit International Public, 1894–. Paris, cited as *R. G. D. I. P.*

Richardson's *Messages and Papers of the Presidents.*

Smith, H. A., *Great Britain and the Law of Nations*, London, 1932.

Special Claims Commission of 1923, United States and Mexico, *Opinions*, 1931.

United States Supreme Court *Reports.*

INDEX

Bei Fragen zur Produktsicherheit wenden Sie sich bitte an:
If you have any questions regarding product safety,
please contact:

Walter de Gruyter GmbH
Genthiner Straße 13
10785 Berlin
productsafety@degruyterbrill.com